A SELECTION FROM
THE 10TH ANNUAL

J.P. Morgan
Summer Reading List

WITH BEST WISHES

J.P.Morgan

Be the Change

ALSO BY LISA ENDLICH

Goldman Sachs: The Culture of Success

Optical Illusions: Lucent and the Crash of Telecom

Be the Change

LISA ENDLICH

COLLINS BUSINESS
An Imprint of HarperCollins*Publishers*

HarperCollins books may be purchased for educational, business, or sales promotional use. For information, please write: Special Markets Department, HarperCollins Publishers, 10 East 53rd Street, New York, NY 10022.

FIRST EDITION

Designed by Nicola Ferguson

Library of Congress Cataloging-in-Publication Data
Endlich, Lisa, 1959–
    Be the change / Lisa Endlich.—1st ed.
        p. cm.
    ISBN 978-0-06-128768-8
    1. Philanthropists. I. Title.
HV27.E53 2008
361.7'40922—dc22
2008019582

08 09 10 11 12   OV/RRD   10 9 8 7 6 5 4 3 2 1

For Mark

you must be the change you wish to see in the world
MAHATMA GANDHI

contents

introduction

LOOKING FOR THE PATH

I chose to write this book about giving for almost entirely selfish reasons. While I told my publisher that I hoped to compile a book that would give readers insight into the thoughts, philosophies, and actions of a group of successful philanthropists; in truth I hoped to hear their answers myself. I knew it would be difficult to telephone perfect strangers and ask them to tell me about their philanthropic journeys. I thought if I told them I had a book contract and that it was an interview, they would be more forthcoming with me.

What was I looking for? My husband and I had been conducting the most haphazard of philanthropic lives. Although we managed to maintain a semblance of adult life—complete with homeownership, children, and careers—we approached giving away money with, well frankly, less thought than we gave to planning a vacation. We were both active and passive philanthropists. Sometimes we found causes that mattered to us, and sometimes the causes found us. In our passive moments we responded to the pleas of our friends. People we loved and trusted told us their causes were worthy, and we pulled out our checkbook. Once we gave money to a couple of young men soliciting donations door-to-door, and days later they were caught by the police breaking into our apartment

(I had left my keys dangling in the door lock). After the police left, I picked through our belongings strewn across the floor, and could not help thinking that we could do better than this.

We had not examined our values and used philanthropy as a way to express those values and I remained highly conscious of the role happenstance played in most of our giving. In the case of AIDS, for example, my research consisted of little more than attending a dinner party. I had lived in Sierra Leone during college, and I had thought about my experiences there for decades afterward—felt them as acutely as the day my plane left Freetown—but had done nothing. Then by chance, at a friend's dining room table, we met a physician whose life was devoted to the research and treatment of AIDS in South Africa. Within weeks we had written him a check, and within months we had hauled our family to Durban for volunteer work (never for a minute losing sight of the fact that surely the cause of preventing and treating AIDS would be far better served if I had looked at a few photos and sent the airfare to the hospital in Petermaritzburg). But what would have happened if we had gone to the movies that night instead? Surely, there was a better way—a more thoughtful, rational, directed approach—to giving.

There is no question, I was looking for the easy way: I wanted to find insightful philanthropists, record a few interviews, take them home, discuss them with my husband, and then use these as our own blueprint.

It was not to be. What I found is that these phenomenally successful givers had become so because they did not, at some crucial moment, turn their heads and walk away. At a basic level it is no more complicated than that.

In each of the stories that follow, there are moments when millions of others might—in the face of raw human need—have failed to notice, been overwhelmed into inaction, written a check, or simply walked away. As each person tells of his journey, there is a personal moment of revelation in which the course of their giving is altered forever. There was nothing profound that happened, nothing is hidden that others could not see just as clearly—in no case was the moment monumental—but once seen by these philanthropists it forever stayed in view.

Bill and Melinda Gates had their philanthropic direction set by a dense 1993 World Bank report. In their early philanthropic days, the couple read the 329-page report, which measured the economic burden on developing countries of a myriad of infectious diseases that had long since been eradicated from the developed world.[1] As Bill Gates explained later, "In my view—and there is no diplomatic way to put this: the world is failing billions of people. Rich governments are not fighting some of the world's most deadly diseases because rich countries don't have them. . . . I first learned about these tragic health inequities some years ago when I was reading an article about diseases in the developing world. It showed that more than half a million children die every year from "rotavirus." I thought, " 'Rotavirus?'—I've never even heard of it. How could I never have heard of something that kills half a million children every year!?"[2]

Like the Gateses, everyone profiled in this book can point to a moment when their compassion turned into giving; and their giving, into full-blown philanthropy, where something touched them so profoundly that they could not turn away. Nothing is special about rotavirus. Millions have it. Millions know about it. Some have tried to help. But for the Gateses rotavirus was their point of no return.

Each philanthropist here saw something where others (either literally or metaphorically) turned the page, turned off the television, or put it out of their minds. In 1986 Paul Tudor Jones watched Eugene Lang tell the story of his "I Have A Dream" program on a segment of *60 Minutes;* from that day until this Jones has worked to improve education for kids in Bedford-Stuyvesant. On a hot July day in 1985, a billion and a half people watched the LiveAid concert, heard about the agony of Ethiopia's famine and saw the images of human suffering, and then went on with their daily lives. Many wrote checks. The rest just enjoyed the music. But Donna Berber, who was in the Wembly Stadium audience, let the concert resonate inside her for fifteen years, before devoting her energies and her wealth to improving life in Ethiopia. It is this singular unwavering focus in the face of endless obstacles that is a hallmark of a great philanthropist.

Bob and Suzanne Wright sought to improve the care for their grandson suffering with autism; and then for every other similarly afflicted child. Connie Duckworth, a retired Goldman Sachs partner, could not forget about a group of women and their children, who she saw huddled in an abandoned school building in Kabul, Afghanistan. She then set out to improve the economic opportunity for thousands of Afghan women and their children that she did not see. Every person interviewed here at some crucial moment did not turn away—and therein lies their story.

Philanthropy is not just a matter of money. No one should think for a single moment that money is what has made these people great philanthropists. Nine million households in the United States have a net worth in excess of $1 million, and it took more that a $1 billion to make the Forbes 400 list in 2007. Looking at these numbers, it is easy to surmise that giving is simple for the wealthy. After all, how difficult can it be to hand over hundreds of thousands when you have millions, or even millions when your bank account is piled with billions? Yet, if it were that simple, every rich person would be a true philanthropist.

Exceptional philanthropy comes not from fortunes but from commitment. It is the commitment to become deeply involved and—in the face of personal and professional demands—to take on yet another set of responsibilities. None of the people in this book have enough time. They have demanding careers, households full of children or grandchildren, and an array of personal, professional, and civic responsibilities that would overwhelm anyone. They run companies, boards, and marathons. They represent the UN and the local PTA. Yet, despite overwhelming demands, they are willing to forgo retirement, leisure, and even time with their own families to take up the problems of someone else's family.

The men and women in this book are willing to dream big and risk their reputations and resources to solve intractable problems. There has never been a vaccine for a parasite, yet Melinda Gates is undeterred from committing her time and her wealth to the eradication of malaria. When something works and when it does not, these philanthropists persevere, so strong are their beliefs. Failure is not a deterrent, just a step along the way. The problems they have chosen to tackle are mind-boggling in their scope and complexity. Almost entirely free of cynicism, each has taken on a challenge of epic scale without naïveté, but with a determination to succeed. This is a deeply humble group; not one has suggested that he or she has all the answers, and not one has stopped searching.

Those who appear in these pages moved through stages of giving: from intrigue to interest, from check writing to fundraising, and finally from passion to zealotry—in the very best sense of that word. These philanthropists have become ambassadors and spokespeople for what they believe in so strongly. At each step of the way, they fell further and further in love with their causes. And though our conversations did not delve into their religious thinking, many made reference to the fact that life had led them to a point where they might better the lives of others—and that this was as it should be.

I did not find the path I was looking for, and in retrospect I was naïve to think it even existed. Success in giving does not lie on a path, but in a person; in a gathering of traits that emerged from each conversation. As you will hear, their voices are very different, their backgrounds disparate, and their causes all over the map—but themes emerge. In the pages that follow, I will try to distill the characteristics shared by successful, committed philanthropists.

Despite the yellow brick road eluding me, I found a group of highly reflective individuals who had figured out the nuances of their own philanthropic journeys even before I descended upon them with questions. The explanations were clear in their own minds—the inspiring event, the early efforts, the inevitable mistakes, the need to meld their views with those of a spouse, and finally the huge role that serendipity played in both finding their cause and in finding success.

They paint a picture of a self-made group who have bettered their own lives through a combination of talent, hard work, and good fortune and have, in turn, tried to give others the same chance. Two of the couples who I profiled here parted with more than $50 million within weeks of laying their hands on it. Research shows that those who have created their own fortunes gave away more than twice as much money, adjusted for income levels, as those who inherited theirs. Those who created wealth—and perhaps perceived that they could do it again—gave more easily and far more generously.

In every case these philanthropists have focused their giving on helping those with economic, educational, or health care needs and this is not the focus of the majority of American philanthropy. In 2005, Americans deducted $280 billion, or about 2 percent of the nation's gross domestic product, from their tax returns as charitable contributions. This level of giving has remained steady since the mid-1990s. But this label, charitable contributions, is a catchall for a variety of gifts. In the most simplified terms, for every dollar we write off as a nation, less than 31 cents helps those who are economically disadvantaged. For the extremely wealthy, those whose annual earnings exceed $1 million a year, this figure drops down to 22 cents. Despite the rise of Africa as a cause celebre, and the painful and widely touted fact that almost two billion people on the planet live on less than $1.50 a day, only 8 percent of our giving leaves the country. The extremely wealthy spend 34 cents of their philanthropic dollar on the arts. For gifts in excess of $10 million, 63 percent goes to higher education, with most of this concentrated on private universities, despite the fact that 80 percent of all college students attend public institutions. I am not sure that this is how we, as a nation, view our giving. Yet a 2007 study by the University of Indiana for Google assures us that this is true.[3]

In the pages that follow, a broad range of philanthropists will tell their stories. You will hear of the decades-long process whereby they practiced philanthropy with their training wheels on, giving to safe, established charities close to home before setting out on daring, life-changing, failure-risking causes and ventures. In each case this is the end product of years of work learning to become a philanthropist and an innovator. For each of them, this was a journey and I am grateful to them all for allowing us to join them.

WHERE TO BEGIN?

While the old adage that "charity begins at home" is meant to suggest that generosity toward those closest to you comes first. Sy Sternberg, CEO of New York Life, argues with conviction that *not* giving to those closest to you is the first step toward becoming a philanthropist. Sternberg suggests that the first questions anyone with surplus means should ask are about their children. How much should I give them? How much do they need? Are they kids who can handle money or not? Will giving too much ruin them? And the real killer for most parents: having no money motivated me— wouldn't it do the same for them? Sternberg explains, "I had to cross over to the point where I said that I am not giving all of my money to my kids. This is a very important first pass because until you come to that point, that I am not giving all of my money to my kids, then you have a natural constraint on your philanthropy. Once you have decided that you don't want to overload the kids, you can now create a charitable trust and begin the dynamic process of allocation."

Many interviewed here were driven by just this concern, to keep their money out of their children's hands. These are not parents disappointed with their idle, body-piercing, drug-addled, wayward offspring. Some of those being disinherited are still in nursery school. It was not even a question of whether their children would be able to handle a surfeit of resources. These are parents who feel that if they truly love their children, they should give them a hand, and then let them make their own way.

Most of the parents can draw an uninterrupted line from their middle class or more humble beginnings, straight through to the development of ambition, and right on to success. This is an all too familiar trajectory; but how does this drive become ignited if the starting point is flooded with wealth? Warren Buffet's axiom suggests that, "A very rich person should leave his kids enough to do anything but not enough to do nothing." Even for the vast majority of those interested in giving, whose excess wealth may run into the thousands or tens of thousands rather than billions, the calculations for giving away that which is in surplus to a family's needs begins with the question of inheritance. "I'm not an enthusiast for dynastic wealth," Buffet explains, "particularly when six billion others have much poorer hands than we do in life."

DEEPLY HUMBLE

This is a deeply humble group. Although most of the people I interviewed love their philanthropy second only to their families and friends, almost everyone needed to be cajoled to speak with me. Over and over again they said their giving was not about them, and they did not want to publicize themselves. They were not what was important; it was the cause that mattered. Most wanted to keep their lives, their kids, and their businesses out of public view. When I asked if people who were successful givers do not lead in a visible way, how are the rest of us going to follow, that usually won them over.

This is a group of people in possession of resumes others can only dream about. Most were phenomenally successful in their academic endeavors and managed to translate that into professional accomplishment. Yet, in all honesty, they mumble when mentioning their worldly achievements and refer to them in only the vaguest of terms. Here you will find an Olympic gold medal winner, who instead of touting his multiple sporting triumphs, explains how the self-absorption of world-class athletes troubles him. You will read of the vice-chairman of the fifth largest company in America who never mentions his business success but, rather, worries about school districts providing adequate services for autistic children. You will hear about a philanthropist who remains anonymous while he pours millions of dollars into the research and treatment of AIDS.

These philanthropists do not believe they have the answers to the troubles they hope to ameliorate. Each acknowledges that mistakes are to be expected—they are inevitable—and that they are on a journey to learn, and through this process, to better help others. These are people who have been experts in other spheres of life, who have been sought out for their intelligence and expertise in medicine, business, and technology. Yet each has been willing to admit that at some point on their journey they knew nothing and started at square one. Each and every interviewee mentioned time and time again the need to listen and from that to learn. They believe that failure in philanthropy results from those who come to a problem—with which they have no professional expertise, just a very real desire to help—and fail to listen.

They speak about "we" not in a royal sense but to imply that theirs is not a solo endeavor—that ventures like these need a team, a family, a group of experts, and mutual decision making either with spouses, friends, or trusted advisors. They want to promote the organizations that they support as well as their program directors and staffs. They deflect credit like superheroes with a force field, raining it down on everyone around them, including spouses, early mentors, and other givers, most importantly, the recipients of their largesse.

Even the most reluctant of interviewees changed their tune once the conversation began. I have done hundreds of interviews, and never has it been easier than with this crew. I arrived at each appointment with my notebook, an iPod set on record, and three carefully typed pages of questions. Yet my questioning never moved past the first page, often not past the first couple of questions. Sure I chimed in seeking clarification (What year did you begin? Was that what you expected to find? What happened next?), but getting people to talk about the people and things they love is never very hard. They were like proud parents effusing over their offspring, recalling every triumph and discouragement of the journey. It was far more than any interviewer could have hoped for.

Their giving is not abstract. It is not conducted at a distance. Rather, these philanthropists have made very personal connections with those whose lives they have altered. All can quote the facts and figures of their giving—how many tuitions were paid, how many vaccines were administered, or how many rugs were woven and sold. They know the costs of their programs and have ongoing assessments of their organization's accomplishments. But their voices soften and their eyes glow when they tell the stories of the real lives they have affected. This is what their philanthropy has brought them, a narrative to their own lives, part of the story of how their own existence fits into a much larger picture, how it will have mattered to so many others.

There was not a great deal of standing on soap boxes. I heard no lectures on duty or responsibility. Giving here was self-evident. There was just a quiet self-assurance that this is simply what we do. We are here. We can give. And so we do.

No one claimed to be geniuses either. They did not herald themselves as the great thinkers behind the great ideas. Rather, each can trace a path in which they listened to the needs of a community or a person, for example, a class of seventh graders or a physician working in his lab, and they listened to the ideas of others—and something came together. They were conduits, catalysts, sprinklers of magic pixie dust, but they were not geniuses, and they did not act alone.

There was a lot to be boastful about. Lives have been changed. Lives have been saved. The conditions are ripe for egos to run rampant—yet only humility could be found. There is a lot of ego involved with making money, but giving it away seems a far humbler task.

OVERWHELMINGLY LUCKY

All of the people you are about to meet feel lucky. Not the "oh, aren't we so lucky to live in America" cocktail chatter lucky, but profoundly, down to the base of your soul, when-you-meet-your-maker lucky. Each person articulated in some fashion that what stood between their comfortable, safe life and an entirely different existence was nothing more than a paper-thin line.

In their insightful research, Paul G. Schervish, Mary A. O'Herlihy, and John J. Havens of the Center on Wealth and Philanthropy at Boston College distilled what may be the very essence of philanthropy aimed at helping those in need. They interviewed thirty-three young, high-tech entrepreneurs who were committed philanthropists. Schervish and his colleagues asked the entrepreneurs about their giving, which averaged $5 million in forty-four gifts a year, with an average of seventy-three hours a month spent volunteering their time. To the all-important question of why people give, these researchers found that the answer was luck.

Schervish and his fellow researchers explain that "the experience of fortune as partially undeserved, or as resulting in large measure from luck, creates within the wealth holder a sensitivity that others live equally under the influence of the hand of fate. . . . Their sensitivity to the needs of others derives from the fact that their own fortune resulted, as they often put it, from 'being at the right place at the right time.'"[4]

Luck reared its fortunate face in a number of guises; it was a person or a market, an era or a technology, and even more often it was a confluence of events. "The more religiously inclined among the respondents attribute their good fortune to grace or blessing; the more secular speak of luck and good fortune." Schervish's research found that among this group of extremely wealthy and charitable young people, "there is the life-deepening appreciation that they have received vastly more than their efforts might ordinarily deserve. They call upon the lives of their parents and less fortunate individuals as witnesses to the fact that others have worked just as hard and with no less intelligence and have come away with far less financial security or perhaps none at all. . . . If their advantage did not derive solely from virtue, then others' disadvantage did not result from their vice. This, in turn, produces a more or less explicit sense of gratitude."

Among those interviewed here is a sense of awe at what giving could make possible. Money, for each of these philanthropists, was the chance to give others a chance. They grew up middle class or poorer, and now they had the ability to create security and opportunity for others where none had existed before.

Connie Duckworth often speaks to groups of young women on the verge of their careers, struggling with the pull between the lucrative private sector and their hopes of helping others. She tells them there is no conflict. If you are fortunate enough—and work hard enough to excel in something that pays well—you will have no end of opportunities to help others. Money bestows power, and as Connie explains, it bestows the power to do good.

The corollary to luck seems to be empathy. And this powerful resonance of shared humanity, rather than a sense of guilt or duty, led to committed philanthropy. A sense of hyperidentification seems to be present among these philanthropists. They do not look upon others with the distance that pity creates; rather, they see themselves in another's life. In the midst of athletic training at the highest level, preparing to compete on the world stage, Johann Olav Koss encountered a group of boys who loved sports every bit as much as he did, but who did not even have a ball to play with. He watched this group of twelve-year-old boys in a refugee camp in Eritrea and remembered that he was once one of them—a youth hoping to play sports. His identification with these boys was so deep that his being Norwegian and their being Eritrean was inconsequential. The differences in time, place, age, and nationality all fell away.

HIGHLY ENGAGED

At the outset of this project, I fully expected to meet people who were highly engaged with their philanthropy. I selected them precisely for this reason. These people are altering the lives of elementary school teachers and the young students in their classrooms, of whole villages across Africa, of entire graduating classes in inner city high schools, and of those who have been the victims of terror in Cambodia, Rwanda, and Uganda. But the word "engaged" does not truly reflect the passion that those interviewed here bring to their causes. Philanthropy was the love affair they did not expect.

Each philanthropist acts as far more than a financier for their cause. They have been almost evangelical about recruiting friends, families, acquaintances, and everyone who crosses their path to donate whatever might be helpful. All have created something new through their efforts and have been party to the process of innovation in giving. Melinda Gates shook up the scientific world when she invited them to focus on the diseases of the developing world through her "Grand Challenges," and as a result, more than one thousand scientists responded. With a powerful Web site, Peter Bloom has linked the giving public, or what he calls citizen philanthropists, with every classroom in America. Both Gates and Bloom, as well as the others who tell their stories here, believe that our biggest social problems can be solved only with radical new approaches.

Venturing into an area where they have little expertise and no formal training frightens many people. They fear being uncovered as frauds or simply looking stupid. Those profiled on these pages were either not plagued by this problem, or they were so dedicated to their causes that they did not let it get in their way. The Wrights admitted to knowing next to nothing about autism—until they devoted their lives to it. These philanthropists took on something huge, often far outside the confines of their expertise; undaunted by the challenge and willing to accept mistakes, they simply forged ahead. Maybe in the still of the night, faced with their own demons they had fears, but not in the light of day with their interviewer.

Gathered here are a nurse, a few Wall Street types, veterans of the high-tech world, the CEO of a major network, the CEO of an oil company, a full-time mother, a special education teacher, an Olympic athlete, and a couple of doctors. With backgrounds in the for-profit world, they are underwhelmed by the traditional world of nonprofits and foundations, and their views range from skepticism to mistrust, right through to outright disdain. There is a unanimous sense, and no one passed up the opportunity to tell me, that a revolution is taking place in the not-for-profit sector, and their causes are breaking new ground. Not one of them feels bound by the way things have been done in the past.

These are folks that by and large have not quit their day jobs. The word "philanthropists" conjures up images of those in the final years of life, removed from the hurly-burly, cloaked in bed jackets, or hooked up to oxygen tanks while they consult with lawyers and craft and recraft their wills. Many of those written about here are still in the office, or their cause has become a new office. Most are under sixty. Many are under fifty. This book is for those like them who have a nagging feeling that they should be doing more. It is for those who need to or want to stay with the day job, but have skills, time, or money they would like to use to improve someone else's life. It is for people who know that they had chances that were "unfair": a shot at a great education, a crack at a first-rate job, or even excellent health. And who also know that if they could give others any one of these things, their lives would be better for it as well.

CONCENTRIC CIRCLES

I never discovered a path because one does not exist. Philanthropy seems to run in concentric circles, beginning with that which is closest to us both physically and emotionally, and spreading out to encompass that which is less personally immediate and self-serving.

Many of those profiled here experienced their philanthropy in ever-expanding concentric circles. They started giving to the causes nearest to them—their kids' schools, their churches and temples, their local community service providers, or the research organizations for any disease that had touched their families. This is philanthropy in bite-size manageable pieces, and it is necessary education for everything that follows. Over time they moved away from causes that touched their own lives and on to causes and people who were previously far removed from them. Their circles widened to include KwaZulu-Natal, Bedford-Stuyvesant, Ethiopia, Cambodia, Denver, south Boston, and the Bronx. They entered the worlds of genetic mapping, college counseling, or refugee camps. It was a huge step—from that of giving which benefits the donor, to that in which the donor does not even share a tangential benefit—and one that took them into entirely different realms.

Each person stressed, some more than once, that philanthropy does not require piles of cash or the desire to save the world. Each told of how they began their philanthropy long before they had wealth, by giving small dollar amounts to manageable causes that they easily could wrap their heads and hands around. These first efforts were their apprenticeships. Through these early gifts they learned about what mattered to them and about the most effective role they could play. Local church fundraisers were the practice runs for multimillion-dollar capital campaigns. Early advocacy efforts in the school auditorium were the training for interviews with the national press. But perhaps most important was the notion put forth by Tim Dibble, that without his early forays into philanthropy—and the experiences and insights that this gave him and his wife—they would have been unable to recognize a truly exceptional program when they saw it.

THE LONG HAUL

I may have been looking for an easy answer, but no one here is looking for a quick fix. These philanthropists are not focused on immediate impact. While each closely watches the organizations they support—assuring that they adhere to budgets, that milestones are met, and that measurable results are collected and reported—they know that the most profound changes may be decades away and elude easy measurement. Each person articulated both that the process of changing people's lives was a lengthy one, and that their own commitment would match that challenge. Much philanthropy is transient, our knee-jerk response to a passing need or a tragedy. Such philanthropy involves construction or immediate relief; the giver achieves his goal and with it the huge satisfaction of having helped someone and completed a job. But these philanthropists are involved in a very different kind of endeavor, one designed to alter the course of others' lives. Connie Duckworth summed up the lasting impact her program could have when she quoted one of her weavers: "I weave so that my daughter will not have to."

LOOK FOR SATISFACTION

While many of these philanthropists look like angels, they are not saints. Each apologized in advance of spouting what they knew to be a cliché—that they get far more than they give. They wanted to make it clear: this may be a well-worn saying, but that does not mean it is not true. Donna Berber admitted that she needed to help people in Ethiopia, and her good fortune had given her the means to do so. About this she was explicit. Although others had benefited from her largess, the giving had brought great joy to her own life. Connie Duckworth listed the rewards of her philanthropy. Thousands of women in Afghanistan earned a steady wage while they and their daughters learned to read and write. In addition, she had traveled both literally and figuratively to worlds where she had never been. Others described their rewards as ethereal; life had been enriched.

This gathering does not conduct its philanthropy at arm's length. Their satisfaction comes because their philanthropy is up close and personal. They need to travel to Africa, to meet the graduating high schoolers, on to read the letters of thanks that pour in from classrooms around the country. They want to see and hear and touch their philanthropy, and in doing so they find many of their rewards. Melinda Gates often speaks about her and Bill's philanthropy as a deeply personal matter, and she highlights the importance of their relationships with those they are trying to help: "I think it's important for people to understand that this will be our lifetime work and our commitment; we're going to stick to the issues we're working on now for as long as they take. And that it's brought a fulfillment to our lives in a way that is hard to describe. . . . That you can have this incredible career, and you can do something else that gives back to the world in a way that deeply fulfills your life is something we both want people to have some sense of. It's why we do what we do."[5]

Almost without exception, every interviewee mentioned his or her spouse when discussing their giving. Philanthropy for most was a partnership. It was a journey they were taking together. For some this was explicit. The Wrights run their organization as a couple; ditto the Gateses, the Marquezes, the Aldermans, and the Berbers. For other couples the partnership is more informal; a joint decision-making process involves consulting and supporting each other in their passion.

THEY ALL THINK BIG—REALLY BIG

Arzu Rugs is an economic model that can be replicated anywhere in the world where the local population has artistic skills that economically developed countries value. When she saw the plight of squatters in Kabul, Connie Duckworth could easily have doled out donations. She could have gone into the rug business and paid a surplus wage to those who worked for her. But she saw a much larger endeavor, one that involved whole villages along with their education and health care. Johann Olav Koss began Right to Play with early efforts in Eritrea, and now he has programs in twenty countries. Year Up, a model of education and training, began in Boston; but as I interviewed its chairman, Tim Dibble, he was immersed in finding directors for its offices in California and Texas. The Aldermans' efforts at healing the psychic wounds of terrorism and genocide have spread from Southeast Asia into Africa and Eastern Europe. As of June 2007, DonorsChoose.org reaches every public school classroom in the United States, and Peter Bloom notes that requests to expand the program come in from other countries every week.

Sandwiched between this book's covers are stories about people who saw the scope of the problems they were addressing very early on, and from the outset developed programs that could be scaled up to meet a much broader set of needs. In each tale these philanthropists took on a problem in such a way that the solution had a far-reaching impact. Had Tim and Bernie Marquez chosen a single Denver high school for their scholarship program, they would have given hundreds of kids a shot at college. Instead, they took on the whole school district and now they are eyeing the whole state. So much less would have still been so much. These are people whose real life has far outstripped their dreams, so they have learned to dream bigger.

WANTED TO GIVE TO EACH AND EVERY ONE

While I lay myself open to the criticism that I have learned nothing from my research and that a scattershot approach to giving still prevails in my house, after each and every interview, I wanted to write a check. This may speak to my aforementioned disorganized approach to philanthropy, but I think it says more about the fact that this a group of people who has chosen to devote a sizable part of their lives and fortunes to some phenomenally compelling causes. Their devotion acts like a magnet toward other people's money.

They are successful philanthropists not only because of their commitment, but also because of their ability to articulate and therefore leverage that commitment. All are vigorous advocates of their efforts. While each recognizes that there is much need in the world, they all make powerful cases for the causes to which they have chosen to devote themselves.

By sticking with their deepest concerns, these philanthropists have found the best way to realize their dreams. By not letting go of the passion that never let go of them, they have altered hundreds or thousands or even millions of lives. They have found what can only be described as a calling, and I looked this up, "a strong inner impulse toward a particular course of action." Through that calling they have chosen to devote themselves in service to others far beyond the confines of their immediate worlds. It is as heroic as it is challenging, and their ability to dream big, persist in that dream, and ultimately prevail must be a lesson for the rest of us.

Be the Change

*From fifty-two years of observation, the people who I see in life that are the
happiest, the most fulfilled, and have a sparkle in their eyes are those who
have a huge component of service in their lives and in some form or fashion
give to other people besides themselves.*

— *Paul Tudor Jones, speaking to Darden School Poverty Symposium*

I N 1955, GENE BAUER, A FORMER LOS ANGELES HIGH
school art teacher, and her husband bought a property in the San Bernardino Mountains to use as a weekend retreat. They built a small vacation cottage there, which they later moved into on a permanent basis. Starting in 1957, Bauer began to plant daffodils after she had saw how they thrived in her neighbor's yard. The first year she planted fifty bulbs and was delighted with the result. The following year she planted more; and each year after that, even more, until she planted 35,000 bulbs in 1993 alone. Now she has more than one million daffodils of 500 varieties planted on her hill, some of which have been in the ground for as long as forty years. Fifty-one years after sowing that first bulb, she has covered her five-acre garden, and during a magical three-week spell each Spring,

visitors from around the world visit her home to witness a sea of colorful blooms. Bauer planted every bulb herself, by hand, one at a time. She has arranged her gorgeous flowers by color and has in effect painted her hill with flowers.

Paul Tudor Jones, the legendary hedge fund manger, views Bauer's work as a parable for philanthropy. Forget about beginning with a big splash, a huge press conference, or an outsized donation. Great things, Jones will tell you, are built over decades. Helping other people begins with the first step, of doing just a bit each day, so that at some point when you turn around and look, there is a body of work—something real and important and tangible—that changed other people's lives.

"We started Robin Hood in my apartment right after the crash of '87. At that time there were three or four of us, and we didn't really have any idea where we were going," Jones explains. "We just knew that we wanted to help people in need [to get] out of their dire situation[s]. At that point in time, if you had told me that twenty years later we would have given out something almost pushing $1 billion, I would have said to you that that's impossible. If you had told me that our first grant of $300,000 was going to grow to this year where we are giving away $130 million, I would have bet the under until the cows came home. I don't think we really knew where we were going with Robin Hood. It just began to evolve and take on a life of its own because it was a beautiful thing. You just need to find something that you a have a passion for, something that makes you want to get up out of your seat. That is certainly how I got involved. Poverty in New York City was something just so compelling that I could not just sit by and watch it happen."[1]

The Robin Hood Foundation Web site lays out Jones' case. One in five New Yorkers lives in poverty. One-third of women who are abused return to abusive partners because they cannot find housing. Fifty percent of youth that age out of foster care end up homeless or in jail. For Jones these were facts from which he simply could not turn away.

Jones's philanthropy covers so many disparate efforts, it is almost impossible to know where to begin. His passion and compassion touch organizations from the National Fish and Wildlife Foundation, to the Everglades Foundation, to a wild life preserve in East Africa. But it is perhaps the Robin Hood Foundation for which he is the best known. Many have heard of the foundation because of its phenomenal fund raising efforts, including a yearly dinner that boasts famed comedians and world famous rock bands and raised more than $48 million in a single night in 2007. Others know it because of the high profile board members, many of whom are corporate CEOs or media figures who support the foundation's vast efforts in fighting poverty.

It is not the patina of glamour that surrounds the Robin Hood Foundation but, rather, the challenge of combating poverty in New York City that absorbs Jones. Robin Hood, as the name implies, raises money from its board of directors and a broad cross section of wealthy New Yorkers; and then through careful study of poverty reduction programs, makes more than 200 grants a year to organizations of every size. The foundation is built on a few solid, but once revolutionary, principles. Every dollar donated goes straight to the programs Robin Hood supports, as the affluent board of directors absorbs all operating expenses. Robin Hood searches the city for effective poverty fighting measures and then partners—truly partners—with those efforts to bring about their success. The word "partnership" is loosely and meaninglessly thrown around in the nonprofit world. But for Robin Hood a real partnership means finding talented board members for their grantees, as well as providing pro bono human resources guidance and expertise, legal work, technology expertise, management assistance, and long-range planning. Robin Hood operates up close and personal. The foundation's board could meet anywhere in the world, from fancy Manhattan offices to the worlds' most exclusive resorts. But throughout the foundation's history, this gathering of luminaries has chosen to go where their money goes, and on a quarterly basis they have been meeting at the various sites of the projects they fund, even when it has meant the prison on Rikers Island.

Unlike other foundations, many of which disburse only the IRS-mandated 5 percent of funds raised per year, Robin Hood gives it almost all away. Whatever the foundation takes in each year, it gives out the following year, holding back only a small amount for a reserve. "We're not in the wealth-building business. That dog ain't going to hunt," explains Jones.[2] Robin Hood disburses money to programs that do work in all areas of social services from education, employment, housing, and health care to teen pregnancy and alternatives for youth offenders. "Why put away money for a rainy day when it's pouring out?" asks David Saltzman, executive director of Robin Hood. "New York City is arguably the richest city in the history of the world, and yet the majority of babies were born into poverty last year. Why would we keep powder dry under those circumstances?"[3]

Jones's philanthropy has been an extraordinary journey. Many of the innovations that he brought to Robin Hood have done no less than change the face of philanthropy across the country. Robin Hood has been a major innovator both in evaluating the effectiveness of the programs it supports and in supporting its grantees in every way possible. An M.I.T.-trained economist runs an intensive evaluation process that assesses the impact of every program the foundation supports. Each program is reviewed in terms of the ultimate effect it will have on the earning power of the individuals it seeks to help.

Jones's commitment over the past two decades has extended to weekly visits to Bedford-Stuyvesant in his efforts to raise the level of education and aspiration in one of New York's roughest neighborhoods. "I love education because I love kids," he says. "If I retired, I'd love to teach second, third, or fourth grade. I also like education because I think it has the greatest multiplicative powers in terms of the ultimate good you're going to do for the hours and dollars expended."[4]

Jones may have left Memphis as a young man, but part of Memphis never left him. With his flat Tennessee drawl, he tells of the many lessons he has learned in two decades of trying to bring educational opportunity to a place he loves in Brooklyn.

LISA: You have told the daffodil story as a parable for how people can begin their philanthropic lives. Gene Bauer has said that she had no idea where she was headed when she just began planting.

PAUL: The point is that she started with an attitude of taking one step at a time, placing one foot in front of the other without worrying too much about the big picture. Then she just kept adding single steps. Her body of work is huge, and she's amassed so much over her lifetime, but it was all accomplished by the accumulation of small steps, of just making sure that each day she did something, however small. It brings to mind Confucius' famous saying of how the longest journey begins with the first step. Gene can look back now and see how her journey has brought so much pleasure to so many people, but it was a journey built on a series of small daily steps.

I think the key thing for any young person to realize is it really doesn't make any difference where you start; what's important is you just simply start. And as you start, it's important to realize it's just the beginning of a long, incredible, and unpredictable journey. Along the way, of course, you'll be able to chart milestones and see progress, but it's only at the end of the journey that you'll be able to look back and fully appreciate the enormous amount of good will you've created and good works you've done. And it's really amazing to see the fruits of your efforts in full like that. Sometimes, though, it can be hard to envision this future, especially in the midst of setbacks or roadblocks, which you will inevitably encounter. But no success or failure is ever final, so when you're in one of those rough patches, I think it's vital to ask not so much what is the impact that you're having this moment, this day, this week, or this year, but rather what will be the cumulative impact over a lifetime? And it's astonishing both to contemplate and behold. But it still takes that first step, and that's why I tell young people it doesn't make any difference where they start or what it is they start with, just find something and start. Find a neighborhood or find anything you're passionate about and just start with baby steps. You might think they're not significant, but they're hugely significant in the ultimate scheme of things.

Your own philanthropy, how did it start?

My twenties were my lost years because I was doing everything but thinking of other people. I was completely self-centered, but self-centeredness was the operative ethic in those days. The twenty-year-old today seems to have a completely different ethic than when I was growing up, much less selfish, much more concerned with the welfare of others and the wider world. In my twenties, Gordon Gekko and his "Greed is good" philosophy were revered, and ostentatious materialism was a noble pursuit. But the attitude changed after the stock market crash of '87, maybe because that was the terminal event of the very visible and gluttonous greed of the '80s. After the crash, I think people's thoughts and ideas here in the business community of New York City and on college campuses across the country changed. Helping your fellow man became a really important facet in everybody's life. People realized that it was just as important, if not more so, to help people in poverty than it was to be on the Board of the Met or the Museum of Natural History.

My real philanthropy as an adult, then, began in 1986, while I was watching a *60 Minutes* piece about Gene Lang. The piece discussed how he had gone back and given the sixth-grade commencement address at the Harlem school where he had graduated. While there, he discovered that the college acceptance rate for the kids in this school was less than 10 percent. He was so distressed by those numbers that on the spur of the moment he told those kids that if they graduated from high school, he would pay for their college education. From that promise the I Have A Dream Program was born. Anyway, I saw that piece on TV and was so moved that I called Gene Lang the next day and said, "That sounds like fun for me. I would like to participate." He said, "Great, I've had a few other phone calls. Let's all meet at my apartment next week." When I got to that meeting, there were about six people there, and they had already split up Manhattan and the rest of New York City, divvying up neighborhoods we'd each be responsible for. I was late so of course I got the area no one wanted. They gave me Bed-Stuy.

Had you spent any time in Bedford-Stuyvesant at that point in the 1980s?

From 1986 on I have spent every Tuesday there, but prior to that, no, I'd never spent any meaningful time in Bed-Stuy. Once I was assigned Bed-Stuy, I went to the graduation of a sixth-grade class at, I think, P.S. 85. I went without any background, training, or anything other than the financial wherewithal and the big heart necessary to make a difference. I adopted a class and began an after school program and promised them all that if they graduated from high school, I'd put them through college. That was in May of '86, and that was my first real step toward giving back, of repaying New York City for the great things it had done for me. I came to New York in '76, right after I graduated from college. I did real well here, and I always felt I owed the city a debt. Sponsoring that Bed-Stuy sixth-grade class was my first step toward paying off that debt, as well as my first step onto the road of philanthropy, and it was a profoundly great experience in many ways, but it was also an eye-opening experience.

Then came the Crash of '87. Personally, that was a great day in the market for me, but I was convinced we were going into a depression. I picked up the phone and got both Glenn Dubin and my friend Peter Borish on the line. I told them we had to do something, because we were going into a great depression and people were going to be starving. That's the day, the moment the Robin Hood Foundation was born, and from that moment on, the I Have A Dream Program and the Robin Hood Program have become the parallel and complementary tracks I've ridden on my personal fight against poverty.

We started Robin Hood because there were almost no charities dedicated solely to helping the poor whose ranks, we thought, were about to swell greatly. We were wrong about the depression. That never happened. But what we learned was there were still untold numbers of impoverished people who desperately needed help.

One of the crucial lessons I learned from the I Have A Dream Program was how extraordinarily difficult it is to actually have a meaningful, positive impact on people—unless you have the right skills and technologies. And I learned that the hard way. You can write a check, and you can have an impact, but one doesn't necessarily beget the other; that is, mere money doesn't guarantee a positive impact. I learned this in '91, after I was five years into I Have A Dream.

What were you doing for those five years?

We had an after school program that students came to every day during the week. We hired a program coordinator, who was not an educator but was a great person. We provided a study hall and helped the kids with their homework. We played some sports and had some other organized activities. That was probably the first year or two.

And you are not running this at a distance? You are deeply involved and spending time with the kids?

I went to Bed-Stuy every week. I took the kids on ski trips. I even built a log cabin for them at my home down in Virginia, and I took them there once or twice a year. I was investing an enormous amount of personal time in addition to spending approximately $5,000 per child per year, and this went on for a couple of years, but it wasn't having the impact I'd hoped for.

We had two Dreamers—that's what we called the students, Dreamers; we had two Dreamers who were killed, murdered. By the beginning of 1990 or 1991, we had had probably a dozen pregnancies. One girl, a tenth grader, had a miscarriage at my house in Virginia on one of our field trips. We had another girl who suffered from schizophrenia, who started to hurt herself. Some of these kids were in gangs or doing drugs and were confronting a whole host of social issues which I was ill-equipped to handle. It was an eye-opening experience, to say the least.

All of a sudden, in 1990, some researchers from Harvard said they wanted to evaluate the results of our program for a study they were conducting, and I agreed to let them. I had never really thought about testing for results. I was so busy devoting more energy and more financial and more emotional capital than you can possibly even begin to imagine that it never even crossed my mind to monitor the results. I'd just never thought about looking to see the kind of impact we were having. As far as measuring results, the most I did was have a report card night during which all the students brought in their report cards. After I saw their grades, I'd say, "Come on, can't we do a little better?" I was the ultimate cheerleader.

About six months after the Harvard researchers came to study our students, they returned with results that basically found the original I Have A Dream Program had no distinguishable positive impact; that is, there was little difference between the kids attending I Had A Dream and the kids in the same neighborhood who were going to school and not attending the after school program. In other words, my five years of intervention had a negligible and statistically indecipherable impact. That completely devastated and baffled me. I thought, "Oh my God, I have invested all this time, I've spent all this money, and I have had zero impact on these kids." Most important, I felt as if I'd totally failed these kids. But that sense of utter failure was transformational for me.

It was because of my failure at I Have A Dream that I realized you can spend all the money in the world, you can have the greatest idea in the world, you can throw all the energy and all the physical capital you have at a problem, but unless you have the right technology, the right delivery mechanism, and the right intellectual capital to solve these problems and, unless you have articulated goals and have a proven methodology that will allow you to achieve those goals, then everything else you are doing is simply fluff. My idea of getting these kids through college, while a great idea, wasn't doing anything to help those children, and I realized that until I changed how I was doing things, I would only continue to fail them. It really was my blinding light on the road to Damascus.

I was too late for our original eighty-six kids, but we still had some successes among them, despite my mistakes. We got about a quarter of them into college, which was double the neighborhood average, but it was still far short of our goal. Probably the reason we were able to get as many as we did into college was that we walked those kids through the admissions process and made them believe they could do it. Many of them did poorly, and many of them did well, and many of them dropped out. Our after school program had not prepared them adequately for the various social and intellectual rigors of college.

So things changed. I began adopting new classes, and in 1991, I hired a new after school project administrator and charged her with educating the kids. While I was great at being the kids' best friend, I acknowledged that I was terrible at actually teaching them academic skills, social skills, and a whole variety of coping mechanisms they would need as they matured and went to college. The program's new goal was to prepare these kids academically not only to get into college but to graduate and be able to get a better job with their education, and that was the focus of the new administrator. The year 1991 was a real turning point because this was when our after school program started to be run by a great educator. I Had A Dream became all business, and the business was,

"You're going to become academically proficient so that you'll be equipped to go get a higher education."

When I look back, I see it was naïve and foolish to think that I was going to take on eighty-six inner-city kids and all the social, psychological, emotional, financial, and academic challenges they had, with no training, no expertise, no experience, and no concept of what I was to do. I was doomed to fail before I even started.

My initial approach certainly wasn't a waste of time, because I did learn a lot and we did have some successes, but it certainly wasn't the way to go about solving the problem at hand, which was to try to get those eighty-six kids into college. Again, you can write a check, but that check is not going to do any good unless those students are actually engaged in the process that will make them proficient enough to achieve the goal of graduating from college.

I was able to funnel that knowledge into the operations at Robin Hood. I had five years of experience and $3 million to show that having the money and the desire to solve problems doesn't mean problems will get solved. Just because I'm opening a drug-free hotline doesn't mean it's going to help kids get off drugs. I use that example because it calls to mind the early days at Robin Hood, when we funded what I think was our worst grant ever. We funded someone on a drug hotline who actually ended up selling drugs on the hotline.

The reality is that when you're fighting poverty you're going to have a whole variety of failures in much the same way you do with any kind of business challenge, and we were in the business of defeating poverty. Success required—and requires—constant monitoring, articulation of goals, articulation of technologies to achieve those goals, monitoring of the delivery mechanisms along the way, monitoring how people are doing en route to achieving those goals, and holding people accountable during the entire process.

At the end of the day, the client for us at Robin Hood was a person living in poverty, and the clients for me at I Have A Dream were those children. Their needs had to come before and above anything else. Once I started thinking of it in those terms and with that frame of reference, everything changed. Instead of approaching the problem with a warm, fuzzy attitude of "Gee, I'm here and I'm ladling out soup in this soup kitchen and I feel so good," I approached instead with the attitude of, "What have I got to do to help accomplish that goal? Am I doing something that is going to have a positive impact?" Once you start thinking in terms of the actual consequences of your actions, you devote more careful thought to the best use of your time, your money, your energy, and your love. And once you've adopted that approach, you completely alter, in a more fruitful, positive way, the ultimate impact you're going to have.

Early philanthropy for you sounds like a crucial step to where you are now.

Early philanthropy for me was exactly like trading. I don't think you can be a great trader unless you have had a near-death experience in the market, unless you have nearly lost everything at least once. Hopefully, you do that when you are young. I did that in my early twenties, when I had $10,000 to my name and lost $9,900 of it. I was down to 100 bucks and I thought, "I'm dead, I'm finished for life."

Those near-death experiences are how you learn, and they become the building blocks for later in life. My failure in the early days of I Have A Dream—how I failed those kids actually (and I feel bad for those kids because we should have done a better job)—became the building blocks for what became thousands of future successes in a variety of different philanthropic involvements.

Probably it was really important for me to have four or five of what I consider to be losses. I had a great time with all of those kids. I took them to Africa, I took them skiing; we saw the whole world. Very few inner-city kids have had the experiences those kids had. We added so many different qualitative experiences to their lives. But did they actually gain tools and skills to help them navigate college, which was the purpose of the program? Maybe I enriched their lives, but I didn't do anything to help those kids attain a higher education. I did very little for those first kids, certainly only a fraction of what we did in versions two and three of the I Have A Dream Program.

Are there intangibles that you also have to account for? Are there things that are important but cannot be easily measured?

I'm sure that there are a bunch of positive intangibles. Having someone come over to spend as much time with them as I did, providing them love and a lot of attention—I'm sure that I gave a whole bunch of them a higher faith in mankind because I gave so much of myself personally to them. But I get back to what the original focus of the program was, which was to help them graduate from college. That was the metric by which I was judging myself. I guess what I'm saying is that despite all the positive things that came from our interaction in all those early years, I was largely focused on my inability to meet the explicit objective of that program. That failure had a huge impact on me, and it certainly made me look at helping people in a much different way.

From that experience Robin Hood did everything differently. Was funding now an entirely metric-driven decision?

We try to quantify everything. When we approach our philanthropy at Robin Hood right now, we really do it with a hard edge—we really look at metrics. If it's a job-training program we want to know how much somebody's income has improved, not just in twelve months but also forty-eight months out. Are we truly giving someone a skill set? We also look to see if we are helping someone who already has a job or was going to get a job without our intervention as opposed to someone who actually wasn't going to get a job without our help. There are so many different ways you can peel the onion to measure your impact.

Every year in December we have our Robin Hood Heroes Breakfast; we bring in people we think have been the most emblematic of what constitutes a real hero in terms of helping our fellow man. I'd say that's the greatest hour of my year, and I venture to guess that's the case for everyone who attends that breakfast. At that time, all those intangibles you ask about are on display. We find the very best elements humanity has to offer, and we put them on display. No one is really getting up there and saying our program did x, y, z and we graduated fifty-six people. They're getting up and sharing their personal experiences, and as you listen, you get a concrete sense that at the root of every one of these programs is a binding of all involved, which is formed by sharing what is best in each of us, what is best in humanity. You find at the event that it's a communal relationship of friendship and love that supersedes the more obvious and measurable metrics of "I'm in a job-training program" or "We're providing shelter to homeless families." What comes out at our Robin Hood breakfast is there is this shared feeling of humanity among everyone in this room, where, for example, a formerly addicted crack head who's telling his story stands twenty feet from a self-made billionaire who doesn't even know what crack looks like. The crack head and the billionaire have found this touching moment of shared success because they have truly helped each other. So in that room everyone gets to enjoy the intangibles that come from philanthropy.

At the core, I think all human beings are good. The great thing about philanthropy is it enables you find the most beautiful elements in a person and bring them out. That's why it's such an exciting thing to be involved with. George Fox, the founder of the Quakers, said we should cheerfully walk over this earth seeking that of God in all people. Working in philanthropy allows me to do precisely that.

Robin Hood was considered very cutting edge when you started your evaluative work in the 1990s, and it seems everyone's followed behind you. Have your views changed at all?

I still say that, at the end of the day, the critical thing about trying to help somebody is effectiveness. The more I think about it and the more I'm involved, the more I realize that intellectual capital is so much more important than financial capital, emotional capital, or time on task. You'll just never find a substitute for being able to think through a problem and deciphering the best way to attack it. Of course, the next step is the huge task of implementing those procedures correctly, and this requires great leadership. All the great organizations have great leaders who set and maintain the necessary tone and culture. The culture of the organization is so critically important. When I talk about intellectual capital, I'm thinking about it in terms of who can set the cultural tone for that organization and get everyone believing in that guiding mission statement. The way you get people excited about that mission statement is to convince them the program is effective and is going to have success after success. People really enjoy being part of a winning team; it's just human nature.

The way you get people to work sixty- or seventy-hour weeks is to get them to see that their work is having an outsized impact and to realize that if they didn't do their jobs there would be a huge hole. People give those extra hours and put in that extra effort because they know they're getting some multiplicative return on their time, and that's critical.

By the year 2000, things had changed with the I Have A Dream Program. Originally we took kids in and told them we were going to help them whether they liked it or not. In subsequent years we went out into the community and advertised for seventh graders who were interested. If people wanted to attend, they had to sign contracts which stipulated that they agreed to attend the after school program at least four days a week. If they failed to meet the attendance requirement, we could terminate them from the program. We also told them that if they followed our program, we would give them the financial equivalent of a full scholarship to attend a SUNY college.

A lot of kids dropped out after a period of time, and we said, "Okay, that's your choice." That was version two of our I Have A Dream Program, and of the thirty students we took in each year, approximately twenty or less would finish the program. I realized from those dropout rates that there was going to be a whole generation of students that was lost to the streets because our after school program still wasn't meeting a critical need. It was really just a Band-Aid. It was a terrible substitute for having a kid in a great educational program all day long.

Around 2000, I realized how crazy the situation was. I was still spending $5,000 to $6,000 per student and I was still expending a huge amount of time and effort, but I still wasn't moving the needle like I knew we could. We were getting almost all of our after school program kids into college, and they were staying in college and graduating, but the dropout rate from what was our starting group of kids was still much too high.

The one-third that did not commit?

Yes, the one-third that did not stick with it. It was a failure rate that really troubled me. This program wasn't designed just for the gifted kids or the kids whose parents pushed them or the kids who had the vision to grasp what we could do for them and so worked hard. We had to touch everyone, so that's when I went to apply for a charter school.

This is I Have A Dream 3.0 now?

This was the end of I Have A Dream and the beginning of me adopting what I thought would be a more effective way of showing that I still loved these kids, I still loved Bed-Stuy, and I was still going to have a positive impact on the community. By that time I had been going to Bed-Stuy for so long, I genuinely loved the place. It is a wonderful, wonderful community. But for my resources to have the greatest impact on that community, I knew the best thing was to start a school and stop relying on an after school program. No more Band-Aids. We were going to start from scratch. I had also learned that starting with a kid in seventh grade was way too late. So I applied for a K–8 charter school.

One of the surprising things evident in the I Have A Dream Program was that of all the kids graduating, 80 percent were girls. Boys—look, I can say this because I am a guy—boys are just knuckleheads until they are in their midtwenties. They're so far behind girls in so many crucial ways. I started thinking that the best way for me to have the biggest impact on Bed-Stuy was to start a school for boys. I thought the best way to attack poverty was to start an all-boys' school, because preparing these boys to go to and graduate from college would enable them to be breadwinners and contributing coheads of families. In my mind, that was the easiest, quickest way to have a significant impact.

So we started the first all-male elementary charter school in America. Ninety-eight percent of its students are African American. We put our application in, and then I sought the services of the first coexecutive director of Robin Hood, a guy named Norman Atkins, who had left to start a private school in Newark, New Jersey, and did a brilliant job. He then got involved with another inner-city school in Roxbury, Massachusetts, and again had tremendous success. I got him to provide the intellectual capital we needed, because I knew nothing about running a school.

What I knew by 2000 was that I wanted a boys' school that was going to be as good as any prep school going, including the one I went to and the one my son currently goes to. I went to an all-boys' private school in Memphis, Tennessee, and my son goes to one in

Greenwich. I wanted to be able to compete with those schools, and that was the standard we set from the very beginning. That was the charge. When I say the best, I mean top decile academics, top decile athletics, and socially well-rounded with a heavy emphasis on character development, which is exactly all that an upper-tier school offers. I wanted my son to say that he wanted to go to this school or to actually attend it (which he doesn't, because it is too far away). To make a long story short, we opened the doors to our school, and four years later we came in seventh out of 720 public schools in fourth-grade citywide testing.

The journey began with a loosely articulated process that offered no structure, no focus, no goals, and no accountability, and it wound its way to an educational edifice that provides the best in education and educational services, all because I solicited the help of someone who had a proven track record of the success I hoped to achieve. He knew what it took to get us into the top decile of student performance, to make sure our school had the right technologies, and to guarantee we would have a board of very smart like-minded people, who would provide him with whatever resources we needed to accomplish our task.

Boy, that school's something else. I named the school Excellence.

It's called Excellence?

Yes, because I wanted all people to understand from the second that they walked through our door what we stood for.

There must be huge demand to get into the school. How are the kids chosen?

It's a lottery system. There is no preferential selection (except for siblings), which was my intention from the very beginning. I wanted everyone to know from the very first moment they entered the school that regardless of who they were or how intellectually challenged they might be, we were going to help them be the best they could be. I wanted each boy to know that whether he was a boy genius or was destined for a white-collar job or not, we were going to ask that he give 110 percent toward everything he did in this school. We simply wanted each student to understand that all he had to do was try as hard as he could, and that has kind of been our motto. And it's worked. Of all the things I am and have been involved with over the years, this school has got to be the one thing that has brought me the greatest joy. Excellence is located in an old brick school built over a hundred years ago. It had been condemned and was going to be torn down. It was completely bombed out because of a fire. We rebuilt every inch of it and put a playground on the roof.

This school has transformed the entire community. And one more thing: The academic workload at this school is so much tougher than that at my son's school, it's embarrassing. It is embarrassing how much tougher it is.

Is this the model now? Does this get replicated?

Yes. Not only did we just apply for our second school, which will be an all-girls' school, but we have been an example to a number of people who are getting ready to start schools based on what they have seen at Excellence. Many are trying to establish single-sex schools. We probably have three to five schools a week that come in to see what it is we are doing. The reason Excellence works is because of the culture, which is different from that of most public schools. It is the defining difference. We have established and maintained a culture in which kids come first. I'll give you one incredible anecdote as an example.

We took this school and spent $35 million remodeling it. Norman Atkins was a genius in this phase of the process; he found a variety of sources that, in the end, funded almost two-thirds of the remodeling. He also got Robert Stern, the greatest architect in New York, to design and oversee the renovation. We built a state-of-the-art facility. Next we hired this unbelievable principal, Jabali Sawicki, a twenty-eight-year-old African American, and he is the most incredible twenty-eight-year-old I've ever met in my whole life in any profession. He takes it upon himself to visit a number of high-achievement schools so that he can implement what they're doing. We did best-practices surveys all over the country, and we hired our original teachers. We finally opened the doors, starting with kindergarten and first grade, and the first year everything was great. We were testing in class; all tests looked good and the kids were happy. So you think we'd be satisfied, right?

After the first year, Norman said he wanted to bring in a guy named John King, a thirty-six-year-old, Yale-educated African American. Norman wanted John to help us with our in-class training of teachers. He told me, "I just want to make sure that we have best practices going on and that we're giving our teachers the support they need." To make a long story short, I went to board meetings, and the news was always good. Our tests were good, the kids were happy, and it seemed as if everything was exactly as we'd hoped it would be. We got to the first semester of our second year, and it was the same thing: the kids were still happy and the test scores were still good. When we reached April of our second full year of operation, Norman said, "I just want you to know that at the next board meeting we're going to have a few parents that will show up. They may be a little irate." I said, "What are you talking about?" He said, somewhat nonchalantly, "Well, John wants to let go approximately half of our teaching staff."

I nearly fell out of my chair. I have run a lot of organizations, and I knew how disruptive this was going to be. I said, "You have to be kidding. We can't let go of half of our teachers. I thought we were doing so great." He said, "Yes, but I think we can do better." I said, "I think if you went to any school and told the parents that half the teachers were going to leave, you would have a revolt. Think about this, Norman. If this were your kid's school, what would you say?" He said, "I would be a little disturbed." I said, "Two years ago it was you and Jabali who hired these teachers." He said, "Yes, I was involved, and what I'm saying is that John King is telling us that we're not getting what we need for these kids. And I'm telling you that we need to replace half of the staff. We're just not going to renew their contracts, which were for only one year anyway. And a lot of parents are upset about this, and they're going to be at the meeting. Oh, and the teachers will be there also."

Well, now, as chairman of the board, I was up to my ass in alligators. The terminated teachers circulated a petition and just eviscerated my principal. These teachers had worked their butts off, many of them consistently giving sixty-hour weeks, and they were not getting their contracts renewed. I said to Norman, "I don't get this. What's the deal?" He explained, "The deal is you told me you wanted a top decile school, and you told me you wanted these kids to truly go to college. So if you're telling me that you don't want to do those things, then we can keep these teachers. But if you're still telling me that we're going to be the best of the best and that excellence is truly what this school is all about, then I'm telling you—and John is telling me, and John is the best that I know—that half of our teachers are not delivering; or if they are, it is barely between a B and C performance for our kids. The way that we keep the culture of this school intact is we all agree to a contract at the beginning of the year. It says the parents, the teachers, the kids, the administration, and the board are all committed to Excellence. Right now, we're not fulfilling our end of the bargain. If you don't stand by John, then you're taking a direct shot at the culture of this school."

I pondered this for quite a while and revisited my twenty years of history at the I Had A Dream Program, including the failures, deaths, and dropouts. In the end, I stood by John, stood by Norman, stood by our principal, and took the heat in many meetings from teachers and parents. Jabali and John King hired new teachers to replace the ones we let go, and we've had almost no turnover or attrition in years three and four. As it turned out, maybe we did make some hiring mistakes in the beginning. We were a new organization, and again, as with anything new, there was a learning process. But now we have as fine a roster of teachers as there is, and we know the exact profile of the kind of teachers that we need to have to meet the goals of excellence we have set for ourselves.

What did that do to the culture among the teachers who were remaining?

I think the message was that all of us were being held to a higher standard. That school is—and was—not about the teachers; it's about these kids and who are the very best people to help these kids achieve the goals upon which we have all agreed. I go back to the first version of my I Have A Dream Program, which had the same problem. My first program administrator, who I had for three or four years, was not an educator. She was more like an activity coordinator, and while she was very fine at what she did, I had the wrong person in the wrong position. When you're in the business of helping somebody else, you have to be very precise and explicit about what it is that you're trying to accomplish.

That moment at Excellence was a fork in the road. We could have been a middle-tier, average school. But we had to ask ourselves again: What was the purpose of the school, who were we ultimately working for, and what were the responsibilities and duties we needed to fulfill in order to achieve our goals? The culture of the school is defined by our striving to make all of our kids the very best they can be. Excellence of effort is the key characteristic that drives every single activity that goes on in that school.

To have the chance to go out into the developing world and really see what's going on with mothers and children in villages, for me there's a grounding there and a connectedness to those mothers and to those places. It is, at least for me, it is so easy to say to myself, "That could be me. If I were not born in the United States, that could be me. I could be that mother in that village in Mozambique or Tanzania or Bangladesh."

—*Melinda Gates*

MELINDA GATES'S PHILANTHROPY IS BOTH PAINFULLY simple and unbearably complex. Her belief and the basis of the work of her foundation is that "all lives have equal value." These five words set the stage for everything she does with her giving. She explains the genesis of her work by saying, "Bill and I started our foundation because we believe that people living in extreme poverty and dying of preventable diseases deserve the same chance we all had: the chance to make the most of their lives."[1]

Yet implementing this belief, attempting to rid the world of, among other things—AIDS, malaria, and the minefield of childhood diseases can be complicated almost beyond our comprehension. With this clarity of purpose comes a laser focus on three primary program areas: global health, global poverty, and education in the United States. Through her family's foundation, the Bill and Melinda Gates Foundation, she and her husband set the direction and are deeply involved with the disbursement of billions of dollars every year. With their work in these three areas, the Gateses have shown themselves to be both committed and daring. They are willing to venture into areas that have been neglected like malaria and to take great risks, as with the Grand Challenges, which funds forty-three cutting-edge scientific research projects in areas such as needle-free vaccine delivery and the development of nutrient-rich plants. The Grand Challenges captivated the scientific world's attention, and more than one thousand researchers from seventy-five different countries applied for the $200 million worth of grants.

The Gateses' philanthropy is a phenomenally effective combination of hard-nosed science, deep analytical thought, and profound compassion. Bill Gates explains their dedication: "Global health is our lifelong commitment. Until we reduce the burden on the poor so that there is no real gap between us and them, that will always be our priority. I am not so foolish as to say that will happen. But that's our goal."[2]

As co-founder and co-chairman of the world's largest foundation, Melinda Gates has spent more than $8 billion on health care and poverty eradication in developing nations, and in this process she has found a unique role for herself. She is an articulate and profound thinker about some of the world's most intractable problems. Yes, she is a great philanthropist, and in time she and her husband may go down as the greatest ever. Ironically, however, one of her most important roles involves neither giving away money nor being on the cutting edge of science or development. Melinda Gates has chosen to use her unique position in the world to provide women who suffer the very worst forms of poverty with something they have lacked throughout history—a voice.

Gates speaks for the mother living in a mud hut without clean water for her family. She stands before the world's audience and tells of the plight of women toiling as sex workers to improve their children's lot in life. She speaks out for women who are exposed to AIDS with few means available to prevent themselves from becoming infected. She does not mince words in calling upon rich nations to leave behind their culture-bound attitudes and act to save lives. "Think about saving the life of a faithful mother of four whose husband visits sex workers," she said. "If you're turning your back on sex workers, you're turning your back on the mother of four."[3]

She delivers the message in no uncertain terms, "In the fight against AIDS, condoms save lives," she said. "If you oppose the distribution of condoms, something is more important to you than saving lives."[4] Speaking out for women whose lives have been deeply compromised by poverty and illness was not a role that Gates knew she would play; but as she traveled the globe, steeping and educating herself in the failures of development and health care that plague large parts of the world, she realized there was a void that needed to be filled. "I felt like I was seeing too much not to speak out . . . [I needed] to give voice to the voiceless," she said.[5]

Melinda Gates attributes the origins of her and Bill's unprecedented giving to her mother-in-law. Mary Gates was suffering from cancer at the time of her son's wedding. A highly active community member, Mary Gates had been urging Bill to become more philanthropically active for years. Mary Gates was involved in an array of Washington State charities and was the first woman to chair the board of United Way International. Later she was asked to be a member of the University of Washington Board of Regents, and there she led a successful movement to divest the school's investments in South Africa. But it is also clear that Melinda's philanthropic vision was developed early on in her life and as valedictorian she told her 1982 graduating class at Ursuline Academy, "If you are successful, it is because somewhere, sometime, someone gave you a life or an idea that started you in the right direction. Remember also that you are indebted to life until you help some less fortunate person, just as you were helped."

Although Melinda French and Bill Gates had determined before their marriage that philanthropy would play an important role in their lives, they envisioned this happening many years later when the time commitments of career and family had diminished. But a letter written to Melinda by Mary Gates on the eve of her wedding altered that plan by decades. With words that would ultimately reverberate throughout the world and across generations, Mary Gates wrote to Melinda French, "to whom much has been given, much is expected." It is a simple phrase yet replete with meaning. Mary Gates's letter—which told of the great opportunities the couple would have to help others—resonated with Melinda, who was raised in a family that valued community service and who had attended a high school that required it. This was a message to which Melinda was highly receptive. "It was really quite beautiful," she remembers. "And that was what got us going."[6]

Up until this point Bill Gates had been hesitant to become involved in major philanthropic efforts, "Mom said, 'It's time you did a United Way campaign,'" Gates recalled. "And I said, 'I'm too busy; we're working day and night to write software.'" He did not feel that building a company and disbursing his wealth were compatible activities. "I used to think it would be schizophrenic to say, 'Let's make money' in the morning and then 'Let's give it away,' in the afternoon," Bill Gates recalled.[7] Yet after their marriage Bill and Melinda began their early efforts focused, like most people, on that which they knew well and was close at hand. They picked up where Andrew Carnegie left off, by focusing on technology with the Gates Library Initiative, which brought computers and Internet access to more than eleven thousand public libraries in low-income neighborhoods. They supported programs throughout the Pacific Northwest, in what might be considered their extended back yard.

The Gateses' earliest philanthropic efforts bear an uncanny resemblance to John D. Rockefeller's beginnings. In an eerie parallel, the sheer weight of requests for money steaming through his letterbox tipped Rockefeller, then the world's richest man, into taking the first steps toward setting up a foundation. Rockefeller wrote to his close advisor Frederick Gates:

I am in trouble, Mr. Gates. The pressure of appeals for gifts has become too great for endurance. I haven't the time or the strength, with all of my heavy business responsibilities, to deal with the demands properly. I am so constituted as to be unable to give away money with any satisfaction until I have made the most careful inquiry as to the worthiness of the cause. These investigations are now taking more of my time and energy than the Standard Oil itself. Either I must shift part of the burden, or stop giving entirely. And I cannot do the latter."[8]

From that point Fredrick Gates took on the role of helping Rockefeller to disburse his vast fortune.

Melinda and Bill Gates' story may be more prosaic and lack the fluid prose of a letter-writing generation, but it is fundamentally the same. While waiting in a movie line, Bill Gates told his father of the difficulty he was having in dealing with the vast quantity of requests for money that he received. In the midst of raising a young family and running a company, the young couple despaired of a solution. The retired Bill Gates, Sr., much as Fredrick Gates had before him, offered to help his son with the flood of inquires, thus taking what would be the very first step on the road to establishing the Bill and Melinda Gates Foundation. Gates, Sr. recalled, "My son was expressing a lot of frustration about his ability to deal properly with requests for charitable gifts. He was concerned that people were complaining that he didn't answer their letters, which he didn't have time to do. And I just said, 'Well, look, son, my time isn't all that fully occupied. Why don't I help you with that?' So that's how it all got started."[9]

The Gateses' philanthropy began where philanthropy begins for many other couples, with their own family. As a couple, they decided that they would give away 95 percent of their wealth before they died. "It was clear to us that we didn't want to leave it to our kids," Melinda recalls. "When we started to look at where the largest inequities [are], global health really stood out, because by every measure, if you can improve people's lives through health, you improve all measures of society."[10] The couple had initially sought to focus their efforts on population control, but as Melinda understood, population control comes to societies that have better health care and a higher standard of living.

As the Gateses studied further, they read a World Bank report that delineated the number of people in developing counties dying from diseases such as diarrhea, measles, and tetanus, which had either been eradicated or controlled in the developed world. Both Bill and Melinda were appalled. "The whole thing was stunning to us," Bill said. "We couldn't even believe it. You think in philanthropy that your dollars will just be marginal, because the really juicy obvious things will all have been taken. So you look at this stuff and we are, like, wow! When somebody is saying to you we can save many lives for hundreds of dollars each, the answer has to be no, no, no. That would already have been done."[11] It is with this understanding, that many achievable measures to saving lives, such as distributing vaccines, were not being undertaken, that the Gateses set their future direction. "We could go down the list and see what was killing children around the world," says Melinda. "Very quickly, we came to the point that this was something we wanted to do."[12] With their first bold efforts at vaccine development and delivery, the circles of their giving widened as they turned outward from that with which they were familiar to a world that neither knew existed.

One of their first efforts was to take the vaccines that are routinely administered to children in the developed world and bring them to seventy-five developing countries through an organization they helped to establish called the Global Alliance for Vaccines and Immunizations (GAVI). They began their efforts with a $125 million dollar grant and invited governments and others to join them and, "That led to the $750 [million]. After the 125 we had a dinner for about a dozen scientists at the house, and we both were extraordinarily impressed with their knowledge, their expertise, and their desire to solve problems. And toward the end of the dinner, Bill posed the question, if you had more money, what would you do? and the room came alive. Just to hear what their ideas were was so exciting for us. It was a revelation. And we both walked away from that dinner thrilled because we had been surrounded by people that were so brilliant at Microsoft. And we saw immediately that these were the same type of people."[13]

Since then, the Gateses have given another $750 million to GAVI, one of the two biggest recipients of their philanthropy, and the results are a humanitarian triumph of epic proportions. Speaking about GAVI's work, Melinda Gates explains, "We think 1.7 million lives have been saved just by children getting the basic vaccines that we take for granted in our country . . . . something like diphtheria, pertussis, and tetanus, something every mother in the U.S. gets for her child when they are under the age of one . . . They estimate over the ten year life of this program that we will save about ten million children's lives via those vaccines."[14]

In a true partnership, Melinda and Bill travel the world together learning about every aspect of public health. Like most Americans, their knowledge of disease in the developing world was limited until they embarked on this path. Their journey has led them to the long sorry history of malaria, the painful story of a blight that has been described in medical texts for at least five thousand years and may be the worst with which humanity has had to cope. "It just blows my mind how little money has been spent on malaria research," Bill explains. "What has prevented the rich world from attempting this? I just keep asking myself, 'Do we really not care because it doesn't affect us? Is that what it is?' Human suffering as a result of malaria is incomparable. By many measures, it's easily the worst thing on the planet. I refuse to accept it, I refuse to sit there and say, O.K., next problem, this one doesn't bother me. It does bother me. Very much."[15]

Melinda's philanthropy is extremely personal and involved. She is deeply steeped in the science and speaks publicly about the advances their foundation is attempting to achieve, revealing both her compassion and deep engagement with those she is trying to help. She often discusses or gives talks on the most complex medical and scientific issues involved in the development of vaccines. But when she speaks of her visits to mothers in the developing world, her entire demeanor shifts, her voice softens, and her rapid-fire speech slows down a bit. Here is a woman profoundly affected by what she has seen and the impact comes through in the five words she uses, perhaps the watchword of a philanthropist: "It could have been me." It is the humble understanding that in life's lottery her numbers have hit, and that alone—the true randomness of the universe—altered her lot from the woman seated before her, bowing over her malaria-ridden child, trying to survive on only a couple of dollars a day. Melinda's professional background—with undergraduate and masters of business admininstration degrees from Duke and many years of experience running multimedia soft-ware projects at Microsoft—gives her the business experience to lead a multibillion dollar foundation with hundreds of employees and programs spanning the globe. But it is the part of her that speaks with a softened voice, which identifies with another mother across the mat in a mud hut anywhere in the globe, that is the making of a true philanthropist.

During the first nine years of their marriage, Melinda Gates refused almost all requests for interviews because, "I wanted to have some privacy in our community," she says. "When I took the kids to a preschool event, a mommy-and-toddler event, say, I could be like all the other moms."[16] Although deeply private about her life, Gates opens herself up to women all over the world and shields herself from nothing, not their pain or the poverty or the disease she is trying so hard to eradicate. Everywhere she goes she enters people's lives, visiting their homes, holding their children, and asking dozens of questions that reveal both her concern and her deep desire to find true solutions to the twin afflictions of poverty and illness.

On a visit to Dhaka, Bangladesh, after the Gateses had traveled through the night from Seattle, they went straight from the airport to the Interna-tional Centre for Diarrhoeal Disease Research, also known as the Cholera Hospital. There they saw row after row of beds filled with young children and babies suffering from cholera. Each child lay on a hospital bed with a hole in the center and a bucket below because of the excruciating diarrhea they endured. Melinda Gates walked through the ward picking up these small children who were ill with cholera and gave them both hugs and oral rehydration therapy as she toured the facility. In a photograph posted by the hospital, Bill looks on smiling as Melinda holds a baby tightly in her arms, her eyes closed as the baby rests against her body.

It was not until 1999 that the foundation moved out of Bill Gates Sr.'s basement to a little office over a pizza parlor. Patty Stonesifer, formerly the most senior female executive at Microsoft, was hired to lead the effort. They started small (for them), they started with what they knew, and they started with the world close at hand. The foundation's giving in the first year of existence (1995) was about $30 million. While a seemingly enormous fortune a decade later, the foundation, which had been renamed the Bill and Melinda Gates Foundation, would disburse more than $2 billion in a single year. Over the same decade, the endowment rose from $107 million to $37 billion; and with the infusion of Warren Buffet's personal fortune, the foundation is set to have an additional $41 billion to disburse. In their lifetimes Melinda and Bill Gates will probably give away more than $100 billion. To put their contribution into perspective, each year their foundation will spend about the same amount on global health as the World Health Organization spends.

It is easy to be blinded by the money. But that would miss the point. The greatest philanthropists of all times did not give away in their lifetimes what the Gateses have already offered the world. As a point of comparison, Rockefeller parted with $6 billion before he died, and Melinda and Bill Gates, who by any measure have just begun, have given away almost $11 billion. Bill speaks openly about the advances in computers and software that lay before us and how much he will miss not being involved in the day-to-day life at Microsoft as he transitions to a full-time position at their foundation. Even with this passion for the cutting edge of technology, he finds global health more compelling. Melinda has chosen to devote herself to raising her own children and trying to help millions of other women raise theirs as well. Her commitment to philanthropy means up to thirty hours a week carrying out the work of the foundation. The impact of these two very personal decisions cannot be overstated. Surely the point must be that here are two people who have chosen to use all of their resources: their time, their money, and the platform that their success has brought them to give a world of perfect strangers, what turns out to be the bulk of humanity, a chance at a better life. "When the history of global health is written," says Dr. William Foege, a former head of the Centers for Disease Control and Prevention (CDC) who now advises the foundation, "the tipping point will be two people: Bill and Melinda Gates."[17]

Melinda expresses her admiration for both what the Carnegie and Rockefeller Foundations have been able to achieve. But hers is a very different foundation, made so by the fact that the benefactors are alive. Joel Fleishman in his book *The Foundation: A Great American Secret* explains, "Once the donor has died, and especially when there is no successor family member on the board, it is not unreasonable to assume that the foundation's zeal may tend to weaken. It is the rare foundation professional who has the same obsessiveness about spending philanthropic wealth as did the person who accumulated it."[18]

Despite its high public profile, the Gateses' foundation is very much a family foundation, and as such need only represent the values of the family that endowed it. The board consists of Melinda, Bill, and their largest and only other donor, Warren Buffet. As such, they can be nimble, adventurous, daring, controversial, and take chances that few governments, and few foundations with large boards and long-standing endowments can take. As Bill acknowledges, their foundation can make a $100 million investment in something they believe might work and if the venture fails, no one will get fired. Few governments or nonprofits can say the same. But part of the dynamism of the organization is, as Fleishman suggests, the very real presence of the founders and their unbridled ambition for the foundations goals. This is not just a job for the two of them; it is their life's work, and that sense of making history permeates, infects, and motivates everyone in the organization.

The Gateses have chosen not to let their foundation exist in perpetuity. Fifty years after the last of the three board members dies the foundation too will cease to exist. Melinda readily acknowledges that this is a decision that each foundation has to make; but for themselves, for the Bill and Melinda Gates Foundation, she is certain that this is the way forward. "Part of that involves that we're alive; we're extremely engaged in the foundation. I was trying to think today 'Is there any day that goes by in our household that we're not talking about the foundation?' I think I came up with maybe two days so far this year and they were days we were off on a vacation. But even on vacations, we are thinking about and trying to sort through what the right thing is for this place." She says that limiting the foundation's life " . . . shows the incredible optimism we have, that the problems that we're trying to tackle in this century can be tackled with the current technology and what we see coming along in biotechnology. And that we have real optimism about in our lifetime having an HIV/AIDS vaccine, really making a dent in malaria, and really making a dent in tuberculosis."[19]

When Melinda speaks of her work at the foundation, words seem to pour out of her; like water overflowing, there seems to be too much to tell. She speaks rapidly, almost without a pause, and it is only when I ask her about philanthropy's unexpected pleasures that she seems to hesitate for a moment before discussing what has clearly brought her so much joy.

LISA: Philanthropy has become your life's work. How did it begin?

MELINDA: I think there are a couple of things to understand about our backgrounds. Bill grew up in a family where his parents were deeply involved in the Seattle community and in some of the national issues. They were very involved in the local United Way, and his mom was on the national United Way board. Similarly, I grew up in a family where volunteerism was a big part of our lives. I went to a high school where the motto was "Serviam," which means to serve, and I worked in some of the Dallas county schools, the county courthouse, and the local hospitals.

Bill and I came into our marriage knowing that giving back was going to be something that was part of our lives. We thought it was going to be a bit further out, but as we got started, we decided to move it forward into the years when we are much younger than what we originally thought we would be when we started, and we have had such an enjoyable experience. We started a little more than 10 years ago, and it has been a complete partnership for us.

In the foundation, we have really focused on the belief that all lives have equal value, which has led us to invest in a number of areas. In the United States the focus has really been around the educational equity issue, about all kids graduating high school with the skills they need. Abroad, in the developing world, it is much more about people having access to the life-saving technologies that we have here, such as vaccines and other key medicines that really just aren't available in the developing world.

Can we talk a bit about the approach you've chosen to take? Through your foundation you could have become an operational organization, delivering services yourself or perhaps doing your own research. You could have focused on a single country. You could have focused on a single disease. But instead you've chosen a partnership approach, which includes working with a wide variety of organizations all over the world.

I think once you've decided what your focus is—and for us it is that all lives have equal value—then you start to say, "We're very interested in health in the developing world." Bill and I started from what we knew best. We began by saying, "What are these life-saving technologies that we have access to here in the developed world, like biotechnologies and amazing vaccines?" and then " . . . why do they not have them in the developing world?" How do you start to solve a problem like that?

We started to look at vaccination, what had been done with vaccinations worldwide in the last 50 years, where did it need to go. We very quickly came to the point of saying to ourselves (this is very early in the foundation's life) that this is an issue where we could provide perhaps a wedge, but it really is up to government to fund vaccines world-wide for these children. We could fund research and pilot projects, but ultimately it's a governmental issue. As we went down the list of other health crises around the world—AIDS, malaria, tuberculosis, the biggest killers worldwide—you suddenly realize that even with the size of our foundation, it is literally a drop in the bucket on these enormous issues. So we have to partner with governments.

Our role, as a foundation, is to show ways to take some risks that governments are unable to take or won't take by funding new types of drugs or new vaccines; but then working with government to get those breakthroughs out there. When we realized the scale of the problems that we were interested in solving, we knew that we weren't going to be an operational foundation, but more a strategic-focused foundation in getting lots of partners to the table to help solve these enormous issues.

In selecting your partners, what are some of the criteria, both the substantive and particularly the intangible things that maybe elude easy measurement, that you look for? As a philanthropist, what are you looking for in the leadership of organizations with which you are going to make a financial commitment?

Well, we absolutely look for partners that are interested in the areas in which we're interested. So oftentimes we select a partner who has already started down the path that we are pursuing. For example, they are already working on vials that have a heat-sensing device that helps vaccines remain effective in the developing world, to avoid having the vaccines be spoiled by the time they get to the patient. We'll come in with a partner like that who is well down the road and say, "Okay, how do we take this technology you've got and work with it?" We'll also look at some other technologies to incorporate because we know they know how to do it.

Let's say we are working with a partner in malaria, somebody who's already working on an early malaria drug, but they need the funding to get to the next level. Or, in the case of HIV, getting a whole bunch of scientists who are looking at HIV in a certain way and saying to them, "Okay, but what if these end up being a dead end? What's the next path we need to go down? How do we collaborate in the right way?" So we're looking for people who are willing to take innovative ideas and innovative approaches but fundamentally are after the same goals that we are after and are already on that path. Those are some of the tangibles we look for.

I would say the intangibles are a lot like business. In picking any business partner, you would want someone who has fantastic leadership and thinks about their organization in a very professional way. You would want them to have the right criteria already built into the organization in terms of how they measure people and measure their objectives and measure their goals. So when we go in to meet with partners and work with them, we look for those intangibles, and sometimes we even write those into the grants.

Our granting money to an organization is also tied to very specific milestones. If a partner with which we're working misses a milestone, our job is not to rap them on the knuckles and say, "You missed your milestone." Our partnership with them, assuming they're still on the right path, is to say, "Why did you miss this milestone, and since we have this joint goal, what can we do to help you get to the next milestone and therefore get the next round of funding?" So those are some of the ways that we build measures of success and partnership into the grant making.

Being partners suggests a certain closeness in the relationship between the grantee and your foundation.

Patty Stonesifer [CEO], the presidents inside the foundation, and all of the managers who work for them have very deep relationships with these partners. In particular, in an area like the U.S. school system where we've been working for more than eight years now, we have deep partnerships in the New York City school districts, the Chicago school districts, and other districts. The planning on those grants has become a bit longer now because we spend more time upfront with those organizations. By the time the planning is finished, and they begin doing the work, effecting the change that needs to happen in a school district, they may have planned for as much as a year and a half. By the time the planning is finished, it is their plan, the school district's plan, it is not at all our plan. We're working together to get to the point, that it's their plan, and then they're carrying it out, and we're their partners in that work. I think that's a great way to work if you're really trying to make change.

Have there been any unexpected pleasures of philanthropy for you, things that you hadn't anticipated before you began? You once described philanthropy as deeply fulfilling—I wondered if you could explain further what it's meant to you.

It's really hard to put my finger on just one thing, because when something is so deeply fulfilling, there are so many pieces of it, but let me just give a couple.

To have the chance to go out into the developing world and really see what's going on with mothers and children in villages, for me there's a grounding there and a connectedness to those mothers and to those places. It is, at least for me, it is so easy to say to myself, "That could be me." If I were not born in the United States, that could be me. I could be that mother in that village in Mozambique or Tanzania or Bangladesh. What would I want? What would my dreams be for my children? How would I even begin to scrape together $2 a day to keep my family alive? What would I do? To what lengths would I go?

So I find when I go out to places in the developing world, it's extraordinarily moving. I love that connection with those moms. I try to figure out, given that we have these amazing benefits in the United States, for that mother in Bangladesh living on $2 a day, what is it that I can do from my seat in the United States to give that mother a voice or to help get the systems in place to help her raise her family. Because that's ultimately what she wants to do. So many of these mothers talk about educating their kids. They want to get enough money to get their kids educated so that their children have a chance, a different chance than they had.

Somehow, for me, those conversations and being able to be a part of that . . . and to come back to the U.S. and somehow give a voice to that and be part of that movement and that change, for me, that's what I would describe as deeply fulfilling.

The second and last thing I'll just say about this is the chance to work with your husband as your partner, as your business partner, but also on something that you both so deeply believe in from your heart and your head and your soul and to work on it almost every day together; to me there's nothing better than that. It couldn't be more satisfying.

You started to say people have touched you as you travel.

I met with a group of prostitutes in India. We have a view of prostitution in our country that makes sense. But you go over there, and you start to look at it, and you realize that those women are in that profession because it's the only way of lifting themselves out of poverty. As I sat and talked with them and I asked, "What is it you're trying to do and why are you in this?" Etcetera, etcetera . . . It became so clear, every single one of them said, "I don't want my kid in this profession, but I'm saving enough money." They would talk about the kids they have in college or in elementary schools and how proud they were that their kids had a chance in life. To me that sort of shows the incredible transformation of these women lifting themselves up in unbelievably sad circumstances. They are in that profession, but what they're trying to accomplish for their kids is amazing.

How about mistakes? You have said that when you go into a new program or country, you try to learn from other's mistakes. Over these 10 years what have you learned about philanthropy that others can use?

Let me make a general point that programs must be developed with close knowledge of the local community. The programs have to become theirs to make them work. I think the best example of that is in India, where we have a program called "Avahan," which is really to help prevent AIDS in India, because everyone was so worried, including us, about the spiraling numbers of new AIDS-related cases.

We started with that program, and you can look at it from one view in the U.S., but when you get on the ground in India, it's completely clear—you need an Indian to run it, and the whole organization needs to be Indian. We were very lucky that someone approached us who wanted to do that work. He had run McKinsey in India. He knew how to run a business, a metric-driven system, and he hired all Indians in the country. The fantastic thing about that is now that they've got their work under way, and they have these great results, now as we go to transition it so that the Indian government wants to take it over, who we've already been working with a long time, it's an Indian program and so it's theirs. It's not like we came in from the United States and created something that was U.S. based.

I think that was a great learning lesson for us and for a great deal of our foundation work. As we looked at how we take this green revolution from Asia now to Africa, we started right from the beginning and said, "This has to be an African program on the

African continent with people who've lived and spent their lives in Africa developing this program." I think that is really an important lesson for a foundation to learn in terms of how you do work on the ground in these developing countries.

I guess people don't do that because it means giving up a certain amount of control.

I think so, or sometimes people think they have the answers going in. It's really important to say, "We have a goal, and we think we know where we're headed, but we're willing to adjust along the way." We do not have all the answers going in. You never have all the answers going in, and you better be flexible and willing to learn from the people who are there and living in those conditions.

One of the biggest lessons we have learned is in sanitation, as we start to look at clean water and sanitation. I've been in plenty of slums where people have come in and installed latrines. They are completely unused and locked, and you think, "This makes no sense." The residents have no sanitary alternative, but here are these latrines, and nobody is using them. Well, why aren't they using them? They're not using them because the NGO [nongovernmental organization] that came in, just came in and slapped them down. Those who came in to help said, "Well, they'll be great, and people will use them, instead of understanding the community's needs and getting the community to buy into the whole system and talk about what they needed and what transformation had to take place before you went in and put in a particular type of latrine. Sometimes they're put in the wrong place, sometimes in the wrong configuration, and sometimes they're not what the residents want, in the way that they want them. You have to build partnerships on the ground with residents before you can go in and put an effective program in place; otherwise you will fail.

One of the things that I think keeps people from venturing into new areas of philanthropy is simply the fear that they really don't know enough about something—that they are straying far outside their area of expertise. You are venturing into microfinance at this point. How do you know if this is a good thing for the foundation to do and how do you become sufficiently knowledgeable to make that decision and then direct the foundation's efforts?

We start by trying to do what I call scope the landscape. This is taking an in-depth look at the history to find out what efforts have already been undertaken in the area in which we are interested. We look at all of the organizations that are working in a particular arena, both large and small. We ask, "What are they doing in various countries around the world?" And we meet with lots of them. So our foundation team goes out and meets with a lot of these partners; they go out to the developing work to actually see the work, not just sit in a conference room and discuss it.

They really talk to the organizations about the lessons they've learned over time. What are the things that went well? What are the key mistakes they've made, and what are the things they're still trying to get to and trying to learn?

After we've done that landscape analysis as a team inside the foundation, then we say to ourselves, "Is this a place where we'd like to invest? Is this a place where we think a foundation can have some sort of catalytic role that can help change what is already going on in a particular area?" Take microfinance. There are some fantastic players in microfinance space and they've done amazing work. Look at Muhammad Yunus, who totally deserves the Nobel Prize.

The next thing in microfinance is to say, "How do you take it to the next level? How do you take it to scale? What has been keeping organizations from being able to go to scale?" One of the things that jumped out from our analysis on microfinance is that all the partners told us that they knew how many clients they had, but they didn't know how many clients everybody else had. There's no landscape analysis to be able to say, "How many clients are involved worldwide and which ones are in what countries?" Then, once you know how many people you're serving exactly, what are the different models? People are using very different models which is great in microfinance, but which ones are working and how do you propel those to scale? That would be a concrete example of how we looked at microfinance to then decide where we would invest.

You mentioned conducting in-country roundtables as a learning device. How does that work?

Usually what we will do is bring together partners and experts who are already working in an area in a country that we are looking at entering. It can be governmental partners, it can be NGO's, it can be people working in the private sector, and sometimes it's literally people in the community who are the movers and shakers. We'll bring them all together to a table to really discuss the issues. You'd be amazed as people throw things out at the table how willing they are to speak about what the key issues are and what the areas are that still need to be addressed or studied further.

One of the things I wanted to ask you about is something with which you must grapple with everyday; the issue of immediate needs vs. the long-term solutions. In the case of malaria, the question of bed nets versus a vaccine. You could go down one path or the other, how do you decide where to focus?

Again, because we have this long-term goal—that all lives have equal value—we're saying to ourselves, "Look at the number of people that die or are affected by AIDS, the same with malaria, and the same with tuberculosis." We go down that list, and we know our long-term goal is to save lives. Our ultimate goal—the only way to solve AIDS—is to get a vaccine. We have to get a vaccine for AIDS. The same is true of malaria. So we are focused on the long term, and once we know we have our long-term portfolio covered, when we can say, "Okay we think, at least for now, that we have the right scientific bets down," then we can look at the near term.

Let's take the case of a malaria vaccine. We've got a number of candidates with whom we are working who are well down the pipeline in the research process. There are seven candidates, and there's one that is looking promising. Once that investment in finding a solution is in place, we have the opportunity to say, "Okay, what else is needed right now, what are the more immediate issues?" We need malarial medicines and vector control and that means bed nets and indoor residual spraying. So we look at the near term and ask, "How do we relieve some human suffering today?" while also knowing that whatever we do in a few countries can be a model for other countries on a much larger scale.

We're not interested in going into just one small community; we're interested in making a real dent in this disease. In this case with malaria, we started with Zambia and asked how can we affect a model that could both help with human suffering today in malaria and also be a model potentially for other countries to follow. Then from there, we said, "Let's invest in three more countries to do malaria evaluation and control" to again have some of these models that can go out to other areas. That's how we look at the piece that's more near term. Are we creating and investing in models that can help and that others, such as governments, can pick up to do the work as well in their countries?

How do you make that transition? Getting other people to pick up on something once you've had a successful outcome? In the case of Zambia, you have successfully proven certain techniques would work there. How do you make the transition to the next step? Does it become an advocacy role for you?

We do spend a great deal of our time and money today on advocacy, which is not something we did in the early part of the foundation's life. But it's crucial to what we do now, because we need to be able to spread these lessons learned so that other people can take up these issues in their own country, maybe take up the model, but in a slightly different way as they've all got different nuances for what works in their countries.

We spend more money on advocacy than we used to, and sometimes the advocacy comes in the form of early financial support. We fund some very large-scale programs like the Global Fund for AIDS, tuberculosis, and malaria. That's the fund in which we participated very early and into which we worked to urge other governments to put money into because that fund provides on the ground money for, let's say, bed nets right now and indoor residual spraying. So we'll help with a very large-scale organization like that, hoping that it will bring others in as it did in this case.

We did the same thing in vaccinations. We got into vaccines early and helped form GAVI to get many, many governments to fund vaccine initiatives. They then did some very creative financing to keep this fund going and to be able to get vaccines out to kids all around the developing world. Now there are about 138 million more kids who have access to vaccines today because of that fund. So we will spend time and money working with those funds in an effort to get governments to come in.

How do you convey the message of how important philanthropy is to your own children? How do you teach philanthropy in a family?

One of the things that impresses me so much today is the number of students in college who are thinking about giving back. It seems to be this sort of wave that is happening where kids are saying, "I want to do something more. I've made it into a great school. I have the grades that I wanted to get. Now how do I give back?"

I think many parents start that conversation with their kids when they are young, just literally around the dinner table, and that is a great thing. Some parents start in high school. As I said, I went to a high school where volunteerism was built into the high school. Believe me—that affects you the rest of your life. So if kids have the opportunity to volunteer in their local community in high school or in some of the college programs where kids can actually go abroad and do a global kind of service learning type of program. I think that's enormous in terms of getting kids to think about how are they going to give back during the course of their lives.

Teach for America is another fantastic example in the United States. More kids are looking at that option when coming out of college much as they did with the Peace Corps in previous generations. To have that out there as a model I think is a nice bridge for kids to know that there are different ways and different paths they can go down.

Switching topics a bit. You've become many people's philanthropic idol in the work that you've done over the last decade or more. Do you have people who have been a model to you?

Sure, we stand on the shoulders of giants. When you look at what Carnegie did with the U.S. library systems—that was amazing. Or when you look at what Rockefeller did with the green revolution. We started reading books about that early on and said, "This is an amazing piece of work that Norman Borlaug did with the Rockefeller Foundation and so many other partners." [Borlaug, an agricultural scientist, won the Nobel Prize for his work in high yielding grain plants that increased food production in the developing world.] You read about how they pulled in lots of partners to make those things work, and how they published their mistakes. There are lessons learned coming out of the green revolution that when you try to take it to Africa you say, "Let's be careful not to do this or that particular thing," or "How do we look at it and expound on it in a new way?"

The fact that those foundations were formed around such big problems, with key scientists and a community around them as partners, and then they published their results—that for us was something we absolutely came in and learned from, and that was very inspiring.[20] So that I would say would be models at the large-scale end.

Then I would say for me personally, on a different scale, I've gone and worked in Calcutta in Mother Teresa's Home for the Dying. To hear that when she started, that she literally said, "I would not have started if I didn't take in that first person."

I always try to remind people of this because many people in our community come to me and say, "I don't know where to start. I'm interested in this or interested in that, but I don't know where to begin." I always just say, "Start somewhere. Start tiny. Just start and do something, and it will build and grow, and you'll change what you think you knew or what you wanted. But start somewhere, and it will grow, and you will figure out what it is that you're passionate about and what's unique to you and where you can make a difference."

That is, I think, many people's stumbling block, that first step.

Absolutely.

And the problems are so large so you think, "What can I do—I'm a drop in the ocean?"

This is the thing I get asked all the time by people. They say, "I don't know where to start, I don't even know the first step." They look at us and say, "Your foundation is so large, and you have it figured out." I say, "No, no, you have to understand, we were tiny." We started with two employees in a little office over a pizza parlor. We had an inkling of where we wanted to go, but we tried lots of things. The number of mistakes we made were as long as my arm, but it's nice when you're small, you can make lots of mistakes. It's okay, that's how you learn. Once you get started, you find that you absolutely will gravitate toward whatever you are passionate about, find your unique lever, and do what you can do.

The last thing I wanted to ask you about is what you think makes a great philanthropist. You once said that it is a mix of rationality and empathy.

I think what it really is, is just passion—knowing that you love doing what you're doing and that you have your end goal in mind that you're trying to accomplish. It's just like business. You pick something that you're totally passionate about doing, and then you spend your heart and your mind doing that. You spend as much time learning, as much as you can, and then you put your heart and soul into it to change whatever it is in which you're trying to effect the change. I think those are the people who really, over the long term, end up making a difference.

One of the things I want to emphasize too is that I don't think philanthropy depends on the size of your foundation. It's what you do. I know a woman in the Seattle community who's making a tremendous amount of difference. She's one person, and she's built a small organization around her, and she's changing the way Seattle looks at people suffering from drug and alcohol abuse. She is changing how we work with them and treat them. She's made an enormous impact in Seattle, and she's only been here six years, and it was one person who came here. Yet, I see what she's built around her. Then I see another organization that might be $10 million in size, but it is completely and totally dedicated to something such as foster children, and that's all it's working on, only foster children. They're super focused on that one issue that the people are deeply passionate about and making enormous change. So it's not about the size of your foundation. It's about what the issue is you take on and how you take it on. I see people making a difference all the time in big and small ways, and I think that's really, truly important. We need everything on all ends of the spectrum if we're going to make change in lots of different areas.

CONNIE DUCKWORTH
Arzu

We went to a bombed out school building, a cinder block building and as it was January the temperature was in the twenties. There were dozens of women and children living in this bombed-out building, no windows, no heat, no electricity, no running water, no food, no furniture, trying to live through the winter, squatting through the winter. I looked at these children's faces, and I thought, "Those could be my children." I literally went back on the plane and thought, "I am doing something. I don't know what it is, but I am doing something.

—*Connie Duckworth on her first trip to Kabul, Afghanistan*

ONNIE DUCKWORTH HAS STRAYED INTO NO-MAN'S-land. After a phenomenally successful career as the first female sales and trading partner at Goldman Sachs and the head of its Chicago office, she is now running a rug business, called Arzu, in Afghanistan. This woman who spent decades traveling the world's financial capitals, business class, now travels land-mined roads replete with snipers. And while there was little Duckworth did not know about bond markets, she will tell you that she knew nothing about Afghanistan and even less about rugs.

Yet, Duckworth has set up shop in a country where the average life expectancy is forty-three years, and 86 percent of all women cannot read. The infant mortality rate in Afghanistan is the second highest in the world, and just over half of the primary-school-age children actually attend school. It is a country wracked by twenty-three years of continuous warfare. A generation of Afghans has never known anything else.

Duckworth smiles when she describes how she went from running a business on Wall Street—the most high tech, financially sophisticated environment on the planet—to using the hawala system, developed in medieval times, where money changers in a market stall rely on an honor code and personal reconnaissance. She leaped from a world where she could speak to her employees by Blackberry, Bloomberg, e-mail, landline, courier, fax, or mobile phone to a place where there is no electricity and where she cannot even communicate with her seven hundred employees in the winter months because there are no roads.

While on the face of it, Duckworth's Arzu commissions and sells the finest-quality handmade rugs to wealthy Americans, buried beneath the very businesslike operation is her true mission: She is committed to employing women and educating them and their children in rural Afghanistan at a time when few would dream of doing business there. At a minimum Arzu is changing the lives of every member of every family that it employs. But in a more ambitious moment, Duckworth acknowledges that such a program could be "a possible template for post-conflict reconstruction."

Village by village, Arzu employees travel throughout northern Afghanistan meeting with elders and briefing them on how the organization operates. They look to strike a deal. If a village signs up with Arzu, they will be provided with top-quality wool, patterns, regular payments throughout the weaving process and finally a ready buying market in the United States. In return the village must agree to send all of its children, male and female, to school and send all of its women, regardless of age, to literacy and numeracy classes. In addition, pregnant women (Afghan women have an average of eight pregnancies) must register with Arzu, which will transport them to health care facilities, both during the course of their pregnancies and later for infant care and immunizations.

With her flat Texas twang undimmed by years spent in Chicago, Duckworth is—as she always has been—passionate about women and their role in business. In one breath she talks about how Arzu empowers women by allowing them to become breadwinners in their families, and then in the very next breath, she discuses her timetable for making Arzu cash-flow positive. Duckworth has brought to Arzu everything she learned about business from distribution, production and quality control, to branding and marketing. Yet she faces novel challenges, unlike any other she has faced, with workers who cannot leave their homes, and land mines that stand between her and the product.

I knew Duckworth from Goldman Sachs. She was a poster girl for the progress in American women's lives in the second half of the twentieth century. I knew her to be passionate about economic opportunities for women. But I also knew her as a woman in a suit, wearing heels and a string of pearls, so when I heard of her latest venture, it was actually hard to know where to start my questions.

I first met Duckworth in 1985 when I was a brand new foreign exchange trader, and she was a more seasoned, fixed-income salesperson. We, along with two other female colleagues, had been invited to the hallowed grounds of the executive dining rooms for a conversation with the Senior Partner, John Weinberg. Because the dining rooms were hidden on the building's top floor, I did not even known they existed, and after a morning on the unruly currency and commodities trading floor, they had an unnatural silence.

Weinberg, whose family would be in leadership positions at Goldman Sachs for more than a century, had summoned four female employees to answer some questions. Why were there not more women at Goldman Sachs? Why did women leave? And what could he do about it? I was new to the firm and spent most of my day trying to remember if the currencies were quoted in dollars to the yen or pounds to the dollar and if the number was getting larger, which currency was appreciating. I had no clue why there were not more women at the firm, so I sat silently as a supremely confident, intelligent group of women—Duckworth foremost among them—oh so gently gave Weinberg the hard word. With her trademark southern manners and graciousness, Duckworth explained to Weinberg that things simply had to change: Family life and business life needed reconciling, and the firm could not ignore this challenge if it was ever to have a female partner. There was no mistaking Duckworth's passion and her sense of opportunity and fairness for the shot women should have in this world. She brings this same passion and conviction to giving women an opportunity, whether they are struggling at the bottom of the economic pyramid or working at the very highest level.

Duckworth was hardly looking for a new venture when she began Arzu. Having recently retired with four school-age kids at home, her plate was heaped full. She had already taken on the chairmanship of the Northwestern University Medical Center Board and held seats on numerous Fortune 500 and nonprofits boards. She was in demand as a public speaker and a skilled experienced corporate director. With a resume, the likes of which few women or men possess, Duckworth could have done quite literally anything.

Like other dedicated philanthropists, she could not have predicted how a single event, in this case a trip to Kabul, would touch and ultimately change her life. She was not looking for something, but she was looking. Like almost everyone in this book Duckworth found her métier by keeping her mind and her heart open. She did not come at this with a plan; but in a moment she saw an image, and her course was set. Like each of the others, her philanthropic journey was determined by the simplest reason. She saw a need so profound that she could not avert her eyes or carry on with her life as if she had not seen it.

LISA: When you were a full-time partner at Goldman Sachs with four small children how could you even think of philanthropy? Where was the time?

CONNIE: We would volunteer as a family on things like our town's big spring cleanup, where you would go and pick up trash along certain routes. We did little bite-size things that centered around time that I could be doing something with my children. I would say, for people who are in that situation, where you have a very busy young family and a very busy job, you do the best you can do, because you can't do everything all at the same time. I'm still one of those idealists who thinks you can do everything, but you have to do it in a serial sort of fashion. As my husband and I started making a reasonable amount of money, we have always taken the approach that we would support charitable activities. Even before we could give much time, we tried to contribute financially.

Can we talk a little bit about that for a moment? Where did your giving start? How much did you learn growing up?

My husband and I both came from what I would describe as upper-middle-class backgrounds. We each had a father that was a professional and a stay-at-home mother. In both of our cases, we had grandparents that literally came over on the boat. That was particularly true of my grandparents, where three of the four of them came over. I think we both feel that it's sort of that old story of "only in America" because these were people that left eastern Europe or west Ireland because of real economic hardships and came here with nothing, including no education.

Then they worked very hard so that their children could be educated. So my mother actually had a college degree, which was very unusual. She went to college in 1939. My father started college but dropped out to go into the Army in World War II, like everybody did. Then he came back and went to school on the G.I. Bill, which was exactly the same thing that my husband's father did. So they both went on and got masters degrees and then worked as professionals.

But we were so much better off than our grandparents were. And when I look at other cultures through my new charitable work, I realize how special that really is. In many, many of these developing countries, you are born into a certain economic group, and not only were your grandparents in that group, your relatives from three hundred years ago were in that group. And most likely not only your kids but your grandkids are going to be in that group. There's so little upward mobility in most societies.

You said that you started giving once you earned some money. How did you go about the decision-making process of who to give to? There are thousands of charities out there. I am sure that your alma maters came looking for you, as well as plenty of others. How did you make a distinction between them?

What we started doing during this phase when we really couldn't give a lot of time is we started writing checks, small first and then gradually bigger, to my husband's undergraduate school and my graduate school. I really have the feeling that Wharton was my vocational training. I owe my entire career opportunity to the fact that I went and got an MBA at Wharton, and I'm very grateful for that. And we of course supported our children's schools and our church because those were the things closest to us. In many ways that's the first step.

The things that are closest to you?

Yes. I think all of this is a journey; at least it was for me. Other people may wake up when they're twenty-one and know exactly what they're going to do philanthropically, but I don't think that's the norm. So we started first with what was in our own backyard, so to speak.

Then the next step is that both of our families have had members who died of cancer. My husband's mother died rather young of cancer. My father died of cancer, but importantly for me I have a sister who was diagnosed with terminal breast cancer when she was forty-six. I was forty-three at the time. You look at that and think that's the same gene pool, and I knew that could be me.

I think this theme, that this could be me and mine, is something that is important in our philanthropic philosophy that's developed over time. So as a result of that, we've both gotten involved with different cancer research initiatives. We started to dedicate time, in addition to money.

My husband went on the board of the University of Chicago Cancer Research Center, which does primary cancer research. We have consistently given a fair amount of money there and brought several researchers to the cancer center because of our contributions.

So cancer became for us, through these family occurrences I'd say, that one step removed from our immediate life, a step into the larger picture. Because of our families, it was a topic that became increasingly interesting to us, and so we looked for opportunities where we might give time in terms of serving on boards.

This year I am the new chairman of the board of Evanston Northwestern Healthcare, which is a three-hospital teaching hospital system that's affiliated with Northwestern University. That started in a rather typical way. Goldman Sachs had an expectation that partners would go on some nonprofit boards, and I was sort of teed up to go onto the opera board because we had a partner that was rolling off, and I was going to take the Goldman spot. Then this other opportunity came in separately, and I thought, "I like the opera, but I'm actually interested in medicine and medical care." So I have been on that board for about ten years, and we funded a chair in research and brought a breast cancer researcher in from

Boston to our research institute. That was sort of a step into the bigger picture but still tied with something that was close to us.

Almost concentric circles?

Yes, you drop a pebble in, and you start to see it ripple out. So that was my one board that I spent time on during those active working years.

There are certain things that you're just passionate about, and it could be anything. Mine has always been women's rights and particularly women's economic empowerment. That has been my personal soapbox I think since I was in high school. I did a lot of things at Goldman related to that in terms of basically starting the diversity committee and doing all the family-friendly policies stuff in the firm.

That has manifested itself in many different ways throughout my life, throughout my career and personal life. I was the firm's representative to a national women's business organization called the Committee of 200. Bob Rubin put me into that. It was a professional organization focused on the advancement of women in business and women's business leadership. I served on the board of that organization for a number of years and when I retired from the firm at the end of 2001, became chairman of the board.

As you moved up at Goldman Sachs, did your philanthropic position in the community change?

My position in the community, if you will, changed dramatically, and not only that but my ability to affect change changed. I have a few theories about that as well. There's all that research that women have different giving patterns than men, that they don't write as big a check, that they don't write checks, or that women are funny with money.

Well, I have a personal philosophy that says she who writes the check controls the agenda. That's true in any venue whether it's business, politics, or philanthropy. If you really care about something, and you support it with your money, it's amazing how much you can get done and how much change you can instigate. But you're much better positioned to do it if you're in a position to write the check. Women who are well-educated and who have money but who have not taken up the mantle of that money—to utilize it, to direct change the way they want to see it. . . I think it's a mistake. You might be surprised, or maybe you're not, that so many women just do not engage around the topic of money. Money is power.

I still counsel and mentor a lot of women, and there is a sort of classic decision when they get out of college. Should I go work for not-for-profit, or should I go work for the big evil business world? I always tell these girls, just like I did when I was at the firm, "There's absolutely nothing wrong with going and having a very successful business career. It gives you the income potential to then be able to really put that power behind what you want to do."

It is easier to save the world when you can pick up the pen and write the check. So a lot of time younger women in particular think that if they're not volunteering their time, that they're somehow not helping, but I disagree. I think you can vote with your pocketbook for quite some time, and then you wake up and you're in a position where you have much broader reach because of your success in a career or a business or whatever field you are in. You can actually be more of a change agent.

How did this lead you to Afghanistan?

It's been a journey, one that you couldn't, at least in my case, have sat down on day one and charted out. It's almost like a career path. Its partly opportunistic. Its partly self-directed.

I was chairing the board of the Committee of 200, and I got

a call from a fellow Committee of 200 member who said, "I put your hat in the ring for something." I said, "What was that?" And she said that she'd been in Washington and the State Department was organizing a bipartisan commission on Afghan women, and they wanted a business representative. She said, "You should call Connie Duckworth. She's interested in women's rights." I was very interested in following what was happening with the Taliban with women, just sort of from afar.

You don't really have an international affairs background?

No, not at all. And I had never done anything remotely in Washington. But I looked at this, and I thought, "Wow, this is exactly my sweet spot." Here we're talking about the most abused women on the face of the Earth, which is my passion, and it's in the international arena, which I was becomingly increasingly interested in.

When you sort of look up from your day-to-day life and post 9/11, I think we all were jolted into a new reality about the larger world. So it just was like being in the right place at the right time. I did get the call, and I was asked to join this commission. It's called the U.S.–Afghan Women's Council.

The idea basically was to create a public-private partnership where leaders from different aspects of the private sector were brought together. There were people from health care, education, business, and philanthropy. We were supposed to help ensure that women had a seat at the table in Afghanistan and to bring awareness to the American public about the plight of Afghani women.

Now how were you supposed to make sure that women had a seat at the table in Afghanistan?

I had no idea. It was part of our mission.

This was an internal matter in a country with which we obviously didn't have very good relations.

Right, but we had just forced the Taliban out along with the whole coalition. It just was a topic that was extremely interesting to me, but I didn't have any particular qualifications for this and didn't know what I was expected to do. And that's part of the journey aspect of all of this. We had few conference calls and meetings, and then in January of 2003 we got on a military plane, and we flew into Kabul.

It was the most extraordinary trip I've ever taken. It really was the catalyst, if you will, for this embarkation on the journey that I'm now on in terms of having founded Arzu.

I didn't know how to respond, basically. It was like going back in time two thousand years. It was so different in every way from anything that I had ever experienced in our culture here. Kabul looked like Berlin after World War II. It had just been flattened in the various bombings.

We went to a bombed out school building, a cinder block building, and as it was January, the temperature was in the twenties. There were dozens of women and children living in this bombed-out building, no windows, no heat, no electricity, no running water, no food, no furniture, trying to live through the winter, squatting through the winter. I looked at these children's faces—that goes back to it could be me—and I thought, "Those could be my children." I literally went back on the plane and thought, "I am doing something. I don't know what it is, but I am doing something."

We see the world through our own lens, and my lens is business. So my response, basically, to this situation is that these women needed jobs. Because it goes back to the power of the purse, and my personal belief that economic empowerment is the driver for women's larger empowerment.

And so I hired a young woman part-time who had worked at the UN to help me do some research. I tried to think whether I could encourage industries to bring factories into Afghanistan. The fact of the matter is, particularly four years ago, this was still basically a war zone, and it was just not realistic to expect private capital to come in and invest.

There was no civil society and no education. This is a country that has nothing. It was a disaster of epic proportions on every single level of society: environmentally, health-care-wise, education, rule of law. It's the most heavily land-mined country in the world . . . just huge hurdles.

Through that research, I went ahead and I incorporated a 501c3 with the mission of Arzu, which is to, in effect, try to help restart the rug industry, which had been a very vibrant industry for centuries.

What state was the rug industry in then at the beginning of 2003?

There had been massive dislocation because of almost twenty-five years of war. The supply chain was disrupted, and the reputation of the Afghan carpet on the international markets had fallen way off because the materials were shoddy. The weavers themselves were displaced. Millions were in refugee camps in Pakistan. The whole rug industry was in disarray. But the reason that I hit on that was it was one of the only things that I could see that women could actually do that was culturally acceptable because they could do it in their homes.

How did you come up with the idea, do you remember?

The rug? Basically by starting to look at Department of Commerce data and UN data on industries and economic flows in Central Asia. Even the U.S. Department of Commerce had a white paper that said that the rug industry was probably Afghanistan's best near-term hope for a legal economy. Because there's obviously a huge opium trade, though that tends not to be women.

So I started picking up the phone and calling rug people. I called Stephanie Odegard in New York. She's a very famous rug designer and has done a tremendous amount to really turn around the child labor situation in Nepal. Stephanie had been a Peace Corp volunteer in Nepal, which is how she got involved with Tibetan weavers years earlier. I called people who had written Oriental rug books, people that dealt with antique Oriental rugs, and I just started calling people up.

What were you asking them?

I was saying this is who I am. I'm trying to think of ways to plant some seeds in the private sector in Afghanistan. Can you help me? They all took my calls; they all met with me and gave advice. And that's how I learned about the rug industry.

Because when I started this, truly, I knew nothing about Afghanistan, I knew nothing about rugs, and I knew nothing about international development. But I know about business. I guess the lesson is that it's just like starting a new job, trying to attack one of these social problems that you're interested in. You really don't know how to do it until you start, but you just have to start. You just have to show up the first day, and you learn.

So anyway it was one foot in front of another. I had one rug expert tell me there was no way we could do this, no way it would ever work. What did I know about rugs? Well, he was right. I didn't know anything about rugs, and then I met with the same guy about six months later and went through where we were, and he said, "You know, you have learned a lot in the last six months."

But it's still a big leap from getting advice to actually getting up and running.

That's right. A lot of it was sort of common sense, and, again, I think about this organization that we've created over there very much like a business. It's a charity. I work completely pro bono and all of the proceeds from the rugs go to support the organization and the mission. But mentally I think about wanting it to be very, very profitable because what we're trying to do is to create what people in international development have told me is a "new template in post-conflict reconstruction." The first time I heard that I was like, "Well, we're just trying to do a little rug business." It's bringing private sector thinking to a public sector problem. I think not having any kind of international development background was probably helpful in a way because I didn't have any of the biases about how things should be done. We just made it up as we went along.

So we started with a staff of one half-time person, and later we hired a full-time person here in Chicago. We're now up to a staff of about twenty people, most of whom are in Afghanistan. We have fifteen people in Afghanistan, all Afghanis. That was one of the decisions. Again, we set the ground rules, because we were creating this thing and made it up as we went along. One of the rules for us is that this is not about us. It's about them.

The biggest issue in Afghanistan is the lack of any kind of human capital. This is a country that has a missing generation because of the practices of the Taliban, when education was literally shut down for everybody. Health care was shut down. And so you have a country where people who would be of work-eligible age have absolutely no skills. It's to the point where a high school intern here in the States would probably just have more general knowledge about running something in the workplace than people there because it's completely outside their realm of experience.

What we figured out very early on was that we were going to hire all local staff. Now we had to have a couple of people who spoke English or some English. But most of our staff does not speak English.

We made a decision after the first six months that we really weren't going to work in Kabul, which is where all of the international organizations sit. We were going to go to the rural areas because they really had nothing. A lot of organizations don't work in rural areas for plenty of good reasons. But in a weird way what we found was that it was much harder logistically, but it was easier in some ways because the people were so receptive, so open to getting this sort of helping hand. We developed a working philosophy that we don't give anything away. This is not about entitlement. It's about dignity. It's about equipping people to earn their living.

The women we're employing are very skilled weavers. They've been weaving forever, but they're weaving in the middle of nowhere and absent any kind of market recognizance, with no negotiating power to get high-quality materials. They were completely illiterate and innumerate, so someone would say, "Okay, the wool costs X," and they wouldn't know if that were true or not true.

Logistically, how did you source the material, find the weavers, and get the finished product to the standard you wanted, back here to be sold?

We did it by getting connected to the right local Afghan people through some of these rug contacts that we made here early on. We met people who knew the industry and knew that we should talk to this person or that person. We now have over seven hundred women employed in eight rural villages, plus our very first group in the outskirts of a very slummy area of Kabul.

But again by design we said we're working in the rural areas. These are villages without any roads. These are women who are

behind walls, and they don't come out. And so we've been producing now on the grounds for two and a half years, and we've gradually expanded. It's taken us that long to get to a critical amount
of weavers so that our run rate right now on the production side
is sufficient, assuming we sell the rugs here, for the organization
to break even. After a year and a half, this past year we're about
50 percent self-supporting. The goal is to become completely self-
supporting so that we don't constantly have to be fund raising.

That's the new template for international development. We are
creating real work there, and we're talking not tribal tchotchkes, as
I call them. We're talking about very high-quality, export quality,
high-end, natural-dye carpets that you would be proud to have in
your home.

Didn't Laura Bush say she's got one?

She has two. She has one in the White House in the private resi-
dence. She had a special one made for the office at the ranch. You're
proud to have these rugs. We go direct to the consumer here. The
distribution is the piece of the business that I'm working on now.
We aren't selling to retailers, because we need to retain the margin, or a good portion of the margin, because that's what runs the
project. So we sell direct to individuals.

Once people have seen our rugs at an exhibit or a show, and they
see the beauty and the quality, it then becomes a totally different
buying decision. Then it's "What size do I need and which color
palette?" because each piece is unique. They are all in effect custom
pieces. It's been a real challenge to figure out how to display and
market rugs when they are all individual pieces.

Business has been built by word of mouth, and we have started
to get very nice press. You'll laugh at this. The first year or so
we got wonderful press, but it was all in the financial press, *The
Times, Financial Times, Wall Street Journal, New York Times, For-*

tune, Forbes, those kinds of magazines. We've held back on seeking any kind of editorial press until we have enough production and the quality in place because we didn't want to build buzz about the rugs until we could actually fill the production orders.

In March 2007 we were in *Architectural Digest,* in Designer Discoveries or Decorator Discoveries, page 156. We're proud of that; we've been trying to get in for a while. We've been in *Aspen Philanthropy,* we've been in the *New York Times* home section, and every time we get one of these news pieces, our sales build again and it spreads the word of mouth. We're very much in the mode now of looking at getting editorial pieces in the shelter magazines, and then the next step will be to get some celebrity engagement because then we'll be in the *In-Styles, People* magazine, and that sort of thing.

That's how we've been building the reputation and building a brand. The Arzu brand values are highest quality, cultural integrity, and benefits for women and children.

Can we go back a little bit? I want to ask about the benefits to you and also about how you made the contacts in Afghanistan. You went into no-man's-land. So you come home, you do research, you call people—in the State and Commerce departments. You talk to rug people . . .

You contact people involved with rugs in America, and you eventually get to where people believe that you are credible, and they understand what you're trying to do. Finally, we had one leading expert say, "Let me put you in touch with my contacts in Afghanistan." And that's how we got to the right people in Afghanistan. Then once you're there on the ground in a country like Afghanistan, there aren't that many people involved in the business. And I've been to Afghanistan three times myself. But there were quite a few adjustments that needed to be made early on. For example, an Afghan-American young man I met through his sister, who worked at Goldman, helped us with some of the early difficulties. He went to Afghanistan for us to see what was going on a month into it. We'd say "We need you to do x, y, z" to our very tiny staff on the ground, and it wouldn't come back right, and so it was frustrating for the first couple of weeks, and then the light-bulb went on. They just simply need much more training. We had to go back to square one.

What did he find?

In one particular case, a woman was in effect inflating her expense account. What we're talking about is very marginal. We're talking about $5 or $10, but it's the principal of things. That was another working premise that we just decided early on. We demand honesty. We taught people how to keep receipts. We do detailed pre-budget of expenses for every month. We wire in money to pay for those expenses. It is just basic training. And so we fired her, and I have to tell you that she was shocked that we fired her. I got this long e-mail from her about how she couldn't believe that in a democracy she would be fired. We had to explain, "We put our trust in you, and you've not lived up to that trust." But we've not had that issue again.

We learned that you have to be constantly monitoring and checking everything. We have a rule that requires that the families who weave for us put their children in school. We actually help enroll the children and then we go and pull attendance sheets from the principals and check attendance. You just have to. Its constant supervision and constant monitoring. We've gotten fairly good at that. It's learning how to work, how to understand what to expect, and to frame your expectations correctly.

We started rolling out to each village doing registration, where we'd hire a new group of families, roughly twenty-five to thirty at a clip. We learned that you need to have critical mass in a particular village because in order to monitor effectively, we had to have a person running the operation in that region.

We needed a woman because it's a gender-segregated society. So we had to have a woman who could interface with the women. We had to have a man who could interface with the village elders and the family patriarch, and we had a rug expert who works with them to help inspect the rugs as they are on the loom to examine the quality and give the women tips on how to improve the quality of the rugs.

Given the devastation in the country, how were you able to find this much weaving talent still available?

There is really not a constraint on the numbers of weavers. We have certain criteria. You have to be destitute, and you have to be a skilled weaver. We give a preference to widows. There's virtually an unlimited number of such people, and so the constraint is not finding the talent, but the constraint, at this point, is getting the operations up and running and having the quality control in place.

What were all these people doing during the time of the Taliban, or before they found Arzu?

They were unemployed or more likely they were weaving for some middleman. Part of the problem with the rug industry as a whole is that it's pretty much a horror show globally. *National Geographic* did a big story about two years ago on twenty-first century slavery, and the rug industry was prominently, and unfortunately, featured in that story.

It's horrible, the exploitation that takes place. The women, who tend to do the work, they do the spinning of the wool and the weaving of the carpets, make typically the smallest amount because there are so many middlemen that touch the material and the rugs and take cuts. The women sit in their homes, and the materials are brought to them. The rugs are taken away and sold for them. They're cheated along the way, and the middlemen make all the money.

I characterize Arzu, in a way, as the ultimate middleman. Because we now negotiate direct for the materials instead of the woman having to go into debt, to purchase shoddy materials which take her the same time to weave even if the materials produce a crummy rug as opposed to a very high quality beautiful rug. The labor is the same, but it's sort of garbage in, garbage out. We now negotiate direct for the highest quality materials, and we pay for the materials. We're delivering those to her door, because we've got the negotiating power that she doesn't individually.

What we try to do is disintermediate as many of the middlemen in production just like we're trying to go directly to the consumer because that's how we retain the margin. That's our goal, to retain the greatest percentage of the margin possible because that's what funds the whole shooting match.

Tell me something about what's in it for the women.

We actually have the families enter into a social contract. Again, one of the things you have to understand is that I came from a place that I didn't know how to do any of this. We just made this up as we went along. It's partly common sense and partly how you would run it as a business. The social contract basically has the family commit that we will pay for the top quality rugs in exchange for their commitment to education. We pay 150 percent of market rate, so we pay a 50 percent bonus.

What do you mean by market rate?

The market rate varies depending on the type of weave, the location of the weavers, the complexity of the pattern, the size of the patterns. There are all kinds of factors, but basically there are market rates for a square meter of carpet. So we have paid 150 percent of that. We also provide the materials instead of their having to buy them, typically by going into debt. Then we pay them throughout the weaving process instead of a lump sum at the end, so that they can have a steady income to live on.

How long does the weaving take?

It can take from six months to a year for the large rugs. This used to require that the women went into debt to put food on the table. In exchange for the 50 percent bonus that we provide, this is the commitment the family has to make—all the children must go to school—girls and boys. We'll enroll them in school and monitor for that. And all the women in the household have to take literacy classes that we pay to set up. So we bring the classes to the villages. And that's everybody from teenage bride to grandma, and we monitor for that.

We also say that we will provide literacy classes for the men, but it's recommended, not mandatory. We're very excited because we actually had our first group of men come to us as a delegation in one of the villages and say, "We want literacy classes, too." It's astonishing. These are men in their twenties and thirties who are completely illiterate. Now many, many of our weavers—hundreds of them—have learned to read, and we have continued the classes with the children where most of them are behind. When we started, everybody was in first grade. It didn't matter if you were forty-five or six; you were in first grade. So we have set up certain fast track classes for different ages of the kids to try and get them caught up so that they can then get enrolled in a government school at the right grade level.

Can girls go to government schools?

Yes. So we have to look at each village situation and see what's the best approach for those villagers, for those women and children. When we approach a village—and again now we sort of know how to do it through trial and error—we go first to the village elders and explain who we are and what we're going to be doing and get their permission to work in the village. Then we go to the family patriarch, the man, and we sit down and explain, and then we go to the women and explain it to them. We work where we're invited to work and where they are willing to agree to our education requirement. If people are unwilling to agree to those terms, then we just don't work in that household.

Have you had people unwilling to work for these terms? Is that common or uncommon?

At the beginning it was somewhat common. I wouldn't say that it was the majority, but there were definitely people that were suspicious. You have to build trust because these are people that have been through decades of war, and it has been a hard life for them, I will tell you that. But once we have consistently been delivering what we said we were going to deliver, they have been more and more open to everything. We see the changes and the milestone in these people's lives, and that's what's really rewarding.

I have to tell you that sort of feeds into what do I get out of all of this. And I truly believe that old saying that you get more than you give. So what have I've gotten? One of the things I've gotten is a full-time job, which I didn't anticipate. You just cannot underestimate the amount of time that something like this is going to take.

And I did not envision that almost five years later I'd be working practically full-time doing this.

My goal is when we get a bit closer to break even, we'll hire a president or COO to come and run this thing for me. Because it's a real company, and I'll, of course, stay involved at the strategic level, but it has become a real business.

But what have I gotten? Number one, I have had an incredible learning curve. I have learned so much about foreign policy, Islam, history, and international relations. There's been this incredibly steep learning curve in the broader sense, and then there's also a very big learning curve of running a start-up business. I just find business to be an extraordinarily interesting thing to begin with. So it's been tremendously fun and intellectually stimulating.

Number two, I have met a whole new group of people that I would never have met had I not been doing this. It's opened a whole new network of people from Washington, the UN, and the World Bank to big international organizations like Save the Children. This is a whole group of people that were outside my traffic pattern.

The other thing I've gotten has been this sense of, I guess it's a sense of empowerment and hope for me, and I think this is one element of the project that I didn't anticipate. We named our project Arzu because it means "hope" in Dari. I was thinking of it in terms of hope that we could provide by employing women and giving their children an education, which is opportunity for them and really an investment in the future. But what I've come to realize is that feeling of hope runs both ways.

I've also met a whole new network of people at home that have been professional volunteers giving time and expertise to Arzu in the United States. Most of them were people I didn't know when we started this. But I've called up and asked them to engage, or they have approached me having heard about what we were working on. I think the reason that this has been so compelling to people and people have been so generous with their time and services is that it equally has given us hope here. In a world where there's just wave after wave after wave of bad news, forty thousand people dead here or a hundred thousand people dead in an earthquake. This is what we pick up in a newspaper everyday and read. I think it's beyond comprehension—you can't process the enormity of these kinds of statements. People tend to zone out about it because you just cannot process global poverty on the scale that it exists in this world, so your eyes glaze over. People lose a sense of empowerment here that anything that they actually do can make a difference.

That's why I think people are so fascinated by the rugs themselves, once they see them and see how beautiful they are. We've had many, many people that have found us, heard, read an article, looked on the Internet. We put up pictures of the all the rugs—bad pictures because we photograph them ourselves—nonetheless they just buy. The reason I think it is so appealing to them is that it's such a simple idea. It makes such common sense, and it really empowers people to do something to help, to materially help someone else. That's why I think it's been such an exciting process, to see people's reaction to it here.

We formally interview the weavers, in fact all of the families when we register them, and find out their demographics: the number of children, the deaths in the families, their personal histories. Then we formally sit down and interview them every six months for a life-change assessment. We have the stories, so when we sell a rug, we send a story, and in most cases we have a photo of the woman herself. Some women don't allow photos to be taken, but in most cases we do. We have their base case—the before story—and then we have some of the after story. We have what has changed in their lives, with actual quotes from the women. When people see these, they value their rugs even more.

The rugs are beautiful, and our customers would have bought them anyway as we price them very attractively, because again we're disintermediating as many middlemen as possible. They feel like they're getting a really good rug at a good price. It's a great buying experience. I don't know if you've bought rugs before, but it's like buying a used car. It's awful. You never know what you're getting. You don't know what the value is. You don't know if it's good, bad, or indifferent, or you feel like you're getting ripped off. But this is a very positive buying experience, and it's personal. They are personally connected to the people that made the rug. So it's just a win–win. People feel really good about that.

So I think all of those things are benefits I've gotten. It has been a real adventure and something that I could never have predicted that I'd be doing. One of my former partners told me if I were a guy in New York, I'd have a card table on the corner. It's like how fast they fall.

Are you doing some long-term evaluative work about what happens to people in the program?

Not yet. But that's definitely part of the plan. I think a couple of things: I think there is a business school case in this but not yet. I don't want the case to be "And why did they fail?" I want to wait until we get cash flow positive and then can expand. I actually think that there's a long-term big-picture strategy with this model once we get the economics right with one product and one country. There's no reason that we couldn't do a roll up of other women's craft-cooperatives around the world. Because in every third world country that I've ever been in, there've been indigenous crafts at a very high quality level and a very high skill level. It unfortunately often gets translated into these tribal tchotchkes that are sold in souvenirs stands. That's not to say that you couldn't take the same skill and have it applied to a real export product like a carpet and connect those women's crafts with the biggest consumer market in the world, which is us. I think that there are all kinds of interesting possibilities and many, many organizations that are doing terrific work in many countries. But they tend to be run like not-for-profits. Good mission but not a sustainable economic model, and I think that they can be reinterpreted. I think that there's a lot more that can be done with this model, but we have to get it right in one country with one product first.

I think the other thing that I get out of this is that I think it is setting a really good example for my kids. I think they're really proud of being involved in it. My kids are now sixteen, fourteen, twelve and ten and they've just done a lot of things for Arzu, and I know they're just absorbing it all. Frankly, I think so many people worry, I know we do, about a whole generation of kids that have grown up with much more affluence than we ever did. How do you keep them grounded in reality? Well, this is the reality for most of the people in the world.

Have they ever gone to Afghanistan with you?

No, it is too dangerous, but I hope to one day . . . I hope that we can all go one day.

TIM DIBBLE
Year Up, Big Brothers
Big Sisters of Massachusetts Bay

This is what I think about myself. The line between my having done well and not having financial security is so razor thin that just one nudge, one twist, one turn, one less mentor somewhere and I wouldn't have it.

—*Tim Dibble*

TIM DIBBLE, A FOUNDER AND MANAGING PARTNER OF THE private equity firm Alta Communications, knew what he was looking for, but he did not know where to find it. After decades of acting as a big brother, through Big Brothers Big Sisters of Massachusetts Bay, he was deeply concerned about the lack of economic opportunity for young urban adults. He knew the problem, he cared deeply about it, yet despite a year researching inner city education programs and writing a business plan, he was uncertain where to begin.

Then Gerald Chertavian walked up his driveway, into his kitchen, and presented him with a vision of just such a program. This was to be a one-year intensive training program that would give eighteen-to-twenty-four-year olds from economically deprived backgrounds college credits, a corporate internship, and a new path to follow. Chertavian told Dibble that he would help young adults to cross a technology divide that kept those without twenty-first-century training from rising above the minimum wage barrier.

Dibble loved Chertavian's vision, his program, and his drive, but he did not think Chertavian had a chance of succeeding. Despite his doubts, Dibble invited Chertavian to move into his Boston offices when Chertavian was ready to launch Year Up in August 2000. Chertavian might not succeed, Dibble thought, but Dibble was so impressed with the planning and dedication that Year Up's founder had shown, that he was willing to do what he could to give him a chance.

By sharing an office with Chertavian, Dibble had a front row seat to watch Year Up grow. He met Chertavian's staff, became familiar with the curriculum, and later with the students. By the time Chertavian asked Dibble to chair Year Up's board of directors and become one of its leadership donors, Dibble was a convert. Sometimes becoming a truly effective philanthropist is a matter of finding Gerald Chertavian.

I accidentally spent a day at Year Up in New York. I had not expected to learn about the program or to meet Chertavian. I was in Year Up's office simply to borrow a conference room for a meeting. A February snow storm and delayed flights meant that my meeting would begin hours late, and I ended up having breakfast with a group of Year Up students who were walking through the looking glass—leaving one world and joining another. This was the inaugural group as New York joined the highly successful Year Up offices in Boston, Washington, and Providence.

For a single year twenty-six young New Yorkers would be paid a stipend to learn and work. They had beaten the odds. Through a highly competitive process, which included lengthy essays and interviews and odds as long as getting admitted to an elite university, they had made it to Year Up.

The previous September they had arrived at a nondescript Wall Street office nervous and awkward in the unfamiliar setting. Now as I met them six months later, they were halfway through the program, brimming with humor and confidence. They told me that if I had entered that office the previous autumn, not one of them would have greeted me at the door or probably even looked my way. Yet that very morning as I had wandered lost into their office, I had been barraged with offers of help and guidance.

Hardly able to contain themselves, they offered me breakfast and blurted out their stories. In six months they were shocked at how much they had learned in courses on computer troubleshooting, written and spoken grammar, and even e-mail etiquette. They had learned how to hold a plate at a cocktail party, take a computer apart, and settle a disagreement with a colleague in the workplace. Their teachers had shown them how to listen to a boss and how to make small talk at a corporate function and—perhaps most importantly for young people, they admitted—they learned how to make eye contact. They had classes in current events, and they laughed when they told me that they learned how to talk to a stranger in an elevator. In short they were prepared for the IT support internships they were now undertaking at Lehman Brothers and Merrill Lynch.

They love it all. They loved the way their teachers had stuck with them. They loved the way they had become a group—a real group that cared about each other—not like the cliques in high school, they told me. They loved that their employers treated them like everyone else, that they had all same the benefits (BlackBerries noted first among them) and responsibilities of everyone else in IT support. They loved that they had met top executives on Wall Street. But mostly they loved that their lives had changed entirely, that they had moved so far so fast, and that their expectations for themselves had risen to meet the demands of Year Up.

These young people told me that they lived in the worst parts of New York City, many in apartments overcrowded with family members including their own children. When they missed a day at Year Up, it was usually because they were taking someone to the hospital or a government office. Some described the program as their last chance. At twenty-four, one of the oldest students credited his young son as the motivation for entering the program. One woman said that she had always dreamed of working in corporate America but had dropped out of college and watched her chance disappear. She came to Year Up for another shot at the job market but said, "Once you are in here, you want all the other goals as well. You want the whole package. I would not have imagined wanting to go to college, but now I am going."

Expectations at Year Up are high, and there is a price to pay for falling short. Each student starts the month with 150 points. Any infraction—being late, failing to complete a homework assignment, forgetting to put on a belt, wearing a skirt too short—costs points. Students who have used up all of their points are asked to leave the program. The teachers at Year Up, as well as fellow students in every group, do everything possible to keep from reaching this point, but it does happen. Every day there are lectures and homework, internships and feedback sessions, interviews and learning assessments, and a myriad of speakers who range from Wall Street personnel directors all the way up to Mayor Bloomberg. And they must take it all in, every last detail, because when they are done, when they have started a career and are full-fledged members of a professional workforce, it will be their job to mentor the next class at Year Up.

As much as the group was impressed with having met the mayor and the head of the New York Stock Exchange, it was Gerald Chertavian who they described as their idol and their motivation. He had given them the sense of what was possible and how their lives could be transformed in just twelve months. As the first New York class, he let them know how important their success was to Year Up and to those who would soon follow them. Not one of them wanted to let him down. These students graduated at the end of their twelve months in August 2007. Merrill Lynch hired five from this class into jobs earning $60,000 year. Graduation was on a Monday in August, and they would begin work on Tuesday. One of the young men hired into the Wall Street firm told Chertavian, "Sunday night I went to bed poor, and Monday I woke up in the middle class."

I had not intended to write about Year Up, Gerald Chertavian, or Tim Dibble. But in the three hours I waited in Year Up's office, I was given a glimpse of everything a social entrepreneur and his well-run program should be. Gerald Chertavian happened to be in the New York office the day I inadvertently visited, and we began a conversation that touched on people and places we knew in common, covered the amazing story of Year Up, and ended with his praise for his chairman of the board, Tim Dibble. He described Dibble by saying, "He runs a $1.5 billion private equity firm, chairs the boards of Big Brothers and Year Up, and spends a meaningful percentage of his time helping nonprofits and being very philanthropic. He also has four kids, coaches four soccer teams, and has adopted an African American young man into his family. I have never seen anyone balance what Tim does. To boot, he has run twenty-two marathons and keeps in great shape." Chertavian cannot say enough about the enormous role Dibble has played in Year Up's success. "He really has done it all—mentored students, met with funders, recruited corporate partners, spoken at events, interviewed potential hires, led strategic discussions, and provided financial resources. You could not find a better Chair, and we are blessed to have him at the head of our organization."

In speaking to both of these men, it becomes clear that as much as Chertavian bet on Dibble, the reverse is equally true. Long before either man was a father, they chose to have an impact on children's lives. On Saturday mornings, while their peers were sleeping off the effects of the night before, each of these men were on their way to parks and hockey games with boys who had been assigned to them through Big Brothers. Both men succeeded in this challenging role through their own tenacity, and each provided a home, college tuition, and unswerving support that extended into adulthood.

This is a theme that runs through everything Dibble does philanthropically and professionally. As much as he invests in ideas, he bets on people. Being passionate about the cause is essential. Knowing in his heart why it is important, and knowing in his head how it can be accomplished are essential. But a key ingredient for Dibble is knowing that, in his words, he has a good shepherd for his capital.

At the very root of Dibble's giving is the lesson he learned at fourteen.

Life can turn on a dime, and it only takes the goodness of one person to make that happen. He has set out from the time that he was a teenager to be a force in other kid's lives. And even when the experience was far from perfect, and others might have soured on the intensity of personal mentoring, he just went back and did it again and again.

Dibble speaks quickly and articulately, like a man who has thought this through on a deep level and can now speak about it passionately with others. He is an interviewer's dream, replete with anecdotes and self-deprecating humor.

LISA: My premise is that philanthropy is a journey, and I am hoping to hear about yours.

TIM: I can start at the beginning and recount how accidentally or otherwise we ended up where we are today. I am currently chairman of the board of two not-for-profits. The first is Big Brothers, Big Sisters of Massachusetts Bay, the second- or the third-largest such local affiliate in the country. I have a long history with them.

I am also chairman of the board of Year Up. I have been involved with that program since its inception. . . . I'm on the development board of a program called Right to Play. Think of it almost like a Peace Corps, using sports as the training tool, in refugee camps and orphanages in third world countries.

I want to start where philanthropy started for you. What was the impetus for philanthropy in your life?

I am the product of two sociology professors, so I was a cry for help from the moment I was born. I remember asking my father when I was a young boy, "Dad, what is sociology?" And he said, "I can sum it up for you in one sentence. Some do, and some don't."

And so being the only child of two academics, you're starting off twisted to begin with. And then fast forward to when I was fourteen—my Dad died of cancer. So I was left this fourteen-year-old boy, and you know how awkward that age can be.

I imagine that his death was both emotionally traumatic and also financially traumatic to you and your mother.

Although the financial piece doesn't really factor . . . I guess it does weave into this a little bit, too. At the time of my father's death I was enrolled at a private school in Connecticut called Choate Rosemary Hall. After he died, we didn't have the financial means for me to stay there. The parent of a fellow student, a guy by the name of Franklin St. John, gave the school the money so that I could keep going there. I had never met him. I have still never met him, ever. But his son must have gone home and said, "Hey, this classmate of mine's father died, and I don't know how he's going to keep going to school." And by the way I had never talked to anybody about our financial situation, he must have just guessed. And so Franklin St. John, whom I still have not met to this day, gave the school money for me to stay there.

Having to leave your school at that age would have made matters considerably worse.

Oh yeah, it would have compounded everything. It was just a tough time all around. I didn't know which way was up. So one of the many blessings in my life is that I actually went back a couple of years ago and gave a scholarship in his name. I have talked to Franklin St. John and his son in the last couple of years. Clearly, he was an invisible mentor in a different form, and so many young people would never have had that kind of luck.

Two summers later, when I was sixteen, I was in Boston working at a Chi Chi's restaurant. I was watching TV one night, and I saw this public service announcement for Big Brothers, and I thought, "Boy, I really could have used that. I really could have used that type of mentor at the time." After that, Big Brothers sort of stuck in my head. Then when I was a sophomore in college at Wesleyan University, I signed up to be a Big Brother. Part of it was knowing that it was something that I could have used and part of it was knowing that I was lucky at the age of sixteen or seventeen to have already had some mentors in my life that made a difference.

How did being a mentor work out?

I became a Big Brother in college, for two years, and then I graduated, and I moved up to Boston. Then I became a Big Brother up here in Boston, in the program that I am now chairman of the board.

The first time I was matched in Boston was with a young boy in Southie (South Boston). We were matched for four years until he got to the age of fourteen, where running with the boys was a cool thing and having a Big Brother wasn't cool. He was one of these kids from Southie with cigarettes rolled up in his T-shirt . . . he no longer thought that he had a need for a Big Brother, so our match ended. It was pretty traumatic; it was like breaking up with a significant other. Because I'd spent every week with this boy, and I had invested a lot of time. It was my heart and soul.

I went to sign up to be a Big Brother again in 1990 and was matched with a young boy named Curtis Blyden. Curtis is from Roxbury, but his family is originally from Honduras. His grand-mother, who had a third grade education, was raising him. She had moved to this country and had diabetes issues, major heart issues, respiratory issues, could barely move, and was simply one of the finest people I've ever met.

She was raising him in the heart of the urban core and definitely taught him right from wrong. She was an amazing, amazing woman. Curtis's father was in and out of his life, mostly out. He fought battles with the diseases that are drug abuse and alcoholism. Curtis's mother had died under mysterious circumstances when he was two. He and his sister, who's a year younger, were being raised by his grandmother.

How did it work this time?

Curtis and I just hit it off. I was single at the time, and he was an eight-year-old boy. He was a kid growing up in Roxbury, but I saw so much of myself in him. Eight-year-old boys, they're all the same no matter where you find them. By the time they get to fourteen, their dynamics have changed.

So Curtis and I were matched and just hit it off and became very, very close. And then in 1994 when I got married, Curtis was the best man in our wedding. When we were on our honeymoon, he was the victim of an attempted kidnapping off of a Roxbury playground. Luckily, a passerby broke it up. Most likely he was going to be dragged into a drug deal as a runner.

I'm a little confused. Someone wanted to kidnap him and make him run drugs?

We never really knew for sure. The guy ended up going to jail after they caught him. Curtis was on a Roxbury playground. He was twelve years old, he was a little dude at the time, and somebody tried to grab him, pull him away. A woman stopped it, and they caught the guy three weeks later. It turns out that he was a convicted drug dealer. They never knew for sure, but they thought he picked Curtis out at random, and he was going to make him go run drugs for him.

So we came back from our honeymoon and talked to his grandmother and said, "You know, we really have to change his environment." So we changed his academic setting to a private boarding school. Actually, that ended up changing a couple of times. When he was in high school, his grandmother passed away. At that point he came to live with us and graduated from Concord Carlisle High School in 2000. He became the first one ever in his family to go to college when he graduated from Curry College in 2004. He is actually off right now at the Peace Corps in Mongolia.

I have a couple of stories that I tell when people ask what's it like to be a Big Brother. So I'm a 5'10" Caucasian male in the venture capital business. One morning, after Curtis and I had been matched for about a year, I picked up Curtis and his cousin Rasheed, and a friend of theirs; so it was three young African American kids and myself. Curtis was in the front seat, and we were driving in my car to the park, and I could hear his friend and his cousin in the back saying, "Rasheed, is that Curtis's Big Brother?" "Yeah," said Rasheed. I can see his friend sort of thinking this over for a second. "Hey Rashid, are you sure that's Curtis's Big Brother?" And Rasheed goes, "Yeah, why?" And the friend leans in and whispers, "Well, he almost looks white." You know, it was one of those moments where I had to do everything I could do to stop from howling. I couldn't laugh in front of him because it was so wonderful.

Another moment I tell people about was in the summer of 2000, and Curtis had just graduated high school and was still living with us before college; and in the house we had our five-year-old daughter, Tessa, and our four-year-old son, Ben, and then in July, little Molly was born. So we had Curtis, Tessa, Ben, and Molly. And my kids know that I always refer to Curtis as my little brother. I still do to this day.

A couple of times when we were walking around town in Boston or Concord, somebody would say, "Cute kids, how many do you have?" And I would say, "Three." And Tessa, who was a precocious five year old, would interrupt me and say, "Dad, you have four. You're forgetting Molly." To her, of course, Curtis is one of us. Needless to say, it can be embarrassing explaining why you have forgotten your newborn daughter.

This is the dynamic of our household, and the truth is that Curtis can do more, just by living in our house for one afternoon, to break down the walls of stereotypes for my children than a lifetime of my preaching ever would. That's been very obvious for us. So that is my connection with Big Brothers.

And how did you move through the organization?

I was cultivated to be a board member. John Pearson, the executive director here in Boston, actually recruited me and said, "Hey, if you're passionate about the program, would you come get involved?" I went and sat in on some sort of team meeting with board members, and it was just not for me.

There was not 100 percent board giving at that point. Very few board members at the time had ever seen a match live. So I just said to John, "I can't do this. I'm too impatient. I'm used to for-profit boards where things move faster, and everybody is committed. I can't do this."

How did he change your mind?

He came back about two years later and said, "Tim, you can recognize the problem, or you can be part of the solution. I'm going to call your bluff. Why don't you come help me change this board?" So I've been on this board for six years, and part of that evolution has been to try to help shape and create a board where you have 100 percent board giving, where everybody is committed to the program, where we are increasing our board diversity, and where we are getting all board members involved in at least one of our major committees. Two years ago I was asked to be chairman, which I accepted.

I really want to talk with you about Year Up. I saw the program in New York and was wildly impressed.

With Year Up I am the accidental philanthropist. Gerald and I met through mutual friends. A good friend of his from London was one of my best friends from college.

At the time I met Gerald, he was in the process of selling his company in England. His daughter had just been born, and his mother who was really a very strong role model for him was dying of cancer. So he was coming back and forth to see her.

I will never forget the first time we met. We had traded e-mails and I said, "When you're coming back through Boston, let's get together." So he came through one winter night in 1999. I'll never forget (laugh). It was a February night, and I think my wife was away, and I had the little kids in the house, and I said, "Why don't you come over for dinner?"

When he pulls in the driveway, there is about four feet of snow in my yard, and I look out the back door. He gets out of his car, and he had these mutton chop sideburns and this Euro jacket and these loafers, and it's about ten degrees out and I've got six inches of ice in my driveway. And his wife gets out, and by the way, for as good as you think Gerald is, Kate is better. Oh, she's phenomenal, just phenomenal. She gets out of the car, and she's got these leopard skin boots on with stiletto heels. And I'm looking at these two from my back door, and I'm thinking, "Forget about starting this program. You're not even going to make it to my back door without falling on your keister."

I had been alone with a bunch of little kids all weekend, and I think I had a baseball hat on, hadn't shaved in two days, and had on a sweatshirt and jeans, and Kate and Gerald are making their way slowly up my driveway, looking at me and thinking, "This yahoo is going to be our savior?"

That night he told me about an essay he had written to get into Harvard Business School in 1989 or 1990. It was about creating a program that bridged the opportunity divide and took urban young adults who were falling through the cracks and trained them for jobs predominantly in the IT field. At the end of one year, they would have the technical skills to compete in the modern economy. He told me how he would start this program and how he wanted to serve 10,000 urban young adults.

I sat there at dinner, and I loved this guy's vision, and I loved his passion. He said, "Look, I'm going to start this thing. I'm not going to take a salary, and I'll be the largest investor." He wasn't even soliciting me at that dinner. He wasn't asking for money or help; we were just talking. I sat there and listened and thought, "This is incredibly wonderful, and this guy doesn't have a chance in hell."

If you were so impressed with him, why didn't you think he could do it?

Because of the inertia of breaking through with not-for-profit organizations and the difficulty in getting funding from foundations. I grossly underestimated about ten things as related to Gerald and Year Up. Let me come back to that. I just thought it was going to be hard for him to raise the money. It was going to be too hard for him to get corporate America to buy into the program. I think we were right on the cusp of the stock market crash, and I thought that would make things worse.

I had seen a lot of great programs get to a little bit of scale and very, very few were able to break through. I underestimated, grossly underestimated, this guy's passion and drive and intelligence, as well as his charisma and lack of an ego, which is a huge factor. I underestimated everything about him though he came with an impressive CV. He went to Harvard Business School, and he worked on Wall Street. He started his own business. He had sold at the top of the market. It's not like he came in with no bona fides. But I'd seen too many great, great social entrepreneurs not be able to break through before. That's the biggest thing I underestimated.

The second biggest thing I underestimated is the generosity of individuals in Boston with their time and their money to support this guy. These generous people said, "I'm not going to just write a check, I'm going to write a big check. And I'm not just going to write a check, I'm going to spend time with this guy and help him get going." So that was another thing I underestimated.

I thought it would be an incredible challenge to hire people, particularly teachers who would take a salary of half of what they could get anywhere else. I don't mean in teaching, but in doing IT and general business consulting. Gerald has created, and they have together created, this passionate place where people don't leave. Actually, it's a little bit of a problem the other way . . . in any business, for-profit or not-for-profit, you need some natural attrition, and they don't have any. So there's a culture about the place that I underestimated.

I underestimated how Year Up's corporate partners would adapt to this. I thought they would look at this as charity. You only get a little bit of charity from these guys that is not in their charter. I think that—none of them have ever said this—I think they all started by saying, "This is charity," and after six months, they thought, "Wow, we get this incredibly well-trained, motivated workforce that doesn't turn over, and we pay no recruiting costs. And by the way, this really helps our diversity. Where do we sign up?" So all of these elements I misjudged. Shows you what a visionary I am.

Look, I thought MTV was a bad idea.

See that one I got. The biggest thing I underestimated was Gerald. I would say although he is by no means alone, he is a truly exceptional leader in this field. I've never seen a person so accomplished who is so open to constructive criticism. He literally doesn't take any of it personally. I think he really understands and embraces the volunteer board and that anything we say, even if it's wrong, we're trying to help.

That goes back to your point of no ego.

No ego, but he's a competitive bastard. I'll give you an example. We're in this capital campaign right now to raise $18 million, and if we raise $18 million, one of our biggest donors will give us another $1 million, so $18 million equals $19 million. So we're sitting here with about $16 million right now, and he's killing himself. He thinks it's going to be a failure if we don't get the $18 million.

I said "Gerald, I have to walk you off the ledge. I understand how competitive you are; I understand how $18 million equals $19 million. You set the goal, and you have to hit it. I understand that. But a $16 million dollar capital campaign for a not-for-profit that's five years old is unheard of. It's absolutely unheard of. So I promise you when we're on our deathbeds, when we're lying in the hospital looking at each other with seconds left, I'm not going to look at you and say, "If only we'd raised that $18 million." So that's the only place where it sort of catches up with him. But even then, when I spent a half hour talking to him, he said, "You know what, you're right." [Postscript: Tim and Gerald raised the $19 million, months after this conversation.]

So how far along was he on that first night when he laid the program out for you?

This was fifteen years in the works. Actually I think it was longer. He went to public high school in Lowell Massachusetts. He is from a strong middle-class family, and his parents are very, very supportive. But I think right there he saw in high school, "I could take AP courses, and I could get into Bowdoin, and the rest of my classmates don't all have that opportunity."

When I met him, he had already begun to talk to civic leaders, academic leaders, and business leaders. He was thinking this through. What makes a good core curriculum? What are the human services issues I have to deal with? Do I have to have a crisis counselor on staff full-time? What will corporate America want in terms of trained IT professionals? He was really starting to think through this.

Then how did your involvement begin?

When Gerald was back in London, he called and said "Hey, any ideas on where we can get started? We don't have any money yet, but I'm moving back to Boston, and I need to figure out some office space." We [Alta Communications] were moving from downtown in the financial district with six thousand square feet of office space to the Hancock Tower where we had thirteen thousand square feet. I said, "We have all this empty office space. Why don't you just come in here? Take it. It won't cost you anything."

If he had called a year earlier, we would have been in that old space and had no room for him. If he'd called maybe five years later, we would have filled all those offices with our own staff. So part of it was pure timing. And so he came here, and we sort of had this handshake deal. He had great business experience and operational expertise that would be relevant to some investments we were looking at here. We let him take the space and did not charge him for it. But in return, if we saw some investments that came through that were germane to what he had done, we just wanted him to help us look at them. That was sort of the deal.

So informal consulting in exchange for rent?

Yeah. It was a handshake. Again, showing you how high-minded I am, there was something in it for us. At first I had no plans to give him any money, to get involved, or to do anything. So I was just watching this whole thing bloom on a daily basis. It was interesting. I just watched him hire a couple of teachers, and they started to put together a curriculum and started to interview the first couple of students, and he asked if I would be a mentor to one of these students. A big piece of the program is mentoring.

Each student has a faculty mentor, a volunteer mentor, and a mentor on the job. When Gerald said, "Tim do you want to be a mentor to one of our students?" it was so ingrained as part of me at this point as to who I was, that I said, "Of course I'll do that." So along the way, I just watched this whole thing grow here and thought it was terrific.

I just got to watch Year Up grow and was so impressed with how the program was working and the output of what it was starting to become. I was just blown away. You know, I say I'm the accidental philanthropist because I didn't go looking for Year Up. It literally came up my driveway and sat in the office next to me, and I got to watch it.

I think the one thing that really made it click for me was that I was so predisposed to believing in what their program is all about. They are just creating opportunities by setting up a mentoring base for young urban adults that otherwise would not have it. Mentors and opened doors of opportunities had played such a big part in own my life. How many kids have somebody write a huge check to their private school when their father dies and they have no money?

But you were just observing, not officially involved?

I hadn't given a dime, but when I signed up to be a mentor with a young man, it really got me engaged in the program. I got to see it firsthand. It was right about that time that Gerald said, "Hey, would you like to go on the board here?" At the time the board had nothing in place, no governance, no nothing. It was just three of us meeting in a conference room here just brainstorming. It was three white guys. We were all thirty-five, forty maybe, no diversity, but it was a place to start. I didn't commit a dime, did not commit a dime. I just said, "I'll help you out."

The more you spend time in the program, the more engaged you become. In particular, I watched that first class, and I watched my mentee go in. I saw how the students carried themselves, how they gained confidence, how they learned to speak in public, and what they could do technically with computers, etc. I watched what came out the other side. The transformation was staggering, just staggering. Probably the thing that got me most was a young woman that I had met at the beginning of the program who was horribly shy. She was incredibly bright, incredibly nice, a really, really attractive, sharp young woman. But she was horribly shy and had horrible body language and posture. Twelve months later she gave the graduation speech—it just blew me away. I was fighting back the tears, and needless to say I was fully cultivated.

So for Year Up the cultivation engine is becoming a mentor and going to these graduations. What I was seeing is story, after story, after story of individual students whose lives were dramatically changed, and I have long ago said to Gerald, "You could shut this program down tomorrow and still know that it was a huge success." That's how I was naturally cultivated. The board started to grow from four to five and needed to have a chairman. He asked me to do it, and I said, "Sure." And then we went to work on getting a board that had diversity by gender, by ethnicity, by background, by skills, and that's what we have now.

I'm now in an interesting spot. I say this with no self-deprecation intended. My job is to monitor and guide and grow the organization but also to replace myself. This is going to be a national program. There is no question. So Gerald needs a chairman with national gravitas, and as much as this only child would love to flatter himself that he is . . . he's not. You have got to get some CEO of a major Wall Street firm, actor, writer or politician etc. to lead Year Up in the next stage.

If you had to name the most important thing in starting out in philanthropy, what would it be?

I'd say the biggest thing we did that worked was we started to give early when we didn't have a lot of money. We weren't giving big money, but it was a big percentage of what we were making. And so it got us in the game at a younger age, and it got us engaged. It put us in the position to recognize Year Up when we saw it, when we finally saw it, because we had been involved with other programs and learned what to look for and what to avoid. If my wife and I had been doing nothing at the time Year Up rolled around, we would not have had the perspective to see how incredible it was.

I didn't have to have any grand vision to become engaged. The problem was there for Year Up to fix. How do you solve the cracks between workforce development and education for urban young adults? By the way, I had seen this firsthand with Big Brothers. I knew what the problem was and I was passionate about it. Maureen and I were going to do our own thing with an inner city education program, and we spent a year writing a business plan. In talking to people we came to a conclusion there's enough other stuff out there. Let's find something else to channel our resources toward rather than starting something of our own. Guess what? A year later Year Up just fell into our laps. I would love to say that I had this grand vision and that I was the architect of Year Up, but it was completely the opposite. This guy came in and impressed me, and I just watched him grow.

Once you have figured some of this out for yourself, how do you pass your thoughts about giving on to your kids? I think this is something that preys on a lot of people's minds.

The answer is, "I don't know." I've heard all different types of approaches. You start a family foundation, kids start giving at a young age, and so on. I'm not sure that I like that approach.

My daughter is eleven, clearly at the age of reason, and she clearly gets some of what's going on. When we went to Mongolia to visit Curtis in the Peace Corps, we walked around a village, and her jaws were open. At home my wife has been working really hard to help rebuild our sixty-year-old elementary school, and it seems like a big deal in Concord, Massachusetts. When we walked by the school in Bulgan, Mongolia, a sixty-year-old Russian-built school that the kids in this village go to, and my daughter's mouth was open, and she whispers to me, "My school really doesn't look so bad." As I said to my wife, "That's worth the trip right there."

I'm not necessarily a believer that my daughter at fourteen should be giving away money. If she makes her own money, and she wants to give it away, that's great. I don't know if it is normal that a fourteen year old would have allocated money like that.

My parents never had any money, but they also never preached that I had to do anything. As a child, it was more what I saw them do versus anything they said. As I mentioned, my father passed away when I was fourteen. Maybe that was going to be when the preaching was going to start, but it didn't. So I just watched what they did and how they thought and how they were involved with people locally or in the big picture. It was part of the DNA of our household growing up that you thought about other people. In my case they were very involved with civil rights issues. It was part of our household, and you could just soak it up.

When I was growing up, I think at about thirteen, I had to start working. Didn't matter what it was, but I had to start working, and it didn't matter whether I made money or not. I just had to get out of the house. So we'll try to do the same with our kids. I would be perfectly happy if my daughter wanted to go to Year Up (if they would take her) as chief bottle washer and coffee getter and copy maker. That clearly, by the way, would be a job that . . . she won't realize it at first . . . would come from staggering privilege. It won't dawn on her when she grumbles every morning at 5:30 when I wake her to come with me on the commute where she'll bitch and moan, and then fifteen or twenty years from now it will hit her, "Oh My God, what a window on the world that was."

It is a very long-winded way of saying, "I have no idea." The kids definitely see us, they see Curtis, and they see us doing Big Brothers. They see us doing Year Up. They don't really understand Year Up yet, but they understand that once every three months some handsome young inner-city kid that is dad's "mentee," whatever that is, comes over for dinner. I think if you ask me in five years [about my kids], I'll be on some road with them but don't think it will involve them giving money away, for quite some time.

Your philanthropy is a very public thing—board chairmanships, fund raising—do you ever wish you could do it another way?

Yeah, but there is a reason why we do this. We always used to give anonymously, always. It was just like this old Yankee thing. We didn't want our name out there. And then selective programs, including my alma mater, have asked us to put our name out there. They said, "We think if we put your name out there, the following ten people will look at it and may become influenced." It is natural for people to say, "The Joneses are giving X; we can probably give X."

I would say this—I think we are now leaning toward putting our name on things, for that very reason. There's no question, there's absolutely no question, that giving travels in packs. And there's absolutely no question that, forgetting Tim and Maureen Dibble, that philanthropists look at the donor's roster and the board list and say, "Alright, those people will be good shepherds of my capital."

What about for the purposes of your own fund raising? Isn't it difficult to raise money if people don't see your name attached to some dollars as well?

No question. We just got a $5 million dollar grant for the capital campaign at Year Up. I met with a representative of the donating family, who's very passionate and committed to what Year Up is doing. When I met with him, I said, which is true, "My wife and I, if you include all of our pledges and donations to Year Up, will have spent more on Year Up than anything else in our lives." Does that make us great people? No, but it does mean that we're committed to the program.

I think what you find in Boston is that there is a very large group of individual donors who are very open to giving back and not just writing checks but getting intellectually involved with what they're doing. These are people who truly understand the difference between buying a table at an event and creating capacity building in an organization for the long run. I personally think it is an incredibly nurturing environment right now in Boston for not-for-profits that is led by a number of great visionaries running these organizations.

When I go off and ask for money for Year Up and Big Brothers and a bunch of others, I will tell you that almost every time when I'm asking for money from somebody who is between thirty-five and fifty, who made it themselves, they will give something. Maybe not always in the amounts that I am asking for, but I know they are always willing to listen, and they are giving somewhere. They're just of a generation and a mind-set and an ilk that they're going to do something with that money and they're going to give back and it's just not going to be to their alma mater. When I go ask for money from people who were given the money, who were beneficiaries of a generational trust, I almost never get it. It's actually to the point where I don't even bother anymore.

Researchers have found that many of those with self-made wealth are influenced by the sense that luck had a huge role to play in their success.

This is what I think about myself. The line between my having done well and not having financial security is so razor thin that just one nudge, one twist, one turn, one less mentor somewhere and I wouldn't have it.

It sounds like your philanthropy is very local.

It is very local.

How do you make that decision? Because there's a huge world out there of dire problems that cry out to us.

There are a ton of global issues, and we try to think about them, perhaps not so successfully. It is funny because I am the child of two parents who were huge big-picture people. We have to solve the world's problems. We have to bring about political change. I still have the picture of my father putting the daffodils on the bayonets outside the White House in the 1960s. So that's the era they came from. Big, big change, tectonic shift at the top, and I could not be more different. I want to solve the problem that I think I can solve.

With Curtis there are some big issues, and it's not always roses, but I know I can have an influence in that one life. With Year Up I know if I give a six-figure challenge grant, that I can get it matched, and that's going to lead to twenty new students in that classroom. I know that of those twenty new students, sixteen will graduate and of those, fourteen or fifteen will get full- or part-time employment at a $34,000 average salary. I know what the output is. I can do that math.

Every investor wants measurable outcomes and metrics, and I think Year Up, Big Brothers, and everyone should be held accountable by those. And part of our giving and part of the job of the CEO is to legitimately measure, track, and monitor those in a straightforward way.

The second item for me with philanthropy is that it has to come with the head piece, and then it has to come from the heart. The heart can only come with the interaction. Yeah, you can see Sally Fields late at night in the UNICEF ad, and you can write a check, but until you go touch it, feel it, see it, you just can't fully understand a program and how/if it works. I think for us we are saying, "We will focus where we can provide the most leverage to benefit the most people, which is in our local community—where we can touch it and see it."

If I go off and ask for money for Big Brothers, I can talk about my story with Curtis. They may not give money, but they will at least know I'm passionate and knowledgeable about what I'm asking for. Year Up will be our way to branch out beyond Boston. Our dollars will no longer be net, net spent in Boston. They're being spent right now in Washington, DC, Providence, and New York. And next year we'll be spending in San Francisco, Atlanta, or Dallas and so on. Year Up will drag us along from local giving, being Boston, to local giving, encompassing the U.S.

I know you like to measure the success of programs like Year Up. But aren't a huge amount of the benefits beyond measurement and off in the future?

There are some terrific ones. One thing I was going to say about metrics is that people can get too hung up on it. I've been in more than one meeting where the donor, typically it's a foundation, has said the cost of $14,000 a student to educate a graduate at Year Up is too high, and you have to bring that down. Keep in mind that includes a stipend for students so they can live. I love Gerald's answer. At first I thought it was defensive, and now I repeat it over and over. This is Gerald talking, "I'm on the board of Bowdoin. I'm a trustee at Bowdoin." Bowdoin is viewed as one of the elite colleges of New England, or we'll take any of the colleges across the river here [pointing to Cambridge]. They're taking the cream of the cream of students, and they're deemed efficient for taking the cream of the cream and educating them for $40,000 a year. So if you want to explain to me why we're being inefficient at taking more at-risk young adults and educating them at $14,000 a year with a stipend, I'd love to see how we could do it better.

That is where the importance of anecdotes comes in and of knowing the organization up close. I have a mentee who graduated yesterday, an awesome young guy. His aunt has raised him because both of his parents have been out of his family with drug and alcohol problems. Two of his good friends have been shot in the last year. He got to Year Up because he saw another student from his neighborhood that got into the program, graduated, and got out that way. How do you possibly measure the fact that that one graduate got another young man to go this route?

I hope that some of the magic with Year Up will be twenty years from now when they have created a new boy network. So if you are a young African American woman from the Bronx, and you just don't know where to begin trying to break into the corporate world, well guess what? Your neighbor's cousin works for Lehman Brothers, and you go sit with her, and all of a sudden you've got an entrée and an interview. That to me, more than anything else, that is when the viral benefits of Year Up will have really taken off.

I guess maybe the punch line with both Big Brothers and Year Up is that we have worked closely in the kitchen. We have two great executive directors, and this is where we write our biggest checks, and this is where we spend the bulk of our time; forget even that Curtis lives in our house. I'm on my third mentee at Year Up. I know probably about three or four students well from each graduating class. I know what they're doing. I know how incredibly well it works. And with Big Brothers, as obnoxious as it sounds, I probably can't be more closely affiliated with the program than having Curtis live in our house. So that's why with these two programs, we are so involved with our time and our money.

I'll tell you another anecdote from yesterday. There is a student from the Year Up graduating class of January 2006 in Boston who grew up in Sierra Leone and was trying to escape all the violence in that country. He and nine other people were driving a car trying to leave the country, and the car crashed. Eight of the ten died. He survived, and he came to this country. His name is Abdul Dijani. So he graduated in January 2006 and was working in a great job. He was shot in January of this year five times in a case of mistaken identity. Mistaken identity, shot five times, lost his leg. Health insurance wouldn't cover the cost of his prosthetic leg, so the Year Up staff passed the hat and paid for it. And now he's back at work full time. They have a new award, which is the Dijani Award, for courage. At the graduation this week [August 2007], he got up and spoke and gave out this award to a student in this graduating class. He was up there with this huge smile on his face, talking about how lucky he was. This kid grew up in Sierra Leone, ran away from the war, was in a car crash where basically everyone else died, was shot five times because of a mistaken identity, has a prosthetic leg, and he's talking about how lucky he is. The anecdotes from any Year Up graduation could fill your whole book.

LIZ AND STEPHEN ALDERMAN
Peter C. Alderman Foundation

While the death of most people is the end, Peter's death was the beginning of life for so many people all over the world.

—Yousif Hanna Rofa, MD, Iraqi psychiatrist and Peter C. Alderman Foundation master

IN THE DUSTY CENTER OF SIEM REAP, CAMBODIA, WITH ITS faded French colonial facades, lies a run-down government hospital complex. This collection of low whitewashed buildings serves as the major medical facility for this impoverished province of nearly 800,000 people. An enormous sign stands sentry, warning in English of "Severe Epidemic Hemorrhagic Dengue Fever," and while I had no idea what that meant as I approached the hospital, I was relieved that I had left my husband and children in the car. The temperature was over ninety degrees, and the air clouded with car fumes and dust as many patients calmly sat in the open courtyard with their families, enduring what looked like it would be a very long wait. A guard stood watch. But even as I passed through the entrance, stepping over a single chain that provides the hospital's defenses, he never looked at me. I was searching for the Peter C. Alderman Clinic, an island of psychiatric refuge in a country devastated by unspeakable war and genocide. Unfortunately, I showed up at lunch. Three days earlier I had met Liz and Stephen Alderman for the first time, and now I found myself standing in front of the clinic they had founded, with two hours to wait.

The Aldermans are the family next door. He is a doctor, and she a teacher, and they raised three children in suburban New York. The story of how this wonderful couple, settled into late middle age, came to establish mental health clinics in Southeast Asia and Africa is an astounding testament to that fact that passion alone can drive philanthropy. For the past five years they have devoted their lives to training physicians and psychologists from countries devastated by the ravages of violence and civil war in the best-known practices for treating post-traumatic depression. In conjunction with mental health professionals, many of whom have attended their Master training courses, the Aldermans have established psychiatric clinics in Rwanda, Uganda, and Cambodia. The unrestrained enthusiasm for the work they are doing pours out of both of them as they chart their six-year odyssey and the deep satisfaction it has brought to their lives. As each donor in this book has explained, and no one personifies it better than the Aldermans, real philanthropy transforms the lives of both giver and recipient.

Yet Liz and Stephen's philanthropy began, not in joy, but in the most tragic pain. Their youngest son Peter, for whom the clinic in Cambodia and indeed all of their efforts are named, worked for Bloomberg LP and was visiting the World Trade Center on September 11, 2001 for a technology conference at Windows on the World, the restaurant located on the 106th floor of the North Tower.

In the months after Peter's death, Liz and Stephen learned of Dr. Richard C. Mollica's work at the Harvard Program in Refugee Trauma, and they approached him. As Mollica recalls, "The family called me up, and they said, "What can we do? What can we do to make a difference for other people who have been through the experience of violence? Because we're so upset and so shocked by the loss of our child, our young boy.""[1]

A sign on the Peter C. Alderman Clinic indicates that afternoon hours resume at 2:00 p.m., and so I begin to tour this ancient city with my family. Most cities in developing countries with large tourist populations, like Siem Reap, are a painful collision of two worlds. The road from the Siem Reap Airport to the center of town resembles the strip in Las Vegas with a parade of gargantuan international hotels. Yet during this lunchtime I leave the town center in the other direction, toward the Tonle Sap Lake (the largest in Southeast Asia) and instead of Sofeitels and Le Meridiens, we drive for miles down a corridor of homes made entirely of tree branches and mud elevated on stilts because of the annual rains. The stilts are nothing more than sticks and with any kind of deluge, it seems that all would wash away.

When I returned to the Provincial Hospital, the same guard seemed oblivious as I headed toward the reopened clinic. In a room that showed the stains of a leaky roof, I met with three serene nurses that told me of the dire need for emotional healing in their province. The clinic's space was not much more than a couple of hundred square feet, and in it doctors and nurses try to assuage the psychiatric wounds of people who have witnessed some of the worst atrocities of the twentieth century. There are more than 4,000 visits a year to this site, and because of the constraint on space, they have recently opened a satellite clinic. The clinic staff I met with were ecstatic. They love the Aldermans, and since they had been alerted to my visit by an e-mail from Stephen Alderman, I too was the recipient of their enthusiasm. The clinic, they told me, has enabled them for the first time to treat people who had given up on their lives, with no place to turn. Every morning and afternoon they see patients who are later followed up with both home visits and sessions at the monastery with Buddhist monks. By crowding into the small space with everyone sitting almost shoulder to shoulder on the floor, psychiatrists are able to hold regular group therapy sessions. It is an all-encompassing program, combining western medical practices and medication with local religious beliefs.

The Siem Reap clinic is the Alderman's model, the first success story that is now being replicated in Uganda and Rwanda with partnerships that include the national governments, the Harvard School of Public

Health, Partners in Health, and local medical schools. "Harvard had run a clinic in Cambodia which went under during a political upheaval," says Stephen.

> "The clinic turned into a part-time, voluntary operation. It had lain fallow for a couple of years. After meeting Dr. Lonh Borin and Dr. Dy Ben Chhym at our second Master Class, we asked whether they would like us to take the program over and restart it. They were very excited, and so I traveled to Siem Reap. At the time the staff of the clinic, all of whom were volunteers, consisted of four social workers, a psychiatric nurse, Dr. Borin and a driver. We were willing to pay everyone's salaries, but we couldn't do everything ourselves. So I went around to the government, to the local Buddhist monastery and asked, 'What can you do for us? How can we work together and get this thing running again?' We were able to create a partnership. The government agreed to provide the building and psychiatric drugs. The Buddhist monks volunteered their time and facilities to provide weekly group spiritual healing sessions for the clinic's patients."[2]

Through their years of work with people who have suffered from the after shocks of trauma, Liz and Stephen have learned what the very best research in this field has revealed. There are three things that help with the grief and pain that accompany such experiences: altruism, work, and spirituality. Yet, even before knowing this formula, the Aldermans had begun to apply this remedy to themselves. Their dedication and full-time work on behalf of those who have suffered from terror has been the very prescription they give to the patients in their clinics. "It takes you outside of yourself," Liz explains. "You start caring about others. The altruism is terribly important. I didn't think I would ever, ever feel good about anything again, but I feel good about the work that we're doing. It doesn't take away the grief. Nothing will ever take that away. It doesn't heal the sorrow, but it helps us to function, and to be productive, and to do some really important good in this world."[3]

Peter Alderman lived a joyous life, and his parents, siblings, and friends have continued to honor him and commemorate his life. The organization they founded is now in its sixth year and is remarkable for that fact alone. Of the 300 foundations established in the wake of September 11, 2001, only 10 percent remain. The logo for the Peter C. Alderman foundation is a drawing of a copper beech tree, and the real tree stands flourishing in the Alderman's garden, planted there by Peter's friends.

LISA: Had you been involved in philanthropy before or was the work with the foundation entirely new for you?

LIZ: Absolutely, new terrain for us. I had been a special education teacher, and then I'd been a stay-at-home mom, which I loved. I felt it was truly a privilege. Steve is a radiation oncologist and had run his medical office. We were a very ordinary, typical family, just totally involved with our family and our kids.

After Pete was killed, I got very involved in Families of September 11th, the largest family group, and I was the co-chair of the Memorial Committee. That was born out of my need to do something for Peter. I was always involved in my kid's lives, and just because Pete was gone, that need was still there. It turned out to be an extraordinarily frustrating experience. It was all about power and money and influence, and the promises made to the families were never kept. After doing that for six months, I felt that it was just bringing me more pain.

I'd always believed, and tried to teach my kids, that people could make a difference in this world. After this experience I lost that feeling. It was simply too frustrating. So Steve and I decided that we needed to create our own memorial for Peter. But Steve and I have been married for forty-four years, and we've never agreed on anything.

STEPHEN: Yes we have. [laugh]

LIZ: [Smiling] Steve was thinking in terms of endowing an academic chair somewhere.

A medical position?

STEPHEN: No, something that had something to do with terrorism. Here's what I thought. After September 11 I was amazed that these guys came out of nowhere and that I knew nothing about them. I remember watching TV. We were down in Washington visiting Pete or Jane when they bombed the U.S. embassy in Nairobi. I knew the name Osama bin Laden, but that's all I knew. I kept thinking, "Where did these guys come from? How did this happen?" I knew nothing about these people. That's what led to my wanting to perpetuate a chair, not in medicine, but in the social sciences. My chief aim was to commemorate my son, to propagate his memory.

LIZ: But I thought, "That's not Pete to endow a chair somewhere." I was thinking more of a small playground in an area that needed it. We were not thinking really big at all. We didn't have a frame of reference to even begin to come up with ideas.

I was barely sleeping in those early months and purely by happenstance I watched a *Nightline* episode that featured a Dr. Richard Mollica from the Harvard Program in Refugee Trauma. They talked about the fact that there are one billion people, one-sixth of the Earth's population, who have directly experienced torture, terrorism, and mass violence, and nobody was dealing with the emotional wounds of these people. As I'm watching the broadcast, I see three young Afghani children that have been orphaned by our bombings, and I just wanted to put my arms around them and bring them home and give them a good life. As I'm watching the broadcast, I'm beginning to realize that there's a lot more that we could do.

Pete was killed because of terrorism, and there was nothing we could do for Peter. But if we could help people who survived the event but were still unable to live their lives, if we could bring them back to productive lives, then that was the most fitting memorial for Pete.

In June 2002, we ended up contacting Richard Mollica, who is a Harvard psychiatrist with a divinity degree, and within ten days we were sitting in his office in Cambridge. It was the first place that we felt emotionally safe since Peter died.

Richard had this dream of creating a Master Class, where he would bring together doctors and psychologists from post-conflict countries to training seminars and then send them back to their countries with enhanced knowledge on dealing with trauma and traumatic depression. Their patients would be people who were normal before the event happened but because of trauma had been left unable to live their lives. But he could not get funding because this was an experiment.

The techniques were experimental?

LIZ: No. What he proposed to do had not been done before. The whole idea of training doctors in post-traumatic depression and then sending them back to their own countries was a new concept. Richard had gone into countries and done training, and that he'd gotten funding for, but it had never been with a very diverse mixed group of people.

STEPHEN: The concept is train the trainer. Everybody walks around training the trainer. What we had were some psychiatrists, some general practitioners because there aren't many psychiatrists in many countries as you know, and psychologists. They had the skills. They were trained in psychotherapy and other therapies but the question was how to apply this to victims of mass violence and torture, essentially to highly traumatized populations.

Let's backup for a second. What happens to people who have been hit and hit and hit by war experiences such as being raped, watching family members be killed, or having children die in their arms from starvation. I can tell you from my experience in Cambodia if people had one war experience, they had seven. The end result of these experiences is a constellation of emotional problems stemming from the trauma, anxiety, and pain. They simply get to the point where they cannot get out of bed and don't give a damn if they live or die.

What we know from small studies is that if they were normal before this happened, 80 percent of them can be returned to functioning lives. Men go back to work, women take care of their families and their households, and children go back to school. So they were salvageable. Their lives can be returned to normal. Can they be happy, who knows? I am not a Park Avenue psychiatrist, but we know they can return to their lives and families.

Mollica evolved eleven points of diagnosis and treatment, but they had to be adapted to the context. It is essential that the diagnostic instruments that you use are culturally appropriate. For example, if your sixteen-year-old kid doesn't light fires in America, he's okay, and that's a good thing. But if this kid at sixteen doesn't light fires in Uganda, then that's a problem because there are cooking fires and heating fires. Every teenage kid I know in America mumbles when they greet you, and they don't always look at you, and again here that is okay. In Uganda this is called Ma Lwor, which is depression. You've got to make the diagnosis appropriate to the culture; otherwise you can't treat it. So there are two instruments for diagnosing trauma-related depression that we have validated and translated into different languages. Post-traumatic stress disorder is part of the human condition, but it is important to recognize that it looks different in different cultures.

Then the treatment is the rest of Mollica's eleven points. What we know is that psychotherapy is a good thing to do. It's an excellent thing to do, but it's not enough. Just like with diabetes, if you just go to the doctor's office and get your insulin regulated but go home and become fat and don't exercise, your health is at risk. We need participation. A patient can heal himself, but you have to give them the tools: how to allay your anxiety, how to suppress your rage, how to get outside yourself.

Mollica ran a multi-year project in the 1980s at a place called "Site II," a refugee camp on the Cambodian-Thai border. It was a terrible place with about one hundred and ninety thousand refugees in a closed camp, a displaced persons camp. It was just a horrible place. He studied people who had suffered severe trauma and what he found was that there were three activities that mitigated the impact of post-traumatic depression—spirituality, altruism, and work.

When you torture a population, the chief emotion people feel first is humiliated.

LIZ: And this goes across every culture.

STEPHEN: It is the human condition. I took me awhile to figure this out. I thought, "Why should people who have been tortured feel humiliated? They haven't done anything wrong." The reason is that it takes away people's humanity, their individuality. So these three things, and I thought they were magic for a long time, let you start to become yourself again and to get outside yourself.

So spirituality, altruism, and work allow you to become a person again?

STEPHEN: Yes, work is obvious. The altruism and spirituality is a little less obvious. What they are, as best I can see, is a way to stop you from obsessing about how you feel about what was done to you. You still feel the same way; you may still want revenge, you may still hate people, you may still have to fight somebody for a scrap of food; but you're not obsessive about it. This is called "social capital." Once you start thinking about your relationship to the people around you and the institutions in your life, then you start to redevelop yourself. Then a country starts to rebuild itself.

The World Bank has articulated this well. When you try to

rebuild a post-conflict country, the bricks and mortar are simple. But to get people back to having faith in each other and in their institutions, that's the tough part.

LIZ: One of the things that was amazing is that we learned about this study long after we had started working with Dr. Mollica. Looking back, I realize that this is something that, and again I can only talk for myself, that helped me to be able to get through the day. First of all there was the work of our foundation. It was a reason to get out of bed every day. When Pete was killed, I had two options: One was to kill myself, and I don't mean that literally; I mean just crawl into bed and never get out. The second was just to continue to put one foot in front of the other. The work was so important. It was a reason to function.

The altruism, in terms of the knowledge that we were helping others, became terribly important. There was that need to do something positive, and for me I call it "spirituality and humanism." Certainly, all the work that we were doing is all about humanism. So for me as an individual, undertaking those three things that were found in the refugee camp worked for me.

How did your Master Class program begin?

LIZ: Steve and I strongly disagreed on whether to take the money from a victim's compensation fund for 9/11.

Steve wanted to take it because he felt that we could do a lot of good with it. I felt that this was blood money. How do you put a price on your child? This was the buy out bill for the airlines, for the insurance companies, and I was adamant against taking it. We even went so far as to talk to an attorney to find out if we could get divorced, and Steve could take the money, and I could sue for accountability. Because once you accepted the money, you had to forfeit your right to sue any entity in the United States.

After much going back and forth, we were in Cambridge again for another meeting with Mollica, and he spoke about how much good we could do with this money. Back at our hotel room at the Charles, I began to think, and it wasn't what Richard said that affected me.

I never cared whether I left a mark on this earth—my mark was my children. Peter was too young to have made that decision, and I began to think that if we could go ahead and turn this—because at this time we knew that we were going to support Richard—but if we could turn this into a really successful foundation, then this would leave a mark that Peter existed on this earth. It would leave a mark all around the world, and it would be a profound and indelible mark. As soon as I started thinking in those terms, I said, "Okay, let's go ahead and accept the money."

STEPHEN: It was 1.4 million dollars. We didn't need the money. Peter was not married with a family like so many others.

LIZ: We accepted the money, and we began the foundation with that money.

Your first action with the foundation was the first Master Classes. So that was in 2003, 2004?

LIZ : September 2003.

In Italy?

STEPHEN: Yes, Orvieto. We always hold the classes every year in the same place.

The doctors who join you and Dr. Mollica for the course, where do they come from? How are they gathered? And how have they changed over the five years?

LIZ: Richard Mollica runs the Master Class. He directs it. We're like the producers. We became very involved. We were a very different kind of donor, which surprised Richard at first. He was surprised when we showed up at Master Class and became involved with the program.

Richard through his global connections initially knew the people to bring to the first Master Class from his relationships. He brings in outside staff who are experts in areas like psychopharmacology or empathy, and Richard of course lectures.

STEPHEN: He had been teaching on this subject for twenty-five years. He had contacts spread everywhere.

LIZ: Each year we bring two doctors from each country so that when they return to their country, they have a support system. We train MDs, psychologists, and government administrators of mental health programs who are also doctors and a fair number of GPs [general practitioners]. So far over the four Master Classes that we've had, we've trained seventy-eight doctors from nineteen countries on four continents. It is a very intensive program, and most participants come back for three years running.

The doctors are required to do certain things to have the privilege to come. We pay all expenses. We pay for their visas, for their airfare. We pay for their stay in Rome until we go to Orvieto. We do it in Italy for a number of reasons; one it's central to where the doctors are coming from. Two, it is easier to get them into Italy in terms of visas. Three, it's a beautiful place. These doctors need healing themselves. Four, it's less expensive than trying to do it here in America.

They come for a full week. It's a very, very intensive week. We live together, we eat together, we sleep together, we take our coffee breaks together, and we sit in on the lectures together. The doctors must bring to Master Class two case studies. In the mornings we break down into two groups and go over the case studies because this is the way physicians learn. In the afternoon there are all different kinds of lectures and seminars.

When they return to their countries from Master Class, each

participant must train ten more health care workers on how to identify and treat post-traumatic depression. It's not the easiest thing to do, because as physicians in underserved countries, they have incredibly busy schedules, but it's the next echelon of training. They will train teachers, social workers, village elders, or the local midwife—people who come into close contact and are trusted by the victimized populations. So it is another level.

The trained masters also must act as representatives for change with their governments. That's not always easy, but we've seen some miraculous things happen. Now we have a cohort of approximately 300 people that have been trained in this way.

STEPHEN: As Liz told you, in the beginning Richard picked the original participants, but that quickly changed. Now our master candidates come from our own students themselves. And we have developed some of the most amazing friendships, everyone in the group has.

Over the years these doctors have been lied to again and again. They have been promised the world and given nothing to help them treat severely impacted populations. We now have a certain credibility with them. Our bona fides with them are that for four years we have lived with them, financed them, and been their friends, and they've been ours. For example, from Master Class III, there's a doctor, who's an Iraqi, and he is terrific. He's a class act, this guy. He's a lecturer in Northern Iraq, just a lovely, lovely guy. Our kids Jane and Jeffrey have met him, and he's begun to know our family, and through pictures and whatnot we know his.

He and I communicate by e-mail all the time. I send him old man jokes, and he sends me back old man jokes. Some of the Iraqi jokes are very good. At 4:00 during Master Class week there was a break, and the two of us used to go for walks around the conference center grounds. And one day he said to me, "You know, in the first Gulf War my sister had just gotten married, and she and her new husband were vacationing in Baghdad, and they dropped a bunker buster bomb, and they killed her." I said, "I am so sorry. What a horrible thing to have happen." Then he said, "Last year my brother was walking down the road, and he made some American sentries very nervous, and they killed him." I stopped walking. I couldn't believe what he just told me. I said to him, "How can you even look at me? Here we are together, and every day you and I have been going for walks. How could you do this?" I guessed he really hadn't thought about it. These are people who are not American doctors. These are people who live very close to the bone. Everything their patients have suffered, they too have suffered. He stopped for a minute, and he looked at me and he said, "It's a miracle, isn't it?" He's a good friend, he's an excellent friend. And it is a miracle.

LIZ: At the last Master Class on the second to last day, one of our African doctors after dinner got up and put a cassette in the cassette player, and it was just this beautiful soulful African music, and he got up and he started to dance. I have to give you a little background first. It was a rough Master Class, because during this Master Class, the doctor who Steve was just talking about, found out that his best friend, who was a neurologist was killed, murdered, assassinated walking down the steps to his hospital, and he was beside himself. A second doctor, who was from the Middle East, got a call from his wife, and she tells him "Don't come home; you are now on a hit list." Well, he has to go home. He has daughters, and his wife is there. How could he stay and ask for asylum in Italy and leave without his entire family? It was a heavy-duty Master Class. One of the physicians tried to seek asylum; she worked in one of the camps in Uganda.

It was a particularly emotional Master Class. The second night, Dr. Davis puts on this music and started to dance (he's from Rwanda), and within three minutes all the African doctors that are there are dancing with him. All of a sudden a very proper, middle-aged, Bosnian GP, a very square, solid looking woman gets up, and she starts to dance. She's doing her own dance. Then we have an eighty-year-old professor, and he gets up, and he starts to dance. Within ten minutes everybody in the room is not only dancing, but they are laughing, and they are hugging each other, and I'm there with the camera like a crazy person, and tears are just pouring down my face. I looked at this and said this is a microcosm of what this world could be. You had Black, you had White, you had Asian, you had Sunni, you had Shiite, and you had Jew—name the religions—they were there. It was a coming together of people, and they came together because they were all healers. It didn't matter what their background was. We even had at one Master Class, a Serb and a Bosnian share a room. They thought it was the funniest thing that ever happened. This is something that gave me such sustenance.

As I said, we did this to leave a mark for Peter. As time has progressed, it's absolutely important that this is about Pete. But I care so much about the people that we are helping that it's become bigger than Peter. The motivation that was all about Peter has become much broader-based.

STEPHEN: This is truer for Liz than it is for me, but when we talk about the clinics, we can talk about some of the promises we have made.

LIZ: The first clinic was in Cambodia, and this is the model that we are following. We believe that the most important thing is that we be culturally appropriate. We want to enable Cambodians to help Cambodians. As Americans, we cannot go in there and solve their problems. The Cambodian Clinic is run by Dr. Borin, who's one of our Masters for three years. She runs the clinic, as a psychiatrist.

Dr. De Ben Chhym who's also one of our Masters for three years is the provincial minister of health for Siem Reap province. He's our tie with the government. Wherever we go, we want ties with the government. What we're doing is creating public private partnerships, and Steve will talk about that. That is very, very important to philanthropy, at least certainly in the kind of work that we're doing.

The government of Cambodia gives us our clinic space. It's on the grounds of the Siem Reap Provincial Hospital. They give us our space. They also give us our psychotropic drugs and some of the consumable supplies that we need. It comes to what they figured out to be about $7,000 a year. Everything that the government gives us are gifts in kind. No money changes hands, so there's no chance for corruption.

When Steve was there, he created a relationship with a local monastery. All of our patients that attend the clinic are offered spiritual group therapy, spiritual healing at the monastery, once a week. In Cambodia it is particularly important because the Cambodians believe that when they have post-traumatic stress disorders or traumatic depression, it's because the household gods are really angry at them or have deserted them. You could imagine a Western psychiatrist saying, "Tell me about your childhood."

We've tied in the predominant religion, as 90 percent of Cambodians are Buddhist. We've tied in the government, and we've tied in our Masters. In its first year our Cambodian clinic had 4,000 patient visits. That's not 4,000 patients, that's 4,000 visits. They did close to 400 home visits, which are really important, and Steve can tell you about that because he went on them. But they had a fourteen-month waiting list. So we opened a second auxiliary clinic down the road, where a doctor sees patients three times a week, and he's supervised by Dr. Borin from the clinic and a social worker. It's cut down our waiting list time, and it's also increased our catchments area. All of that, in Cambodia, cost us $21,600 a year.

STEPHEN: The Buddhist experience, the spiritual healing, is very good for us because patients continue on after they are discharged from the clinic. This way you can see who is succeeding and who is failing. You can bring them back in before they get really bad.

How do you measure how successful you are in a clinic? How are people monitored? If they've been discharged from the clinic, how do you know what happens to them?

STEPHEN: Kids are relatively easy because they're in school. You can look at their attendance, their grades, and their social behavior. Adults are more difficult, and the way you have to do it is to monitor substance abuse, spousal abuse, ability to work, and suicide. If they have a job, how's it going? I have been on home visits in Cambodia and seen how this works firsthand. On one home visit there was this guy who was sitting in his front yard, and his sister was with him, and his wife was at work; she's a teacher. There are actually two guys. One guy lives down the street, and we've been seeing him, and he has stopped drinking, and he got a job. This guy stopped drinking for a little bit and was looking for work, and then all of a sudden he wasn't working anymore. And we said, what is happening? Are you working? Are you looking for work? What are you doing?

He's sitting around the house, and his sister says he is drinking. He has no money, so we wonder, "How does he get booze? His sister says, "As you know, he is the nicest guy in town; he walks into a bar, and everybody gets him a drink." So we really don't understand what's going on, and we said to him "Are you taking your medication?" and he says, "yes." His sister looks at him and says, "no." We say, "Why aren't you taking your medication?" He said, "Well I do take them, once in a while." And his sister says, "No, you don't." We go back and forth like this, and it comes out that his wife dispenses him the medication, and he is positive she's trying to poison him. The upshot of it is we have his sister now giving him his medication. The guy has a job now, and he's happy.

So the Cambodian Clinic is doing great. The Master Classes are going fine, and through this process there is an opportunity to have a bigger impact.

We had two Masters in Cambodia, one was the Provincial Minister of Health, Dr. Dy Ben Chhym. We're all friends. We've known these people for four years and have e-mailed back and forth and whatnot—so that we were instantly credible.

LIZ: We're only building clinics where we have Masters in twelve post-conflict countries. We're continuing to grow.

STEPHEN: Listen to my wife. She wants clinics all over the world. The foundation through either the clinics or trained personnel have impacted 55,000 people. And it's going to be more, a lot more. Our catchment area in Siem Reap is four hundred thousand.

Clinical medicine is retail. The way you treat people is person by person and in this setting also family by family. If you do it long enough and you do it right—you're going to return whole villages, whole communities, back to social function. This is public health, and it is delivered on a wholesale level.

LIZ: Without treatment this problem goes from generation to generation, and you have to break that cycle. A child growing up in a home with parents suffering with traumatic depression is going to have a set of problems from his environment.

Poor mental health as well as good mental health probably spreads in the village as people see other people up working, living.

LIZ: If you treat a child, and you can be very, very successful with children, don't bother unless you can also treat the mother. If you return a child to the family where the mother has traumatic depression, everything that child gained will be lost. Ideally, you want the whole family, but the most necessary one is the mother.

STEPHEN: Yet on a macro level we are influencing public policies. For example, in Uganda there is a hospital that was built with

World Bank resources called Butabika National Referral Hospital. Its job is to empty the refugee camps of 1.7 million people from northern Uganda. The assistant to the executive director is our Master. He is influencing public policy. He is getting the politicians to exert the political will to put the economic resources where they need to be. Less than 1 percent of health care budgets of post-conflict countries are spent on mental health—this is changing. We're helping change it.

For example, we've had three Masters from Rwanda, and one became the Minister of Mental Health. We were invited in by the government to set up a clinic there in eastern province because they were particularly hit by the genocide.

These are people who have had the double whammy—the genocide in 1994 and then a generation of their parents being taken prematurely by AIDS. There are children called "cotos"—children on their own—and also defined as head of household under seventeen years of age, that have been hit by a double whammy, knocked on their keisters; you should pardon the expression.

We met a woman from Harvard School of Public Health, Theresa Betancourt, and she is from Alaska, and she's somebody who's nuts about kids. She did her dissertation on child soldiers in Sierra Leone. Then not so long ago she went to Gulu in northern Uganda and dealt with internees and returnees of the 25,000 children who had been kidnapped and pressed into service. Now she's gone to Rwanda. We financed her to do Phase One studies. Theresa's work combines qualitative and quantitative analysis. She looks at the big picture qualitatively. Then she focuses and does randomized control studies to answer small questions.

In six months, based on what she finds, we will then be able to do best practices psychiatric care for children that have been impacted by both the genocide and HIV/AIDS. We will know definitively what that is, at least to begin. We will then do a five-year longitudinal study. We will be able to define the mental lesions of mass violence but also correct them.

LIZ: This is something that has never been done before.

STEPHEN: There is something going on in mental health. People like Paul Farmer have shown that poverty and illness are a cycle, and if you break the cycle—if you treat the illness, then the poverty goes down. Somebody with anemia can't work. Take care of his malaria, correct his anemia, and you've got a productive person.

The same is ultimately true with mental illness, yet it is stigmatized. People's perception of mental illness is that it's forever, that it is incurable. The question is, "Can you cure it?" and we've talked about this before. We talked about this 80 percent of the people that are coming back. Are they going to be wonderful husbands and fathers? We don't know that. Are they going to go to work and contribute? Yes. So we can break the cycle.

LIZ: But it's desperately important that you do your research, that you have your numbers, and that you are absolutely sure of the efficacy of what you're doing. For us to be treating people and not be studying outcomes would be absolutely foolish.

STEPHEN: We are spending our lives on this. We are spending hundreds of thousands of dollars of our money and other people's money. It would be stupid if we didn't look for outcomes. We must be evidence based. But we believe that NGOs cannot treat disease. Charity is not the way for a country's illnesses to be solved. Philanthropy is not a sustainable model for a health care system. They have got to build capacity so that they can do it themselves. We have to teach them how, but then they've got to follow through.

You are a foundation with $1.4 million, and while that is a lot of money, given all you want to do, it is not a lot of money.

LIZ: You know, Peter had the most incredible group of friends that you could ever, ever imagine. There is not a week that goes by that we don't see them, hear from them, phone calls, e-mails. The toughest part of it all is that we're invited to all the weddings. I always vow that I'm not going to cry, and I always do. They have formed a group called the Friends of Peter Alderman (FOPA), which is an arm of the foundation.

STEPHEN: Their motto is, "For Pete's Sake."

Oh my . . .

LIZ: They formed this group, and there were eighty original members, and they each paid $50 to join—just to cover mailings and stuff like that—it's a one-time thing. It has grown substantially. They decided that they wanted to be able to do something as a group. They hold an event every year, they have had five so far and raise approximately $30,000 net, and then they decide how they want to spend it. And so they voted for the last couple of years to support the Cambodian Clinic. The Cambodian Clinic had a leaky roof, and they couldn't see as many patients during the rainy season, and so on the spur of the moment these kids got together, and they held a Ping-Pong tournament at a bar downtown, and they raised money for the roof. This has been terribly important because they are the future. They are the future, and so this will go on.

STEPHEN: These events, by the way, are not funerals. They are celebrations. My oldest, who was six years older than Peter, said, "When I grow up, I want to be like Pete." Pete really knew how to enjoy himself. Pete really knew how to cultivate his friends, and we still see these kids.

But the foundation is better off with us dead than alive. Our wills are such that for our three kids, it will be split a third, a third, a third. So the perpetuity of the foundation is assured. It will be endowed with a third.

Okay, but for the next forty or fifty years while you are still here . . .

STEPHEN: Aren't you nice? We are sixty-six, so we have got to get this stuff done quickly. We don't buy green bananas.

Also we have a Board of Trustees. One guy was Pete's boss at Bloomberg and the last guy to talk to Pete from the Towers. His name is Kevin Foley, and he knows lots of people, and we see them all. We use our Board. We have lunch in the city a couple of times a week, and we talk to anyone and everyone about what we are trying to do.

The other part of this is for our soul. The best part of all of this is people we meet. Not necessarily the funding people but others. For example, we have met with Juan Mendez, the head of the International Committee for Transitional Justice. He's a lawyer who spends his life working on human rights. He is just a fabulous human being, and it is an inspiration just to listen to him talk. He's on our Advisory Board. Jack Rosenthal from the *New York Times* Foundation, just another fabulous guy. We've made friends with people who we think are just wonderful. This is not fund raising. These are people who help the organization.

The reason I am asking you this is because your expansion plans and desire to have clinics in so many places suggests to me that you're going to need funding.

STEPHEN: Our budget for the last couple of years, for the clinics, the Master Classes, research and everything has been about $240 thousand a year. Right now we're intact; in other words we have not spent more than we've made.

LIZ: We will continue to expand. Steve has just returned from Uganda, and it is clear that we will need funding for both ongoing programs like the Master Classes and the clinics and for emergencies when they arise.

STEPHEN: On this trip we laid the foundation for an annual conference to be held each summer in a different East African country. It will be similar to the Master Classes with training for physicians and psychologists. We are hoping to get forty attendees this summer from different African nations. The five days will cover the history of trauma and genocide in East Africa, handling complex humanitarian emergencies and their psychological consequences and what we know about the most effective treatments and therapies. It is important that we are able to plan long-term events like this, which will hopefully be able to increase collegiality among countries that have not always worked together in this area, but we need to be able to respond to crises as well.

One of our Uganda clinics is just ten miles from the Kenyan border. When I was there two weeks ago, it was clear that there were no mental health services at all available to the Kenyans fleeing their country. Our staff is now spending three days a week trying to do what they can in the face of this humanitarian crisis. I am so glad that we could be there to help because right now there is no one else around.

BOB AND SUZANNE WRIGHT
Autism Speaks

You will have many, many chances to make contributions of time or money to different worthy causes. In some special cases, you, too, will have to ask the question, "If not me, then who?"
—Bob Wright, 2007 commencement speaker at Holy Cross College

MANY PEOPLE TRAVEL THROUGH THE CONCENTRIC circles of philanthropy, the movement from that which touches them personally to that which affects the larger world, over many years or decades. For the Wrights, this journey was just a blur. In 2004 Bob and Suzanne Wright were concerned, involved grandparents helping their daughter with their grandson, who had an undiagnosed affliction. By 2005 their family was privately struggling to deal with the specter of autism, something about which they had known almost nothing. By 2006 the couple had brought together autism organizations from around the country into their newly founded Autism Speaks and had plunged into a national awareness campaign. And by 2007 Suzanne had addressed the United Nations, and Bob had testified before Congress on the need for research into this developmental disorder. In a period of just two and a half years, Bob and Suzanne Wright established the largest national autism organization dedicated to research, fund raising, awareness, and lobbying. They raised tens of millions of dollars, helped push through a $900 million piece of national legislation, and merged the largest autism organization in the country into a single highly visible organization. It was a path taken with almost frightening speed, and yet the Wrights will tell you that they are not moving fast enough.

When families are in crisis, they often turn inward, pulling together in search of a solution for whatever pains them. For Suzanne and Bob Wright this is exactly what happened when they found out that their daughter's son, their grandson Christian, was autistic. Christian was the first child born to their daughter Katie in the late summer of 2001. A healthy thriving six and a half pound baby boy, he was born at Columbia-Presbyterian Hospital in New York City, where Bob Wright was a long time trustee.

Katie was a knowledgeable and vigilant mother and noted how her son hit each of his early developmental milestones such as eye contact, smiling, first words, and recognizing people around him, on time or even early. As happens with some autistic children, Christian appeared to develop typically, vocalizing, interacting, and showing the affectionate behavior of a toddler. Then approaching his second birthday things began to change. Christian's behavior altered, at first subtly and then in a more dramatic and obvious fashion. He grew silent and withdrawn as he stared into space and took little notice of those around him. He began to scream and hurl himself onto the ground, and soon he became obsessed with drinking baby bottles of milk, up to a dozen in a day. His pretend play, the conversations he had often carried on with Barney, the purple dinosaur, disappeared. Katie Wright describes her son as entering a "very swift cognitive downward spiral," where he went from speaking hundreds of words to just a few, from waiting for grandma at the front door to silence. Suzanne Wright calls autism a "kidnapping"—the process by which a young child is taken from his family.

Suzanne had watched her adored grandson rush into her home, dole out hugs, and blabber his baby words. When she drove with him in her car, he named each truck he saw driving by. Then one day it stopped. By the fall of 2003 she was extremely worried. Where there had once been smiles for grandma, she now drew blank looks.

Katie and Suzanne took Christian to the pediatrician, but they were told not to worry. The doctor suggested that since there was a new baby in the house, and the family had recently moved homes, the emotional turmoil might have unsettled the young boy. Give him a bit of time was the advice. To Suzanne, who had raised three kids and moved often as Bob moved up the ranks at General Electric (GE), the advice did not ring true. Katie Wright, in hindsight, has said that she regrets taking this advice, that she knew something was wrong, and should not have let someone who knew so little about her child suggest otherwise. She describes trusting this advice as the "biggest mistake of her life." She wasted six months as her son slipped into silence. By early 2004 Katie Wright was out of time and took her son for a thorough evaluation at Columbia.

As Christian's problems began to unfold, Bob Wright sat at the pinnacle of corporate America. He was the chairman and CEO of NBC/Universal and vice chairman of General Electric. He had been a trustee of the Columbia-Presbyterian Hospital for two decades, and the hospital gave his family everything they could—which turned out to be not much more than a diagnosis and a few suggestions of therapies they might try. "We have given him [Christian] every conceivable test we can to find a medical problem, and we are sorry to tell you that we cannot find one. Therefore he is autistic," Bob Wright remembers being told by the Columbia doctors. "They said it that way because what they really meant was that 'We can't help him.'"

The hospital was not remiss. Little is known about autism, and trial and error was the best strategy they could offer. The Wrights were sickened by the unscientific, unmedical, entirely haphazard approach that parents are forced to use to find what works for their kids. Time was slipping by, and the single thing that autism experts agree upon is that early intensive interventions—with behavioral, play, social, occupational, and speech therapies—as many as five times a week is the most effective protocol.

But which therapies? Since no one knew what worked for each child, months and years (let alone thousands of dollars) could be wasted as parents experimented with different therapies.

For most families of autistic children this is a confusing, tortuous path, with a myriad of dead ends, astronomically priced consultants and medical practitioners, and few certain answers in the end. For Bob Wright, the journey was exactly the same and entirely different. He did not need to begin with the Internet, the local pediatrician, or the yellow pages. It was at Columbia that Christian had received his diagnosis, and it was to the head of Columbia, Dr. Herb Pardes, that Bob began to ask questions. What do we do? Where do we start? What therapies work? How will he progress? Yet even the head of one of the best hospitals in America, a world-renowned psychiatrist, had to admit that there were few answers.

Bob and Suzanne began to travel the country in search of therapies and physicians that might help Christian. They are the first to acknowledge that this luxury was theirs because of Bob's financial success. Although they had money and connections, the process was still harrowing, uncertain, painful, and unclear. All they could ask themselves is "How do people do this?" This was a near impossible journey for a family with every advantage. How do millions of others make the journey? They soon came to understand that depending where a family lives, the cost of the services a young child like Christian would need could be anything from $10,000 to $100,000 a year. As they sought answers for Christian, they became aware of the paucity of knowledge and resources surrounding autism. The Wrights were deeply saddened at what they found and swiftly moved from grieving grandparents doing everything they could to help their family to national activists in a matter of months. As Bob points out, many parents dealing with autism are either exhausted, broke, or both. As grandparents, they were neither.

Before autism, the Wright's philanthropy was both generous and conventional. As he traveled upward on his corporate trek, the pair, who married in Bob's law school days, increased their involvement with groups like the Junior League, GE's service program, the Elfin Society, and the

United Way. Wright lent the power of his office to fund raising, and Suzanne gave her time to support local community causes. Every year they gave the maximum that GE would match and encouraged others to do so. They had been good community members and corporate citizens, but nothing in their pasts signaled the way this husband and wife duo would take on what they call an epidemic. Bob and Suzanne had always been very private about their family during his years as a highly visible executive, and they chose to draw a strict line between their private and business lives. Autism put them over the edge.

The Wrights are a study in contrasts. As they talk about autism, Bob focuses on legal challenges that will improve educational opportunities for kids with autism, a Web site that would link everyone with relevant knowledge from researchers to parents to educators, and the magnitude of their fund raising challenge. Suzanne talks about the pain families suffer and the injustice of how autism has until recently been largely ignored. But both focus squarely on visibility for autism. Without a national profile there is no money. Without money there is no research, and we remain in the dark.

Both Wrights are well versed in what has become the fastest-growing developmental disorder in the United States. More children are diagnosed with autism than with AIDS, cancer, and diabetes combined. It is a lifelong affliction that affects a person's ability to interact socially, but little is known of its origins.

So the Wrights went into battle. They gathered resources and researchers. They gathered allies and advocates, and then in February 2005 they established Autism Speaks. In two short years, they have tried to take on every aspect of autism. They began with a massive media blitz, a manageable task for the head of one of the major networks. This was followed closely by a national advertising campaign sponsored by the Ad Council. They focused on changing laws so that school districts would be mandated to be more responsive to the needs of an individual child. They gathered autism organizations around the country and, using what they would call a big-tent approach, merged resources into a single national structure and have poured funding in medical and scientific research. They worked to lobby state legislatures to change the requirements for insurance companies and lobbied Congress to pass what would be known as the Combating Autism Act, the most comprehensive piece of legislation dealing with a single ailment. They have developed a Web site that serves as a source of information for parents on every aspect of autism, and they did it all in two years.

When I sat down with Suzanne and Bob Wright at the end of this whirlwind, I was struck by the fact that neither of them feels they have even begun. They both speak, interrupting each other with a constant string of anecdotes, as if they are in the earliest planning stages.

LISA: Can you just give me a little background? I'd love to tell the story of how your philanthropy started and then led to Autism Speaks.

BOB: I went to the University of Virginia Law School, and we were married while I was there. After graduation my first job was with General Electric, which was helpful to me in my military obligations because I was going to go . . .

SUZANNE: He was on his way to Vietnam.

BOB: Yes, basically. So I went to GE's factory in Pittsfield, Massachusetts, and it was a typical hundred thousand population town that embodied all that is good about community service and involvement. All of it was heavily supported by General Electric and its retirees.

Was this officially supported by the corporation or voluntarily?

BOB: The company encouraged community service participation. GE provided space and picked up the bills for expenses and also had matching grants. So it was both a supporter and economic contributor but a very strong advocate. GE allowed people to take the time off if necessary and encouraged people to do that to become part of the community. I quickly became very active in United Way right off the bat.

I went to a high school out in Long Island where I was yesterday. It is called Chaminade, and it is where I really learned about community service. It's an all boys Catholic school out in Mineola, Long Island, and it's a wonderful school. It's been around since the 1930s, and everybody that went there was very middle class.

SUZANNE: I think our Catholic education really reinforced in us giving back. They had a mission of giving back, and that's just what everybody did. My dad was a cop here in the city, and my recollection of giving back came from Bishop Fulton Sheen.[1]

In our house growing up, we would have to put half of our allowance into a little Lenten box that my mother had. At the end of Lent we would count up all of the money as a family, and then we would go over to the church and give it to the priest. It was a little like the UNICEF boxes but long before they had them. So that was my earliest recollection of giving back. My parents giving back to the church and the poor people that Bishop Fulton Sheen preached about.

BOB: All during my time with GE, I was always involved in the United Way. When I was the head of GE Capital in Stamford, I was the head of the United Way in Stamford. Then I became head of the tri-state United Way, which is New Jersey, Connecticut, and New York; and that's a big organization. That's all before the United Way blew up with its expense account issues, which was really a sad moment. That's the sort of thing that we did wherever we were. I always used my office. I always lent the credibility of the office I had to whatever organizations were where we lived and were important. But that's the kind of philanthropy that we grew up with.

Autism Speaks is a fairly big break with your more traditional philanthropic past.

BOB: What we're doing now is different from our past, and it's driven by an event, by our grandson. And as much as this is hard to say, and it doesn't sound right, but it's really not about Christian. Christian has all the medical care and help that there is available. It isn't about him.

When we were trying to understand what happened to him, people would tell us to go here or go there looking for therapies and medical care. And we went here or there, and I saw something that I just couldn't believe. I could not believe that in 2004 you could have the most prevalent significant childhood developmental disorder, and no one knew either the cause or the cure. There were no organized treatments, insurance was limited, and medical care in some places was nonexistent.

It was a crime to see doctors not even be able to treat these children in hospitals because of the insurance battle. If you don't have insurance, you're really limited as to where you can go. You can only really go to emergency rooms or charitable hospitals.

But the case of autism is really worse than that. Medically it's a stigma. Once you're diagnosed with autism, many doctors won't see you. On one hand they say your medical problem has nothing to do with autism, which is pretty funny because then we go to doctors who say, "I'm sorry, because your son is autistic, I'm really not able to treat you. There's definitely a relationship between autism and the medical problem, and I can't see him because I'm not experienced enough to do that."

Can I wind back for a second because I want to get to the genesis of starting Autism Speaks. A lot of families have health care problems or other issues within their families, and they turn inward, as family members try to help each other. It is a natural response. Your family had a crisis, and yet you turned outward looking to help others.

SUZANNE: We turned inward as a family until we got through our grieving period, and then I was so horrified to see other families with this terrible situation that we had to act. In this country 1 in 166 kids are afflicted with autism, and it is 1 in 104 boys. I could not understand why the country wasn't screaming. How could that be?

When I was growing up here in New York, 1 in 3,000 people caught polio, and we had a national health crisis on our hands. Everybody gathered around. The country pulled together and did something about it. Now we have had that with AIDS, and we did something about that too, as a country. With breast cancer, we took action as a country; with prostate cancer, as a country. But the children with autism were not being heard—period.

As a mother and a grandmother, I was so shocked, and I still am shocked that this could be going on, and no one was paying attention.

So your original mission was presumably your own family? What I want to know is how this goes from being a problem in your own family to taking on the issue at a national level. How did you make that transition?

BOB: Two things happened to us. We traveled around looking for every service we could find for Christian. We were meeting with doctors and looking for therapies. Christian's got all these gastrointestinal issues, and we are just trying to get some help. I'm also talking to my friends and other people and saying, "I can't believe this situation. We really ought to find a way to deal with this."

I was trying to get familiar with the organizations that were out there to address autism, and it was very thin on the ground.

I've been on the board of Columbia-Presbyterian Hospital for almost twenty years, and I said, "I can't believe this." I spoke to Herb Pardes (MD, CEO of Columbia-Presbyterian Hospital), and he said, "This is a terrible situation." He told me that it is like schizophrenia was twenty years ago; he's an expert on schizophrenia, and he said, "Bob, it's just a mess. We know what the problem is; but we don't know what to do about it. We believe it's genetic, but we don't have any independent research money here, and we don't have doctors trained in it." I said, "Herb, I can't believe this." At this point they were interested in starting a diagnostic and treatment program for autism, but the program was not in place yet. Their recommendation was to go get behavioral, occupational, and speech therapies. But they did not have any particular recommendations in Connecticut, which was where my daughter was living.

SUZANNE: It was very primitive, very hit or miss.

So you were really on your own?

SUZANNE: Totally. Katie and I had to go out on our own and find everyone we needed for therapy. There really was no organized approach. We were watching him slip away, disappear in front of our eyes, and there was no sense of urgency. This was happening everywhere, and if that is not a national crisis, a real emergency, I don't know what is.

BOB: I was learning how little there was when I got a call in August 2004. Bernie Marcus [founder of Home Depot] called me up. He's somebody I had a relationship with, but he was not a close friend. This was just before I was leaving for the Olympics in Athens, and he said, "Bob, I hear from some of your friends, my friends, our friends that you really want to do something in autism. I really want to talk to you immediately." I said, "I'm going to Athens tomorrow." He said, "When?" I said, "Tomorrow night." He said,

"I'm flying to New York. I'll see you tomorrow morning. Can I come to your home?"

So he arrives at my house in Fairfield at 9:00 in the morning, and he's got Gary Goldstein with him, who's the executive director of the Kennedy Krieger Center in Baltimore. The Center is a very large public charity, which is affiliated directly with Johns Hopkins University. He took me through his experiences, and he said, "I've been involved with autism for eleven years or twelve years." It's a long story. He tried to help some people, and he thought this was someplace where he could make a change, and he ended up building a facility for treatment. "But," he said, "I've not accomplished my goal. My goal is to move closer to understanding the cause and finding the cure, and part of the problem is that there is no awareness. All the money I've spent, the tens of millions of dollars, and there is no awareness to show for it. If you really want to do something here—I encourage you to do it on building awareness. Without that we can't get anything done." He said, "I could write checks. I could write my entire fortune here, and it still wouldn't make a difference."

So I said I would think about what we would do and how we would do it. That began a period of going back and forth talking with Bernie and Suzanne. We spent a lot of time with Bernie and Gary. I came to the conclusion that he's right, that I agreed with him, that awareness was really the issue.

From my own fund raising experiences in the past I know; you need awareness to raise money. And you need money to do research. You need research objectives to connect to the politicians and to connect to governmental agencies and hospitals and insurance. These things all go downstream. It's a waterfall.

It was very clear to me that it would be silly for me to get into autism and to simply follow Bernie's path when he's basically telling me, "Don't come my way. It's just too expensive, and I can't make things happen." So I said, "Alright, I'll take on the awareness. We'll really go after this."

We then began a negotiation with Bernie on how he would help us. In the end Bernie agreed to put up $25 million, to fund the early years of Autism Speaks. This would make funding available to do things that we could not raise money for, to do things in advance of raising money. That was very important to me. I wanted that assurance that we could make commitments and honor them without having to start raising money that first afternoon.

The second thing that hit me in the fall was that there was no organization, no national organization for autism, and that in order to have an awareness campaign, that we really should try to merge with existing groups, or merge existing groups together. It became obvious very early that there were only a few groups that were trying to both raise money and invest in research. Other groups were acting more as facilitators and gathering points like the American Society of Autism.

They were information hubs for parents?

BOB: Yes, and it was very rough. Then there were smaller groups that were really just about the care of their own children, and maybe they had a particular focus point, but they were small. They had no national reach, and they had no Washington clout. There was a little bit in New Jersey and some in California but not too much.

SUZANNE: There were splinter groups across the country, NAAR [National Alliance for Autism Research] and CAN [Combat Autism Now], who are with us now, but they didn't have any power. They were powerless. They did as much as they could, and they did a fantastic job with volunteers helping each other to get some recognition. They started fund raising walks, and they did a lot of great things, but what they didn't have was a voice in Washington. That's where you have to go to get heard.

When I went to Washington for the Combat Autism Bill, one

hundred senators said "yes." They couldn't say "no" because when they had the facts in front of them, it was undeniably an epidemic, and nobody was doing anything about it. It was really a crime. Before this nobody was there to say to the Congress, "Hey listen, these kids have to be heard. We have to do something."

Hillary Clinton is smart. She's now got a bill for another $350 million on top of the $1 billion already approved in the Combat Autism Bill, because she knows I went to Barack Obama. We said, "Barack, guess what? Hillary is going to own autism. There's millions of votes here. We need to know where you stand." He showed up at a breakfast with forty people, all autistic families and spent two and a half hours with us. Barack's on the list now. He's going to help us with his platform. We are going to every presidential candidate and saying, "We want to understand where you stand on autism. It's an epidemic so either you're with us or you're not with us." That is why we needed a national organization, to have the clout to do this.

BOB: The first step was we independently created Autism Speaks. I did it with lawyers, and with top outside counsel and accountants, just like it was a business. Then I said, "We should merge with the Autism Coalition, because they had some good board members, and they had connections to a lot of other groups. So that became the first of our mergers. Then later on we merged with NAAR, which was a very well established group headquartered in New Jersey, but pretty much in the Boston, New York, Long Island, Westchester, and New Jersey area. Then lastly we merged with Cure Autism Now. It's a West Coast–based organization. Every one of these organizations had a different character, different mission, and a different geographic focus. So that was the business side of this. It was to try to be a big tent, and meanwhile in parallel we were doing awareness as much as we possibly could. I was trying to get press, I was trying to get events, I was trying to get the Ad Council. These efforts were all running in parallel.

Starting out we had to set objectives, and I was convinced two years ago that in order for this to be a successful organization, we would have to raise a $100 million a year—year in and year out. The organization would have to go beyond us and become self-sustaining. That $100 million would have to be replicable to be able to support both awareness and research and later family service and information. Awareness was initially the biggest cost, but it will become a smaller cost every year. We needed something in the neighborhood of $50 or $60 million a year of money to go into research. Our estimate was that in 2006 the National Institute of Health's total focus on autism, their real autism-related research, was $60 million. That is out of a $30 billion budget. They say it's $100 million devoted to autism, but they assign multiple diseases to lots of studies. When they add it up, it's a $100 million budget because they count up everything multiple times.

How did you come up with $100 million as the amount you would need?

BOB: Some of this was also a conversation I had with Suzanne and with Jim Simons, the founder of Renaissance Capital. Jim Simons had not taken a public position on autism. He was very quiet about it but was doing marvelous things. We did spend a lot of time talking to Jim to see if he could come with us. He didn't want to do that. He wanted to drive his own research. He was perfectly happy to share his results, to keep us apprised, and he has helped financially. In conversations with him, he believed that you needed to spend about $60 million a year to really be a factor and reach a critical mass in research. He's focused on the genetic work, not exclusively, but significantly. Jim has been very helpful to both of us in organizing our view on genetics, cell biology and the genome, and other areas that I certainly don't pretend to have any formal training in.

We also elected to take on family services, which was something we didn't initially focus on when we formed Autism Speaks. Family services is the business of trying to help families during the lifetime that they have to deal with autistic people; so it's very broad. It isn't building buildings or schools, but it is dealing with insurance. It is dealing with education. It is dealing with the treatments and hospitals and other medical institutions. It is dealing with a home. It is dealing with what happens to adults with autism.

All those things are our focus right now, and it's part of family services. We're going to start isolating funds for family services because I can see tremendous leverage. We can really accomplish things. This will be a permanent part of this organization going forward. Hopefully, it will be actually one of the most visible parts of the organization. I just see low-hanging fruit all over the place.

For example, a lot of states have laws that can be interpreted in a more positive way than they have been about housing for people with disabilities. A lot of states say you must have housing; other states say if it's available. Other states say that you have to have a certain type of criteria. We're close in a lot of states and just encouraging people to build housing and understand that they can get a fair rate of return from that investment will be a big help. I think this is an area that will grow over time for us. It is still on our horizon. It is the next piece we are going to get into after insurance.

This is not a cure. Autism is a lifelong affliction so you don't really get better and if your parents die, who takes care of you? If your parents have no money, who takes care of you? There is a tremendous deep, dark side to this situation. Many people with autism lose their benefits with the states. They do not have housing when they become adults even though they may not be able to live alone. These are not Down syndrome people who can live in group homes or live individually and take jobs. The autism spectrum has a lot of people who can't do that.

SUZANNE: What are we doing with the education? I think this is another groundbreaking area.

BOB: Education is a crucial issue. It is the ability for parents to get a plan of treatment established for each child that is meaningful in their school district as opposed to just accepting what parents are offered by the school district, which is generally very little.

We formed a legal group to address this [Federal Legal Appeal Project Initiative]. One of our board members, Gary Mayerson, is a very prominent lawyer who represents families with autistic children and appears on their behalf in front of boards of education and states and local groups. Now this is where you get power here. We are now well known enough that he went out to major law firms around the country and said, "We need you to help us with appellate work in representing families with autistic children and taking these cases to appeal. Would you be interested in supporting us?" The show of hands was unbelievable.

He went around soliciting pro bono work instead of soliciting money?

BOB: He went to firms like Akin Gump and O'Melveny and Myers to give you an example of two very big national law firms and asked their lawyers for help. Their partners said, "I'll take a look around and see if anyone wants to do this work pro bono." Then some of their partners said, "We don't have to take a look around, I'll do it." Others said they would take a look around, and they found out that they had ten or fifteen partners or associates that raised their hands to help us with this litigation. A lot of them had been clerks at the U.S. Court of Appeals level and in the Supreme Court, which is where we have to go. This sort of plays into my own background.

This is not to take on individual cases. This is to take on the laws that exist?

BOB: No, this is to take on cases that are about laws. In other words, you have to represent families, but by winning the cases, the laws themselves are changed. I call them our Special Forces unit. Counties and school boards are going to be shocked when they see who's on the other side of the table now. The good news is that they're so enthusiastic. They came back to us and said, "Forget the expenses. We'll cover the expenses too." Generally in pro bono cases, you don't pay for the lawyer's time, but you pay their expenses. We're out now scouring the country for cases that we think have great appellate capability.

SUZANNE: Gary just won a major case in Tennessee. This town in Tennessee spent $3 million or $2 million to fight this case. They tried to avoid spending $60,000 a year to send a child to a special school. The county was so afraid of autism that they spent $2 million to fight it and lose.

BOB: This single county in Tennessee spent $2 million in court fighting Gary and the family he was representing in their demands for adequate education for their autistic child in the public schools in that county. In the end the county gave the family what they had demanded, and they made them sign a nondisclosure. That's what happens. Then the next family comes along, and they go right back to square one. That's how this game works. That's why you have to have appellate cases.

Most school boards have the ability to engage litigation costs outside the budget of the school board. So they don't have to report the spending to the voters. And the voters don't have to approve these things. That's a real major problem. They can spend almost anything they want as long as they get the county approval for the spending without having to report it to voters, whereas states limit the reimbursement of lawyers representing families, keeping the cap on some of them as low as $4,000. So the state limits reimbursement of a representative of a child and does not limit the amount of money that the board of education can spend.

SUZANNE: That's why they spend the millions they do.

BOB: It's a very intimidating issue. That's why we want to get to the federal appellate court. The reason you want to get to federal appellate court is it becomes national, and families no longer need to take on their school boards alone. We want the Second Circuit Court of Appeals here in New York to rule. That's a very prestigious one and that would be very important. We want the sixth circuit, and we want about two or three others. Then what happens is if there's disagreement, it goes to the Supreme Court, or if there isn't particular disagreement, other courts will look at those courts and tell the school district that this is law. The lower courts will say, "You don't have to go to the Supreme Court. We have read the opinions and that is the law." So you win either way.

Now there's going to be different points involved in each of these cases. They're not all going to be the same, but they are going to head down a path that says you cannot do this to these kids. You cannot offer these kids a couple of hours of therapy and call it a day and think you've met your educational obligations.

SUZANNE: That is what they did to us, to Christian, and we're living in the wealthiest county in Connecticut—Fairfield County. They offered us a couple of hours a week of therapy and that was it. We had to leave and went to New York City. There was nothing there for us, but we could afford to leave it. What about all those people who we left behind? I thought to myself, "How could this be?" Christian is now at a school that costs almost $100,000 a year.

BOB: This is the part that I think is really gratifying. There is a tremendous amount that we can do that goes beyond just raising money.

SUZANNE: Because we will be getting justice for these families.

BOB: There are some analogous issues here to cancer. There are two hundred types of cancer, and autism is a wide spectrum. Most children who have autism are born autistic. There's no immediate test for autism, but the condition manifests itself so early that the conclusion is that you're born with it. But there are some children—somewhere as high as 30 percent—who have regressive autism. In other words they don't manifest the typical symptoms of autism early on. They can actually appear to be very ordinary and then all of a sudden lose all their faculties for communication, along with picking up a bunch of other problems. This happens somewhere between the age of two and three generally, maybe a little later but in that area.

That leads you to the conclusion that all children are not born with autism. With cancer, the majority of people with cancer are not born with cancer. There certainly are well-known cancers, such as childhood leukemia where a person is certainly born with cancer, but melanoma and lung cancer . . . those aren't thought to be cancers that you inherit. Rather the environment you lived in has drawn out the genetic problem that's caused it. Genes and environment are totally locked together. In cancer, most of them are in later life. In autism, most of them are in early life. You don't get autism when you're forty.

The point is that we need money that looks at the whole autism spectrum. We need to try to isolate genes that are present in a person with autism versus a person without. All of this was theoretical five years ago, but now it's all very practical. We have met researchers at Cold Springs Harbor Laboratory. The geneticists, Michael Wigglers, the most active geneticist in the United States today, is saying, "I have the tools now—I just need the money to use them." It's very exciting. There are going to be answers on the table in the year 2010. That's the exciting part. That doesn't mean you get cured, but it gives you a pathway.

SUZANNE: It's coming out of the darkness into the light. It's just beyond belief what's happened in four years. I have just been to the United Nations. They asked me to speak there, and it was standing room only because it was about the epidemic of autism worldwide. Two weeks ago we had a resolution passed unanimously in the United Nations—we are about to pass it in the General Assembly—to have an International Autism Day, April 2, in perpetuity until this darn disease is gone. In the history of the UN, there have only been three other such days devoted to AIDS, diabetes, and disabilities. We are going to get worldwide attention, because this is around the world.

BOB: It is not hard to see how you bring autism to the national agenda. The numbers speak for themselves. Most of the people that are associated closely with us are there because they have autism in their family. We make a generalization here, but I think it would stand the test of . . . some test. For every autistic person, there are twenty people that know a lot about that person; most of them are relatives. But some of them could be people that work in the household, or they could be godparents or friends. But twenty would be a rough number. We don't know exactly how many autistic people there are in the country. Let's assume that it's between 1.7 million and 2 million. That would mean that upwards of 40 million people in this country know a lot about autism through the experiences of a particular individual. So it isn't difficult to find people that are connected in some respect.

It looks like it's almost a new business for you. It looks like you left one industry and almost created another.

BOB: I consciously tried to do it that way. Then I'm at least comfortable with the metrics. I'm comfortable with the process and how we're doing. I don't want it to slip into something I'm not comfortable with. Autism Speaks isn't a business, but if it were, we would be having an IPO because we've accomplished a lot. You can be in a not-for-profit situation and use all your business skills, and I have found that in my entire business career with the United Way, I used every one of my business skills. I have tried to bring board members and supporters to Autism Speaks who want to do the same thing. We do need wealthy people. For the organization to thrive we need their money, but if we can get them intellectually interested and contributing their expertise as opposed to just writing checks, then they actually become part of some of the goals and to take some responsibility for achieving those goals. I think you get a lot of leverage that way.

How this process has changed you, immersing yourself in philanthropy at this level, how has it affected you or your family?

SUZANNE: I think we've always been so focused as a team. When autism happened to our family, and it was such a tragedy that we just took that focus and put it into Autism Speaks. We've always been partners in everything we've done. He's always treated me as an equal partner, so when we decided to do this, it was just an extension of what we've always done as husband and wife. We just took it on like we've taken on so many other different jobs Bob's had or moving or raising a family. It's just something that came to us pretty naturally. When we decided to do it, we never looked back; we only looked forward and said, "This is what we really are committed to do."

You have traveled a long way in three years.

SUZANNE: I never thought it was going to be anything but what it is, and there has to be so much more.

BOB: We feel our time is limited. Because whatever prestige I have will dissipate, and I have to use every minute I have here, to get Autism Speaks established and meeting its goals. At some point it will dissipate, and it won't be an issue because we'll be strong enough to operate without that historical prestige. I look at it as a timeline here. There's a very short time here. You just have to really accomplish a lot quickly. I just force myself to think we have to get this done before next week.

One famous Ethiopian saying goes, "For every one dollar comes twenty Americans." Everyone has their voice; everyone knows what's best—we don't.

—Donna Berber

When extreme poverty breaks your heart—you can no longer turn your back.

—Philip Berber

THE TERM "ENGAGED PHILANTHROPY" CANNOT BEGIN TO describe Donna and Philip Berber's involvement with their foundation, A Glimmer of Hope. The English-Irish couple, longtime residents of Austin, Texas, have immersed themselves in helping the rural poor in Ethiopia. Engaged philanthropy, a term so in vogue over the last decade, describes the practice of devoting time, money and expertise, of becoming far more involved with giving than simply writing checks. But for this forty-something couple and their three sons philanthropy has led them to spend every summer traveling in rural Ethiopia from the time the boys were tiny. For Donna the immersion has been even more complete. She has lived in dirt huts with thatched roofs sleeping side by side with twelve other adults as rats traipse across her pillow at night. Her giving has led her to walk miles to waterholes in the blazing Ethiopian sun, to be eaten by bed fleas at night, and to live amidst the hunger and poverty she is trying to alleviate. Does she need to do this to help those halfway across the world to live a better life? No. Is she better able to understand their health and education needs, the way their days are dominated by the gathering of firewood and water, able to evaluate if her funds are being spent in the right place? Can there be any doubt?

Donna and Philip Berber met and married in London where Dublin-born Philip was a software entrepreneur. The couple spent their early adulthood absorbed with their business and raising their three sons. They often sent small checks to various causes, but giving was such an inconsequential part of their lives that neither can remember now who or where they donated to in those early years. The Berbers were an average striving couple. Their income grew, their family thrived and life was good—except for one thing. Donna had been at the LiveAid concert in 1985. She had stood among the 75,000 fans at Wembly Stadium, and the sounds of that day reverberated for decades inside her. "The calling to do something and make a difference, it was always there," Donna says. "If anything, it got louder and louder as my life got quieter and quieter and more comfortable."[1] Like so many of the other philanthropists profiled here, the Berber's philanthropy was born of simply not being able to look away.

Neither Berber grew up with much money. Donna was raised in London, and when she was eight years old, she, her brother, and her mother witnessed her father's death in a small plane crash. Her mother went back to work to support the family after he died. "I didn't have a joyous childhood," she says. "Quite an unhappy one really. It was very strenuous; very, very hard financially and emotionally. Having seen and experienced so much turmoil, I had empathy for the pain of others."[2]

Philip grew up in Dublin, as one of five children, with a father who was a small business owner and thus the provider of a variable income. Growing up in a terraced house like so many that cover the British Isles, it was hardly inevitable that he would become an Internet entrepreneur in Texas two decades hence. After graduating University College in Dublin, he went to work in London for Systems Designers, developing aerospace software. "When both Donna and I grew up, our families were scraping by. For me, when the telephone didn't work at home, it wasn't because of a technical fault, it was because we couldn't afford to pay the bill. My father was an entrepreneur and had some good times and times where it was difficult to pay the bills."

In a life-changing moment of insight, Philip realized that the technology he was developing for military and aviation use could be brought to bear on the financial markets. The optimizing software could be sent out to search financial markets for the very best price at any given second, rather than searching for a military target. In developing such a program, Berber was cutting out the middleman, the long-established Wall Street broker, so commissions were slashed as well. For the average Joe trader, the guy seated behind the personal computer in his den who makes ten to twenty trades per year, this tiny advantage was not worth much. But for day traders, who were coming into their own in the 1990s with accounts that might ring up ten to twenty trades a day, this service was invaluable. Philip said, "My bosses said, 'The Ministry of Defense isn't interested in trading stocks.' " "I said, 'I know that, but someone is.' "[3] Before he could do anything with his moment of insight, he and his young family were transferred to Houston.

Philip founded CyBerCorp in his son's bedroom with a PC and a company account balance of $230. Four years later, in early 2000, he sold the company to Charles Schwab for $488 million. His timing could not have been better as the market for Internet stocks crashed two weeks later. Even before he sold the company, Donna had begun to explore options for what she might do to help in Ethiopia. Philip had sold an equity stake in the company, and Donna intended to take some of the proceeds and "do something in Ethiopia."

It is essential to put this in context. After Philip sold CyBerCorp, the couple donated $100 million in Schwab stock (which declined in value with the stock market as it was sold off by the foundation) to get their efforts in Ethiopia under way. It was an act of monumental generosity. This donation earned them a place on *BusinessWeek's* list of the top fifty givers in the United States and placed them as one of the top ten on the list in terms of the percentage of their wealth given to philanthropy.

I wanted to interview the Berbers because they began to give away a massive fortune from almost the first moment that it materialized. They were young, just forty-one. They were not in possession of a mansion, a private jet, or vacation homes scattered across the globe. Yet quite literally, without hesitation, they gave away $100 million. They had no philanthropic past, no period of giving with their training wheels on. They went from zero to sixty in a few short months, and I wanted to know how it happened. "We really wanted to make a serious commitment—I think it was about commitment—and wanted to take a reasonably large proportion of our funds to do that," Philip recalls. "We did not sit down with any accountant, who would've surely advised us otherwise, nor any philanthropic advisors. Frankly, I didn't even know how to spell philanthropy before I got into this. We just, from a place of heart not of head, wanted to make a significant commitment and to venture down that path and see how it unfolded."

The Berbers reacted differently as fortune rained down upon them. For Philip this was long-awaited good news. He had been an entrepreneur for decades and finally had his payoff. The money was an acknowledgment of his success and the assurance of security for his family. The toys it would buy would be fun as well. For Donna the money did not accompany such undiluted joy. She loved her life and knew that with this windfall things would change in many ways.

The Berber's philanthropy can perhaps best be described as intimate philanthropy. They have come to know those they give to. They have lived in their villages, visited their programs, and kept in constant contact with the various projects they fund. They hoped to develop a direct conduit from Austin into Dembi Dolo, and that is what they have created.

They have been iconoclasts in their work in Africa. They sum their philosophy up in a few words, "First—ask; don't tell. Second—help them to help themselves." It is very telling that Donna's first step on her philanthropic journey was to hire a local guide. Her very first action was not to fill an air-conditioned office in Austin with well-meaning Americans. Instead, she hired a national out of the Ethiopian Embassy in Washington, a man who would know and understand both worlds intimately. Working closely with local Ethiopian groups outside of the capital city, the Berbers have ignored the huge international NGO infrastructure. They have deliberately focused on small, manageable projects, on water, irrigation, schools, and health and veterinary clinics that can be brought to completion for a reasonably low cost. Like Duckworth's Arzu Rugs, A Glimmer of Hope has gravitated to isolated locations that for logistical reasons have remained hard to reach by outsiders. Also similar to Arzu, the foundation has focused on making investments rather than gifts. A Glimmer of Hope might provide the capital for a water pump, but in a contract with its recipients, it expects those who benefit to manage the installation and maintenance of the equipment. Philip maintains the mind-set of someone who has run a successful business with efficiency as one of his paramount goals.

Barron's commissioned Geneva Global, a philanthropy consulting firm, to look for ten of the most effective philanthropic organizations in the United States. Lists abound of the largest givers, but here was a different view on giving. As Geneva Global CEO Steve Beck points out, "Ranking philanthropists based on dollars given is akin to ranking the world's great investors by the amount of stock they bought rather than their returns; it celebrates the input without regard for the impact."[4] This was a search for those organizations that had shown a sustained commitment to their cause over a number of years and did it in the most effective manner possible. A Glimmer of Hope and the Peter C. Alderman Foundation, as well as Eugene Lang's I Have A Dream Foundation all made Barron's top ten list of those who have learned to give wisely.

The Glimmer of Hope foundation relies heavily on listening to those in need and using their ideas and proposals in an effort to give grants where they are needed most. "We went to the poorest villages and asked the people what they wanted most," Philip says. "Ethiopians may be poor, but they are not stupid. I am sorry to say that the bulk of international aid starts in an ivory tower somewhere in Washington, and then the expats tell the Africans what they need and want."[5] The Ethiopians told the Berbers that they wanted water, schools and jobs, in that order. So Philip went to work, studying everything he could find on irrigation, agriculture, and African poverty and politics. Then A Glimmer of Hope, through its own tiny office in Addis Ababa, solicited proposals, short one- to two-page requests for funding. This funding would come with caveats: Groups receiving funds from A Glimmer of Hope sign a contract that stipulates that only 5 percent or less of the funds will be spent on administration. The recipients must take ownership. If they wanted A Glimmer of Hope funding, they would have to bring their own energies and resources to the table as well. Philip describes the process, "We buy the brick; they build the wall. We buy the pipes, and they dig the trench."[6] It is a partnership from the first day, and the Berbers ask for quarterly reporting, again a short report of a page or two—no tomes—to keep a close eye on their projects.

In the tiniest microcosm of their philanthropy, Donna met a woman in 2007 struggling with dire poverty. Her husband had died of AIDS, and she had seven living children. Every Tuesday she carried fifty pounds of grain from the market to her village on her back. It is a thirteen-hour trip, and when Donna met her, she asked how she could help. Without asking this question, Donna would have given the women food or medicine, or she might have assumed that the woman would ask for clean water, but instead she pleaded for a donkey. Both Berbers started this process acknowledging that they knew nothing and that the most important thing was that they listen and learn—and seven years hence neither has changed their stance.

A Glimmer of Hope has no fund raising machine. The couple has established an endowment, which they spend a portion of every year. As the foundation runs down its endowment, Philip has said they will replenish it from their family's wealth and then spend that down as well. And while other donors, most prominently Susan and Michael Dell, have given generously to A Glimmer of Hope, it does not need to make raising money one of its causes.

Interviewing people like Donna and Philip is a job made easy. She does not struggle to answer any of my questions. Her philanthropy took two decades to incubate, so she has had time to think it through. Philip's respect and admiration for his wife and the journey she has led him on is instantly obvious. A man of strong opinions and keen insights, Phillip approached the couple's philanthropy with a businessman's mind and an almost spiritual belief in what they are doing. "What I feel is a healthy, custodial responsibility and stewardship around all of this wealth, and it's about doing the right thing for families also and being in service to others," Philip explains. "At a more spiritual level, it feels like there are no accidents, and things unfolded as they did, and we get to serve our purpose in a much higher and more meaningful way by being engaged in this way."

LISA: A Glimmer of Hope is so huge. I wanted to ask you what led up to it. It's a pretty big undertaking to start a $100 million foundation working halfway across the world. Were you two involved in any major philanthropic efforts before jumping into your efforts in Ethiopia?

DONNA: A little here and there, a little contribution to this, a little contribution to that, but no more.

PHILIP: What we would do, like anybody else, was receive these mailers to give $50 or $100 to different causes. Some of them touched us in one way or another, and we gave. It was totally unstructured, reactionary, and unresearched just an emotive response to some of the mail that was coming through.

So it wasn't during school or college or early adulthood that your philanthropy developed? I know that you, Donna, went to the LiveAid concert in London. What happened after that?

DONNA: It actually started with the images on television prior to the LiveAid concert, when Jonathan Dimbleby [UK journalist] went on British television and brought out all this footage from the famine camps in Ethiopia as they were called then. They don't have them anymore, thank God.

I remember being in my mid-twenties and looking at these images and just being absolutely torn apart. It was one painful image after another all very compelling, heartbreaking, and heart wrenching. It was one of those things where I so wanted to change the channel but couldn't. That is truly where I think the spark occurred. It gave birth in me to the notion of living in this world and it being much larger than myself.

Watching that footage on television was really the point of pure impact for me which was "Oh my God, I'm living in this world and this too, this suffering, is part of my world."

I was so inspired by a single person, Bob Geldof, who just at the core level, decided that he wasn't going to sit back, and he was going to take charge. As he mobilized LiveAid and BandAid, he didn't actually care how his message was perceived or received. The most important thing was that it was heard.

He's not everyone's taste, but he really resonated with me because his approach was so direct and powerful—this is what's happening; this is what's real. And for all the successes or challenges of BandAid and LiveAid, it really brought into focus and into awareness the enormity of the struggle of Ethiopia at that time.

For me that was the major point of impact, a moment in time, the realization that just one man from a rock band alone could make a phenomenal difference. I had the good fortune of meeting Geldorf recently. We spent a couple of hours in the Hilton Hotel in Houston last July with him, and it was fantastic.

Roll the clock forward, and life is going well. Philip and I moved to Houston from London in 1991 with a five year old and a one year old. Philip was an entrepreneur, and his London company was bought by a Houston-based company, and we were transferred with the package. So off we trundled to America to start a whole new phase of our lives with two small children.

Life was going well, although Philip's situation didn't work out, like most of his entrepreneurial pursuits. It is interesting that he had this big success after twenty years. But as he says, it took him twenty years.

People don't realize that about people who have found success. They think it was the first time out.

DONNA: They think it's overnight, and it really was over twenty years. After four years of living in Houston, we discovered Austin and decided that was really where we wanted to raise our family. We went ahead, and we had our third child during that move to Austin.

Life was getting really comfortable, Philip was starting an online trading company called CyBerCorp, which was doing very well, and I remember it was after a couple of years, in 1999, we sold a very small portion, like 8 percent, equaling about $3 million.

All this time I was living this very comfortable life, but I've got this almost painful, yearning inside of me that is just feeling that my life is too comfortable, that there is more to it than this. As good as things are—this is not what it's about. Philip was very consumed with CyBerCorp, and I was very consumed with the children, and yet there was something much bigger at work in me.

Were you explicitly thinking about Ethiopia, or it's just a more general feeling?

DONNA: A very general, but palpable feeling. So when we sold part of CyBerCorp and got the $3 million I thought, "This is the time to follow your heart, start getting proactive, put something into action. Find out what it is that's gnawing at you." That's when I started my series of phone calls and e-mails.

And you immediately started in the direction of Ethiopia?

DONNA: I immediately started in the direction of Africa. As a little girl, I had a humongous resonance with Africa, so I knew that it was going to be Africa but not much more than that. I started, if you like, my research, and it led me to a café called Central Market in South Austin, where I started chatting to a woman who had just adopted two children from Ethiopia.

And it was in that moment that she unlocked the key for me. All the images of twenty years earlier came flooding back.

It was absolute knowing in that moment that I needed to do something in Ethiopia. So here I've got $3 million in my back pocket, but that could be my life's savings, too. I had no clue what was going to happen from that point on with CyBerCorp, but I contacted the Embassy of Ethiopia in Washington. I called up the head of nongovernmental organizations there. I said, "Hello. My name is Donna Berber, and I'd like to come and see you because I want to open an orphanage in Ethiopia."

And it was this conversation in a café in Austin that made you think you wanted to open an orphanage?

DONNA: It seemed to me, listening to her, that here was a generation of children surviving without parents because of the AIDS epidemic, disease, and the war. In my very western ways of thinking, it seemed absolutely logical that, with $250,000 to spend (as that's what I set aside out of the $3 million), I could do something to help these orphans.

The man I spoke to was Tamaru Abasaba. He was very polite and invited me to come up to Washington, DC, to meet with and speak with him. I went to the Embassy in Ethiopia and had an incredible meeting with this man. We talked about the 1980s famine and just really connected. I remember quite clearly we both sat there crying together, which you don't really expect to happen anyplace on Capitol Hill.

It was a real meeting of the hearts, and at the end of it he said, "You know what you really need to do is go and visit Ethiopia. Go and see it for yourself." And so that's what I did. A few months later, I think it was in September of 1999, I went for ten days. I went with a girlfriend, and we went on a, if you like, fact-finding mission to Ethiopia.

But as fate, destiny, or divine guidance would have it, during the period of me having $250,000 in my pocket, CyBerCorp had sold for an unearthly amount; and all of a sudden I was showing up in Africa with multiple millions in my pocket to find out what, where, when, how, who, and if this really was the place, then what? There were some massive question marks.

Philip, at this point you are not really involved with Donna's research?

PHILIP: Donna and I were responding to our good fortune in totally different ways. So here I was, I have just sold the company for a half-billion dollars and am starting to enjoy the perks and accoutrements of corporate America and being an Internet success. So while I was starting to ride in private jets, and my entrepreneurial ego was being inflated, she was venturing down a different path, a far more humble, meaningful path. She was starting to meet with people in coffee shops and restaurants and making phone calls to inquire about people in need, particularly overseas.

DONNA: To backtrack a little bit, after I did my research and had made my decision that I was going to work in Ethiopia, that this was going to be the place, I remember coming home to Philip, and he'd basically said, "Go ahead, follow your heart. See where it leads, and we'll go for it." This was with the $250,000 in my back pocket and then later with the rest.

I remember coming home after having been at the gym. I was running on the track, and I was thinking, "What am I going to name this foundation. What's it going to be called?" Literally, it came into my head—a glimmer of hope. I came home, and I said to Philip, "Okay, it's A Glimmer of Hope, and it's in Ethiopia."

He looked at me and practically scratched the top of his head and said, "Do you think we could do something more locally?" He said, "Donna, if this was a business, it would be just too challenging trying to get this off the ground." I said, "You know what, Philip, I hear you. Let me sleep on it." And I went to bed that night, and I dreamt about it, and I was there. I got up the next day and said, "I'm going to Ethiopia," and "Are you coming?"

Did you ever consider giving to something that already existed in Ethiopia rather than starting something on your own?

DONNA: At this point we had started to research international aid agencies and NGOs and figured that we could actually find a better way ourselves.

I also think that engaged philanthropy is what it's been about for us. It hasn't been about writing a check and finding someone else who could deliver or partially deliver. It's been about having our own selves, our own equity, personal equity in terms of who we are very much absorbed in the process from that point to this point.

I wouldn't have it any other way. It felt critical to our own personal involvement. It's not damning of anybody else. We just felt that there was another way of doing this that could be more impactful and more effective. The truth as I understand it is about any form of philanthropy in its genuine sense. It's a God-sized hole in my own heart that has to be filled first. Being aware of that is helpful for me, because I see that I'm not doing anything for anyone. My life is better because I am able to do this, and please God let others benefit in the process, and that's the way it seems to work. Going back to the question?

We were talking about how you actually got things going after realizing that your efforts would be in Ethiopia.

DONNA: I had a ten-day trip there that rocked my world. From all the research, e-mails, and conversations I thought I knew what I was going into. But there is nothing like the living, breathing experience. There's no point of reference. There's no television, no media, no story, and there's no photograph that can ever, ever give you the living experience and depth and knowledge and smell and touch and feel of the people, of the place, of the challenges, of the richness, of the beauty, and of the despair. There is nothing.

It was an amazing trip. I got to meet the president and the prime minister. The doors opened for me, talk about the wind behind my sails. It was inexplicable how I felt this energy was moving through me in this place and with these people. I went all over the country and met, as I say, an amazing array of people in government, and I was overwhelmed.

Someone had said to me before I left, "Donna, be sure you can swim; otherwise, you just might drown." And I thought, "No, I'm prepared. I'm prepared." Actually I did drown when I went to

Mother Teresa's [a clinic in Addis Ababa that serves destitute terminally ill patients]. I'd never been touched so deeply in my life. To walk amongst people with smiles on their faces as they prepared to move on with some dignity and grace. I was in awe of the sisters and their hope and gratitude while living amongst squalor and disease and deformity in a way that I've never witnessed. Their belief is that God lives amongst the poorest of the poor, and I think they're right. And it just moved me, and I did drown in that place. That's okay; we need to drown from time to time. We just need to drown and out of that comes something better.

I came back from Ethiopia and talk about a wild, diverse, extreme life. I arrived at Newark Airport after a twenty-four-hour journey. Driving to the Addis Ababa Airport in those days was a real trek. It was a different city then. The capitol is rocking right now compared to what it was. I remember that first trip back to the airport, seeing the mothers sitting on the side of the road in the rain, nursing their babies with little corrugated shacks behind them. It just was more than I could stand.

So I arrive in Newark Airport after this journey, and there's my name being called over the loudspeaker system. I'm coming through Immigration, and I am thinking, "This is too weird." I get to the other side, and there's Philip, bless him. He came to Newark to pick me up in a private jet. I had a five-hour layover, and I was thinking, "God, give me strength to understand this."

Here I come from the most deprivation and squalor and sorrow that I've ever, ever, ever witnessed, and I'm getting on a private jet—like how do I do this? How do I live in these two worlds?

PHILIP: As she walked down from the airplane at Newark, I could sense that something in Donna had deeply shifted. And on that flight back from Newark to Austin, I listened to what she was describing, and in her bag she had brought back video footage from Ethiopia. I sat there that night, quietly on my own, watching my wife on the video handing out loaves of bread to Ethiopians lining the street holding out their hands—gracefully and graciously receiving these loaves of bread from my wife. The tears just started pouring down my face. For this was something I didn't recognize. This was something beyond my frame of reference, and it touched me very deeply to the point that the curiosity was sparked to go and see and feel for myself. What was this that I was witnessing from both what she was describing and what I was seeing on these videos?

What happened after Donna's first trip?

DONNA: I come back home and went completely underground for six weeks. I couldn't really talk to anyone or do anything. The only people I really wanted to talk to was my immediate family who can see that things are not ever going to be the same again.

What were you doing for those six weeks?

DONNA: I stayed in my dressing gown for quite a while. I kind of moved around at snail's pace. I was on the phone everyday to Tamaru saying, "Help me, help me; it's so big, it's so huge. I don't know where to start. I'm overwhelmed with the need. Will you help me? Will you come to Austin? Will you help me with this?" He said, "It would be my honor." He left the embassy in DC and came down to Austin.

With Tamaru everything changed. He understood the world of NGOs. He understood the Ethiopian government. He was a national, so he understood the culture and the people. What better situation could there have been? When he comes down to Austin, Schwab very kindly donated two little office cells to us, and we got to work.

I said to Philip, "If you're going to be engaged in this, then you have to go see for yourself, or you're just not going to get it." He ended up with Schwab for one year, by which time Tamaru was on board, and we were already cooking.

PHILIP: So when I went out there, I went way into rural Ethiopia, southwest Ethiopia, to a very small village called Dembi Dollo. I spent time there, and that was where, for the first time, I saw and touched poverty at such a deep level that I came back knowing it was time to resign from my start-up CyBerCorp and from Schwab. It was time to step away from the game of business and to devote myself to helping these people I had met in rural Ethiopia. I had no frame of reference for poverty and human suffering on this scale.

Poverty to you was what you had seen in Dublin.

PHILIP: Yeah. There were poor people in Dublin, but they all wore shoes, all went to school; they all drank clean water, and they all wore clothes. Here were people drinking brown infected liquid and spending hours in search of it. The children were not in school, and the women were dying on birthing tables. I was taken to a hospital on my first visit, and I had literally not understood that humans could exist in such a devastating level. I didn't understand how these people could survive, and yet they did.

I was looking at the children thinking, "What could be their hopes for their future? Were they just to repeat the same cycle as their parents? What of the mothers that had died on the birthing table? What of the children that were literally dying from diarrhea?" These are our brothers and sisters who happened to have been born in Africa as opposed to America, or developing countries as opposed to developed countries. None of this made sense to me, because I had never been exposed to any of this before.

I did not believe I would be in the position again where I would be able to build a business over five years that would get to the stage of half a million dollars a day in revenue and then be able to sell it for such inflated valuations. Therefore, my days were done in business, and there was something far more important, far more meaningful for me to do with my life, and that was to join Donna on this path that she had shown me. I'm just thrilled and blessed that I married Donna and that she showed me this path.

Now that you were both committed, had the resources and the time— what were your first steps?

PHILIP: What's the first thing you do in business? You do your homework. So we did the research, and the research was appalling. It started with *Lords of Poverty: The Corruption and Disruption of the International Aid Business* by Graham Hancock. This book documents particularly what was going on up to the late 1980s . . . also through the 1950s, 1960s, and 1970s . . . the traditional corrupt, disruptive, and mismanaged international aid business. And as I read through the pages of what had been going on, I felt both sick, and I felt that (Donna doesn't like me to say this) an array of people should've at least been put in jail, if not worse. It was disgusting.

I did more and more research into international aid, and then I started studying charities, international charities, looking at NGOs, analyzing their balance sheets, analyzing their financials, looking at financial ratios and all of those things. The bottom line was really clear: If you were lucky, somewhere between 50 and 70 percent of the money may get to the intended cause, and I'm probably being kind because there's a big black hole in terms of how financials are accounted for overseas.

Now we had pledged $100 million of Schwab stock, and if 30–50 percent of that was not going to get realized, we were going to be responsible for between $30–$50 million being pissed down a big black hole. And in the context of my background in business, and in the context of being custodian and a steward, it was not acceptable to send our money down existing and traditional channels of distribution, because that's what they are.

What we're talking about in the whole business of charity can be broken down into middlemen and channels of distribution, because that's what the industry is. There are donors, there are middlemen, there are channels of distribution, and there are implementing agencies, and then beneficiaries. So I was able to map out the flow of funds through the intermediaries, through the channels of distribution, and I rejected that model completely.

It's kind of funny that we were in Austin, and one of the most famous companies here is Dell, and they talk about Dell Direct. We chose to develop a new, secure, direct-aid model, whereby the funds would go directly from ourselves to the implementing agency. Now that's important as well. If we go overseas and set up a business, we'd probably set up a head office, and then we'd establish distributors and then go about our business. That's what we've done in Ethiopia. We've set up our own NGO, not some third-party NGO. So it's A Glimmer of Hope, Ethiopia, NGO registered in Ethiopia, authorized by the Ministry of Finance. So we've formed our own head office, staffed it with Ethiopians, not expats running around in their Range Rovers with their children's school fees being subsidized, with all the shenanigans that goes on around the overhead of supporting expats in overseas countries. The third step that we took was that we chose to empower and engage local and regional Ethiopian self-help organizations and local and regional Ethiopian NGOs, who had the know-how and the willpower to work with the local communities to implement projects. What they were lacking was primarily capital and support.

DONNA: We wanted to work with local self-help communities like local regional administrations and district administrations.

People who were there in Ethiopia and whose work it was to support local communities. We wanted to work where most NGOs won't go, where there were no roads or electricity. We wanted to engage with people who were prepared to engage in their own future, i.e., if you can't give money, then give your time, give your skills, give your sweat equity.

We wanted to elevate the role of the woman. The women carry the burden of society literally on their backbones. They are the mules of society; and while that is changing in urban areas, it's still quite predominantly true in the rural areas. We were empowering the women locally by having at least one female representative on each local committee so that the needs of the community could be heard. Because it's the women who know the need. They carry it. They are it. It lives through them.

How did you begin?

DONNA: We started our work in a model village in a place called Dembi Dollo in the southwestern region of Oromyia. We created a model village where we looked to provide all the social functions and the basics a community would need. It contained everything a human being would need actually to have a reasonable, humanitarian type of existence.

PHILIP: And from there we reached out into every region of the country seeking to find local and regional self-help and NGO organizations.

DONNA: At that point we had to say to Tamaru, "Listen, for us to have a presence in Ethiopia, you need to go back and create your own team on the ground." So he went back. We have an in-country office where five people work.

Which he could do because he was Ethiopian. He knew the country, he knew the need, he knew things that you would never know.

PHILIP: In business you always want to have domain expertise. He was our domain expert. We needed his and other's expertise to invest in Ethiopia. We don't view this as giving anything away. This is social investing through social entrepreneurs for social profits. That's in essence the model. If you and I were talking about investing, then we would talk about portfolios. What we were doing in Ethiopia was applying the same process of screening potential partners in the same way that one would evaluate potential money managers for your investment portfolio. We are looking for a portfolio of projects and partners who share our goals.

Talk to me a little bit, then, about the criteria. What were you looking for?

PHILIP: The usual stuff. What's the first thing you look for in an investment manager? We looked at their track record in implementing projects. Secondly, we looked at their field of expertise, be it water, health, or education. And what you soon find is that most implementing agencies have a bias or specialization or a particular expertise in one or two of the areas, and that's what we found.

The third factor is that you don't invest in projects. You invest in people. It's, again, the old adages. There's nothing new about what we did other than we took the lessons one had learned in the world of business and reapplied them in the business of international aid. That is the mind-set.

So that's how we were screening potential Ethiopian implementing partners. Once we gathered our short list, we sat with them and began the allocation process. You allocate based on how many people are in the region and the capacity of the implementing organization. There is no point in giving somebody a million dollars if they only have the capacity to implement $200,000 worth of water wells, given their staff and size. So the population gives you a sense of the size of the need, and the capacity gives you a sense of their ability to deliver. Then the third thing is, and this comes over time, relationship and trust.

You don't allocate the whole portfolio to an unproven manager. So what we chose to do is create a pilot. Initially, we chose one community, to see whether it was possible to work with these people through this model. The first project we were asked to do—we don't tell them what they should do—we were asked to build a school for hundreds and hundreds of children in this rural village. For us, that proved the concept. It was possible to fund that from Austin and direct into Addis Ababa through a local implementing agency, and a school was built.

When we went back to visit the completed project, the completed school, about six or nine months later, they took us across the road to the hospital. They showed us that this was the next need, and after the hospital it was water, and so on. What we learned with that first cycle in this pilot program, in this pilot village, was that the community knew very well what it was they needed and wanted. They even knew in which order they needed things the most.

How do you decide how much to give in total?

PHILIP: It's funny because we're doing this right now. We, Donna and I, determine at the beginning of the year how much we're going to allocate to Ethiopia at the start of the year. For example, this year it's about $3.5 million that A Glimmer of Hope will allocate from its own endowment for funding projects.

So this is out of the original donation that you made seven years ago?

PHILIP: Yes, and that excludes all of the overhead. The endowment also pays for that. So what we do is we allocate the funds across the different regions. Then we invite our partners in Ethiopia to propose to us what they need and want to do with that money in the form of projects that reflect the need of the people in the communities they represent.

So let's say that's $3.5 million. Let's say $500,000 goes to a particular region. The partner or partners in that region are told, "Hey, we've got $500,000 for you for the next twelve months. Go to your people. Ask them what it is they need and want. Then come back to us and propose to us." We are a little bit like a venture capitalist, except we say, "There's a $500,000 fund here. Come back to us and propose what you'd like to do with that fund." And they come back with water wells, schools, health clinics, veterinary clinics, etc. We then receive all of these proposals in Addis Ababa, not in Austin, with all of the proposals, there's usually around 300 projects every year. They are reviewed in Addis Ababa by our Ethiopian staff— the partners and the staff.

Then Addis comes back to us, Donna and I, and says, "Here's the whole portfolio. Of that amount of money, these are all the projects, in each of the regions, by type, by how many people will benefit. This is how much it will cost." They do the calculations all the way down to what is the cost per head for each and any project, down to the second place decimal. You know is it $6.38 or is it $7.32. All the way down to cost per head for every project in every region and every village.

Can you give me an order of magnitude. If its $3.5 million and say 300 proposals, how many would finally be funded?

PHILIP: Almost all.

Almost all of the 300?

PHILIP: Yes. This year when were looking at 2008, including money that comes to us from donors, we'll be investing over $5 million in 2008 in Ethiopia.

And $1.5 million will come from external donations?

PHILIP: Yes. And about $3.5 million of that is coming from us. And that approximately $5 million next year will impact over 400 thousand people, and there are nearly 600 projects.

And by impact you mean they will have clean water or will have a new classroom, etc.?

PHILIP: Exactly that.

How do you keep track of the progress of all the projects that you fund?

DONNA: We meet with them every single year. Tamaru meets with them many times during the year, and they send in their project proposals once a year and then quarterly updates. We provide funds to them quarterly, so what happens is after each quarter they send in their reports. We might do a spot check, go and visit and see what issues have come up, what support is required.

For example with water wells, what we'll do is . . . while we don't manage them, we make sure when the water well goes in, that there is support for training, for management, maybe a stipend fee, etc. We'll get a report back after a certain amount of time of how many are working, how many aren't, and it's just a phenomenally high number of wells that are working, in excess of 90 percent, and each one has a useful life, and we're aware of that. At that point we give them their next round of funding.

All different things come up when you're dealing with Ethiopia. Expect the unexpected. But now we're very much in that groove of the foundation of having humanitarian support—water, health education, and veterinary clinics, and we have well in excess of two thousand projects over the last five to six years that have been operational there.

And how do you measure the success of the project?

PHILIP: I would say quantitatively and qualitatively. Qualitatively, we walk amongst the people, look in their eyes, and take note of a myriad of things that I could not show you on a spreadsheet. In the case of water, look how their eyes are whitening up again . . . and the smiles on their faces, I can't show you that in the spreadsheets. Walk into a classroom, and this is a brick classroom not a run-down shack, you wouldn't keep your cow in with children sitting on the floor. This is now a brick classroom with a proper whiteboard and it's ventilated, the windows are open, and the children are sitting at desks. And look into the eyes of those children and speak with them and hear them speaking English in this rural village. I can't show you that on a spreadsheet. Speak to the mother who didn't die giving birth, whereas her sister did four weeks before, because this time there was a health clinic or a doctor or a gynecologist. Walk in the ward and see children recovering from burns, wounds, children recovering from distended bellies and insecticides in their water, and I can't show you that in a spreadsheet. The smiles on the faces of the mothers who no longer have to walk three hours a day to fetch dirty water but now can get it and walk with a plastic container 300 yards from their house to pump crystal clear water. And they now have hours a day on their hands for being with each other and other multiple benefits. Again, I can't show you that on the spreadsheets. These are the qualitative measures.

Quantitatively, we measure it in a number of ways. Particularly, we have our partners reporting back to us once a quarter on the progress of each and every project that they have signed up for. If they are on track and things are moving as they have planned, then we will release the next quarter's funding. It's the same as a business cycle, a quarterly business cycle, because this is performance philanthropy. We will invest in people based on them performing, doing what they said they would do. And if it breaks down, then we'll sit down and try to understand what it is that's holding things up. How can we help? Are these issues resolvable? Is it just a delay? The rains in the south last year delayed the school construction project significantly. We can't hold that against any partner. It rained, and the village was inaccessible. You try to get your trucks through these rivers of mud. It's not possible. So you understand the circumstances, and you don't penalize people under those circumstances. You just wait patiently.

Africa has its own time and timetable, and we Westerners need to understand that. Often we go in with our Western mind-sets, and it creates conflict. And I think what we've learned over time is we're probably partially Western and a lot more sympathetic and empathetic to the African mind-set, and the African way of life, and the African frame of reference. In addition to the partners reporting to us, then our people go to Africa as much as they can to visit on site. And then Addis also gathers up reports and feeds that back up to us here in Austin. That's the spreadsheets, that's the numbers and the quantitative control.

We both go over about once a year. The way it's set up is empowering and enabling our team, our staff in Addis. We have a weekly phone call with our Addis office, Donna does that, and then there are ongoing e-mails and communications on multiple topics in an ongoing basis. For the first six or seven years, we went out as a family, visiting all sorts of rural regions of Ethiopia, really getting to see different aspects of community life in different parts of the country.

More recently, I have become quite focused and engaged with microcredit. Much of what we've done to date is humanitarian aid, and its great, and we'll continue to do so. However, there's a need for economic development if we're going to truly help them lift themselves out of poverty through microloans, loans for small- to medium-sized enterprises, loans to farmers for irrigation equipment, loans to women for start-up businesses, and that's why I was there this year.

That was my theme. Donna, God bless her, decided to go and live the life of the poor rural women in a hut, in a rural village, sleeping on the floor, doing the walk for water, and I'm not sure I can do that. In fact, we've come to learn that there are many Ethiopians who would choose not to do that. Ryan, our son, was out there in the summer, and he was out following up my work in the area of microcredit—meeting with microfinance institutions because we want to expand our microcredit program beyond the first region where we piloted.

When we go, there's always the opportunity to spend time in the village with the children, with the adults, visiting projects, seeing the water wells, visiting health clinics, and being with children in schools. When you walk amongst the people, it reminds you why you do this work.

Having your trusted people in the country must make all the difference.

DONNA: . . . all the difference. We couldn't do it without them. You know, that's the partnership. It's all very well us having good intentions, but if we don't have that level of trust, of competency, then our dreams are not going to be realized.

I'll never forget after the first year, one of our partners wanted to do nine schools, and they did it very efficiently. They came back and they said, "What should we do? We've got about $10–15,000 left over. Shall we return it to you?" Where do you hear that in international aid? You truly don't. I said, "No. Spend it." How beautiful that they would come back and even ask—that just demonstrates the trust element. So we're very, very big on that and keeping our word and being efficient and keeping our promises and showing up every year.

I just came back from Ethiopia last week, where I lived in a hut in Tigray for the best part of a week. So I could fully—internally, on the ground—have greater insights as to what the challenges are for these people. I've visited the place seven or eight times. I've been out to rural Ethiopia many many times, but I have never experienced anything on the level I just did.

I came away thinking I would never know what it was like to be an Ethiopian woman, or an African woman, who gets up and walks four or five hours a day to contaminated water and then schleps the water back and then her day is just beginning after four hours. I'll never know what it's like to carry thirty or forty pounds of sticks on my back for firewood. Let me tell you, I walked in their footprints this last week. I walked in their footprints. And it is so much deeper, it is so much greater than I ever could have known, and my regard and my fury have just been raised to a new level.

My love and compassion have always been there, but I am so ignited with fury because people should not have to live in such an inhuman way; it's not okay anymore. It's not right, people living amongst rats and breaking their backs and walking thirteen hours barefoot over a rocky mountain carrying grains to sell in markets. Thirteen hours this one woman walked, and her greatest wish was not for clean water, not for education for her kids, but for a donkey, for a $30 donkey to change her life. So we bought her a donkey.

It's just not okay anymore. It is time. It is time for people to sit up and stand up and take responsibility and know that God truly lives in the poorest of the poor. They are alive and kicking and doing their best, and a little support is required.

And the future? Are you going to grow this? Are you going to seek funds from others? What is the direction?

PHILIP: In a phrase, A Glimmer of Hope 2.0, that is our theme that we embraced about a year ago. And what that really said is a couple of things. Number one is now that we know a little about global poverty, and a little bit more about poverty in Ethiopia, we realized that this is a huge, huge challenge. And our endowment, however large or small, is not going to crack this. It's not enough. It's not smart to try to do this all on our own, so part of Glimmer 2.0 is . . . we need help.

We've invested $20 million so far and impacted over two million people in the first six years. So we ourselves have inadvertently built sort of a track record. What that has done has attracted some families, strictly local families and some people from the tech sector here in Austin. Michael and Susan Dell are an example of that. We've come to learn that if you share and describe and tell people what you're doing, there are those who would like to join you on the journey and would like to co-invest alongside us in this work, especially because they know that 100 percent of the money is going to get to the Ethiopian partners.

Secondly, we go out of our way to try to bring back photographs, bring back videos, bring back stories, connect them and engage the donor with their work. So yes, part of Glimmer 2.0 is to reach out to others to co-invest and donate alongside us in this work so that we can reach more people more quickly because the need is so great, and so urgent.

Part of 2.0 also says, and I touched on it before, all of our humanitarian aid work is wonderful, but it's not enough. It's a giant Band-Aid. And we've come to view that the other half of this is to really address poverty. It doesn't take much to realize that the solution to poverty is simply to help them make money. That's how people rise out of poverty by economic growth, by jobs, by income. And so we started with the largest single group in Ethiopia, and probably Africa, and that's the farmers. The trouble in Ethiopia is the rains are inconsistent. So rather than stand around and wait to see if it's going to rain to determine whether you and your family are going to eat or not, we've moved into irrigation, the same way Israel turned a desert into an agricultural economy. We are funding through microloans farmers to buy low-cost irrigation foot pumps and drip kits. Fields of rock and rubble are turning into fields of green. They eat, their food is now secure, and they are taking the excess cash crops to market, and they're making money multiple times more than what they borrowed for the pump in the first place. We lent a group of women entrepreneurs money for a bread factory. Basically, they make Ethiopian flatbread in a group of corrugated huts. Now they have a contract with the local Tigray-Mekele University. And they're shipping out these flatbreads as quick as they can make them.

To the cafeteria? For the students?

PHILIP: Correct. And let me tell you it's not just the economic impact on these women. It's empowerment. Women have been the mules of African society for decades or centuries probably, and providing economic empowerment to women provides personal empowerment as well. There's a whole piece on that, and it's wonderful to see. Now most recently we've started to fund small and medium enterprises. Microloans are famous for being $50 to $100, and that's all very, very true. And there's another sector in industry—small and medium enterprises—and we're starting to do $500,000 loans to small and medium enterprises.

What kind of businesses are examples?

PHILIP: The ones we're starting to fund now are tannery, weaving, ironworks. They're usually associated in some way with rural agriculture where they're making saddles or leatherwear or gates; it's all that sort of thing. It's very much handcrafting, rural and agriculturally related small and medium sized enterprises.

One of the last things I wanted to touch on is . . . how this has affected your family?

PHILIP: Our children have been provided with the opportunity of seeing and experiencing a way of life in Ethiopia that is very different to that which they see at home, meaning here in Austin. What I see here is children living in the bubble. I see high school kids driving their cars with their telephones and all the things that are part of our life here. God bless it all. But this has given our children a chance to see beyond the bubble. They've walked and talked and played with children with no shoes. They've connected with people in rural Ethiopia living in huts. They have seen what it is not to have access to clean drinking water. Our youngest was three years old when he started going to Africa, and our eldest was fourteen. He's the one that went back this summer, meeting with the microfinance institutions trying to figure out how we can expand our economic development programs in Ethiopia to help the rural poor lift themselves out of poverty.

I would say that these experiences have changed their perspectives forever, and they realize that there's a whole big part of this world that isn't living the life that they're exposed to everyday.

I think they've seen that we all have a duty to give of ourselves to help people in need whether you're three years old or fourteen. They know that this is what Mom and Dad do.

DONNA: I just wanted to add that I think that one of the most important things a philanthropist can do is truly listen. One of the famous Ethiopian sayings goes, "For every one dollar comes twenty Americans." Everyone has their voice. Everyone knows what's best. We know that we don't. Not in international aid, not unless we're living it on the ground, we don't. We have to respect that these people know what's best. We have to let them decide what their communities need. Once we start and try and impose our thoughts on their needs—it's lost. And that I would say one of the greatest things that I have learned during the process is to continue to listen, and just as soon as you thought you've listened as well as you can, listen more.

PETER BLOOM
DonorsChoose.org

*I think whatever motivates people to give money away should be celebrated.
If part of that motivation is public recognition, that should be celebrated;
and if part of that motivation is a desire for anonymity and privacy, that
too should be celebrated. I've discovered that it can be more satisfying to give
away money when you don't expect to get anything in return.*

—*Peter Bloom*

T COULD ALMOST BE CALLED NEWSPAPER PHILANTHROPY,
the process whereby a successful professional, perusing the newspaper on an early morning commute, or with croissant in hand on a quiet Sunday, reads about a social entrepreneur and then, with a phone call or e-mail, changes his own and the organization's destiny. Most of us read about a compelling cause every day and then turn the page or click onto the next story. But some, like Peter Bloom, pause, think for a while, and then change thousands of lives.

For Bloom it was a 1,400-word story buried in the *New York Times* Metro section entitled "Matching Givers With Those in Need; Some See Web-Based Charity as the Future of Philanthropy." Written in July 2002, Stephanie Strom told the story of Charles Best, a twenty-six-year-old high school teacher, who, through his brand new Web site, had raised $120,000 from 170 donors for a wish list of classroom projects posted by Bronx public school teachers. The cost of the projects, which ranged from requests for books and calculators to soapstone and carving tools and field trips to class speakers, were outside the school district's budget and, without the Internet as a conduit to philanthropists, would have languished as the pie-in-the-sky dreams of a few ambitious and highly committed teachers.

When Bloom read the article, DonorsChoose.org was not much more than a neighborhood program. Only two years earlier Best had been a brand new social studies teacher in the Bronx. Listening to the lunchroom chatter, he quickly realized how much more his colleagues wanted to accomplish than the school's budget would allow. He learned that his colleagues regularly dug into their own pockets to buy paper and pencils for their students, but something like a classroom full of calculators would simply be too much. He knew that many people outside of the school would love to help but were reluctant to send their checks into a black hole, to be gobbled up by overhead or administration. Most helpful souls, he reasoned, would not even know where to start.

Bloom conducts his philanthropy with his heart and his head. He and his wife have been generous but anonymous donors to a myriad of causes. True to his Wall Street background, here is a man who does his due diligence, consulting experts like Guide Star and the American Institute of Philanthropy charity rating guide, to find out where his dollars are going and whether the funds are really needed. He had seen too much well-intentioned giving that was ultimately unfocused and unstructured and yielded few objectives. But even first-rate organizations, Bloom learned painfully, may not be the ideal place to give. "Two organizations that I had been continuously supporting—one helped people with specific handicaps, and the other was a human rights organization—truly did not need the money I was giving. Both organizations, one through their real estate, and the other through a massive legal settlement, were in very strong financial positions. Yet they continued to fund raise, and I had continued to give, assuming the need was real. Both had very compelling fund raising strategies that were hard to resist, and in both cases neither organization needed a dime for the rest of their existence. So that discovery was a seminal event in my own giving, and that lead me to conclude the following: that I would not give money to an organization that I hadn't thoroughly researched."

Yet there was no way to research DonorsChoose.org; it barely existed. The background check that Bloom considers essential to responsible philanthropy was all but impossible. DonorsChoose.org would be a bet on an idea and on a rookie schoolteacher and his ability to execute that vision. Despite Best's commitment and obvious intelligence, he did not have a track record that suggested he could run an Internet start-up business or scale up an organization to cover the goal of serving every school in the Bronx and later New York City and eventually the nation.

Bloom, with his background in technology and a successful career in finance, loved the Internet aspect of the program and the concept of helping public education, but neither of these are the reason he telephoned Best and invited him for breakfast. The article said that after Best graduated from Yale, he helped train Tzotzil Indians as teachers in Chiapas, Mexico, and later taught Spanish literacy at an orphanage in Nicaragua—and Bloom had a sense that he had found the real thing. When the two had breakfast together, Bloom's expectations were confirmed. This was not a young man trying to build his resume with a stint in public school teaching before moving on to a money making job in consulting or on Wall Street. Best had a vision and was deeply committed. Even as Best was cultivating donors and expanding the geographic scope of the DonorsChoose.org Web site, he had not left his day job. He had an idea with almost infinite possibilities, yet he had no money, little organization, and a board of directors that consisted of the first two donors—his aunt and himself. Best had little experience with developing a growing organization. He did not have a background in technology, the years of experience working with nonprofits, or the financial skills like those that Bloom had gained in his years on Wall Street. Bloom and Best brought to their partnership the essential components of effective giving. Best had an idea that donors would find compelling and would sustain their focus. He had the passion to devote his career to achieving its success. Bloom could help him build a fund raising and governance infrastructure and keep the organization focused on its essential mission.

At the time he launched DonorsChoose.org, Best was living at home with his parents. With some of the savings this gained him, he paid a programmer $2,000 to develop a rudimentary Web site, based on his design, where teachers could post their wish lists to be seen by all. He then asked his mother to help him with some homemade desserts and brought them into the teacher's lounge. The deal he posed to his fellow faculty members was simple: You eat the cookies, you go to the Web site, and post projects that you would like to have funded. Eleven of Best's colleagues complied. The first request came from the health teacher who wanted a set of "baby think it over" dolls, the life-size dolls used in pregnancy prevention courses. Requests for SAT prep materials, art supplies, and classroom speakers followed. Best convinced his aunt, a nurse, to fund the first project and then secretly funded the other ten projects himself. His tooth fairy approach to philanthropy brought a stream of requests from other teachers in his school and around the Bronx, and DonorsChoose.org was born. Best was not going to be able to play Santa Claus forever; it was an unsustainable model. So he raided the mailing lists of his prep school and university, and every afternoon for months his students sat and handwrote letters about DonorsChoose.org to the alumni. The kids printed, stuffed, stamped, and mailed two thousand letters and generated the first $30,000 from a couple hundred intrigued alumni.

Through Best's DonorsChoose.org Web site, generous individuals could scroll through a catalogue of requests and then provide full or partial funding for any project they wished to support. Best, with his soft-spoken manner, gives his teaching colleagues credit for making DonorsChoose. org come to life. Seeing his bright innovative colleagues unable to realize their dreams for their classrooms was his driving force. He will tell you that it was all common sense.

Philosophically, Best was very much in Philip and Donna Berber's camp. The Web site did not post what he or DonorsChoose.org thought teachers wanted, despite the fact as a teacher he might have had a very good idea, but rather they asked the recipient. Each teacher, the young Web site founder reasoned, knew best what his students needed. It was to be one of the essential ingredients in his program's success, the direct link between an army of citizen philanthropists and classroom teachers all over America.

After September 11, 2001, teachers in schools located around ground zero began to use the site for disaster-recovery needs. One teacher wrote in to say that she was teaching out of a basement, and the kids' calculators were sealed into a building that was off limits. Would someone fund a new set? Much equipment had been lost or was cordoned off near the site, and 150 proposals poured in from the surrounding area. Best thought this would be the turning point for his nascent project. A heartbroken country was looking for ways to help, and what could be more compelling than kids who were having their education compromised by the disaster?

Best telephoned the local press to let them know about the projects posted on the Web site, yet not one reporter was remotely interested. In frustration, Best cold called *Newsweek* Editor-in-Chief Jonathan Alter, who picked up his own phone, spoke to Best for an hour, and wrote an article that said the following: "DonorsChoose.org may eventually change the face of philanthropy. I know because I tried it." So complete was Alter's enthusiasm that he later joined the DonorsChoose.org board. Oprah saw the coverage and invited Best to be her guest, and the show resulted in $250,000 in donations from forty-eight states.

DonorsChoose.org is located in the noisy garment district in Midtown Manhattan. In two cramped rooms Best's seasoned management team and the droves of young people that run this national organization undertake everything from verifying a teacher and a school's authenticity, to determining a project's costs, to farming out proposals to readers all over the United States who will give teachers constructive feedback, to executing the proposal. No money is sent to teachers. DonorsChoose.org executes the delivery of goods and services for every funded project themselves.

DonorsChoose.org's bright sunny office has an entire wall covered in shelves filled with boxes of envelopes. On a freezing winter day, Best and I leafed through these envelopes that contained the projects being processed. Inside each envelope was a roll of film or a stack of pictures, a sheaf of letters from a classroom full of kids, and a carefully prepared receipt for each project expense, down to the credit card processing fee. As I selected an envelope at random, out fell twenty beautiful thank-you notes written by primary school children whose teacher had requested a pencil sharpener for each child. Pencil sharpeners. A tiny, almost throwaway item costing no more than a few cents at any local stationery store was what this teacher wanted for a classroom of brand new writers. The envelope would soon be en route to the donor, with the receipt that Best's staff got from buying and shipping the product, and a photograph of the class and their shiny new sharpeners. "You can see now how they trust that their money really went to the right place," Best explained to me. "They are looking at an authenticated request, and the proposal has been checked out by one of our volunteers. They know that when they give their money, it's not being handed over as cash to the teacher, that exactly what they are giving for was really purchased, and then they receive photographs and thank-you letters, showing them the impact that they had," Best further explained. "Our donors come back. The feedback is our resolicitation. We get letters and e-mails from donors all the time who are in tears." Two of the biggest surprises for Best were that donors seem to have no regional allegiance. They give money to a project that calls to them, not necessarily one that is in their neighborhood or state. And of all the noncurricular terms searched on the Web site, "autism" is the most frequently entered word.

Bloom's role as chairman of the board of DonorsChoose.org is to keep the organization focused squarely on showing philanthropists of every size a detailed portfolio of the impact they have had in every classroom they touch. The enthusiasm with which he explains that every donor can see how every penny was spent is unbounded. He is justifiably proud of DonorChoose.org's accomplishments, of reaching every state in the United States with its program while having its operating cost underwritten by corporate sponsors. Yet at the same time here is a man who is so moved by the stories he hears that he is nearly overcome with emotion recounting the good that Best and his team are able to do.

Bloom's years of philanthropy led him to DonorsChoose.org, and everything he has learned about giving, about carefully watching where dollars go, focusing on the recipients' true needs, keeping it close and personal, giving quietly with no fanfare or recognition, has been brought to bear on this national organization. "We lead ambiguous lives—often it is hard to discern our impact. Macroproblems like hunger or cancer seem to overwhelm us. DonorChoose.org addresses strategic goals with tactical delivery," Bloom explains. "The program, with its accountability and transparency at every stage, gives a donor a sense of connection and impact that is very satisfying."

LISA: I want to start with the earliest influences in terms of where you think your impetus toward philanthropy came from.

PETER: While working on Wall Street, I had a mentor who organized a philanthropic effort to help Jewish families escape from the Soviet Union. This was in 1990 just at the time when they were allowed to leave, but they required significant amounts of capital to get out.

My mentor organized a plane, and you could buy a seat on the plane, although the money was really used for all of the expenses and logistics that were necessary to rescue a family. We filled a very large plane and brought a meaningful number of Soviet Jews to the United States.

It was a turning point for me because my mentor taught me that by giving money strategically, I could truly change people's lives in a way that I had no concept of before he opened my eyes to the possibilities.

And that was a one-time event for you or something you got involved in long-term?

I think it taught me that you could get a lot of leverage from people coming together to focus on a common philanthropic goal. This was an issue that I cared about because of my heritage, but there was a crisis of the moment that demanded immediate attention and effort. I would equate it to what is happening in Darfur, although that situation is more extreme. There's a current crisis. If we don't address it now, then at some point, inexcusably and tragically, it will become irrelevant.

Where did this experience lead you in your philanthropy?

I began to watch the people that I worked with who were in two categories. There were those who were making their money and spending it on visible material possessions. And there were others who were very clearly committed to giving away money in a way that had a real impact.

What was interesting to me is it actually was age independent. I had some young colleagues, who were very focused on philanthropy. I also had some older colleagues, who you might have expected to be more generous because they'd reached the stage in life where they would be more focused on giving, but in fact they weren't. I observed the people that were making a difference and doing really good work so that I could then model my own behavior on theirs.

What was it that you saw about their behavior that you wanted to emulate?

One thing that I discovered early on that has made a difference in my own thinking about this is that there were people that were clearly passionate about something that I didn't understand.

They often spent the time and effort to educate me about the cause they cared about. Even though that passion could sometimes be overwhelming, I was frequently not only impressed and educated, but felt motivated to give because of the genuine commitment they brought to the cause.

The other thing that became clear to me is that individual solicitation and education was so much more meaningful for me than institutional efforts. Like many corporations, my employer encouraged institutionally supported giving to organizations like the United Way. I felt obligated to give, but it just felt like my money was going into a black hole. Whereas when I talked to people who had an individual cause that they were personally, deeply committed to, I felt a stronger connection to what they were doing.

What kinds of causes? What kinds of things drew you in early?

What drew me in originally were stories about individuals. But I learned that while it was incredibly satisfying emotionally, it did not provide a lot of leverage in terms of my own personal giving. While it felt really good to change one person's life or one family's life, there was so much more that could be done. Then like so many Americans, September 11 for me was really the seminal transition event in terms of activating my own desire to make a difference on a more significant level.

I want to go back before September 11. What sorts of things were you involved in philanthropically?

As a citizen of New York, I was always concerned with hunger. You can't live in New York City and travel a subway without recognizing the crisis of hunger and homelessness. Like most of us, I felt guilty about it, and I would often give money to whatever homeless people I encountered. This assuaged my guilt at the moment, but

I knew it wasn't an effective strategy that actually addressed the problem. The other core issue that's always been important for me is public education.

How were you pursuing these?

I would say in an ad hoc, unfocused, unstructured way. One of the eye-opening things that I got involved with was a high school in East New York that my employer adopted. For a couple of years, I was one of the program directors for that activity. It was a tremendous effort by a group of Wall Streeters to help students in need, but there were some real problems. We had donated rooms full of computers that were barely used. Friction developed between parents and my employer when the parents said, 'What are you doing mentoring my kid? My kid doesn't need mentoring."

One day I took three of the kids that we were supporting out for dinner. These were inner-city high school students, and I had little in common with them. We were sitting around at dinner, and one kid was particularly uncommunicative. Finally, I was able to break through, and we had a really amazing conversation. And at the end one of the other kids whispered to me, "He lives in a car. The reason he didn't want to talk to you is that he was embarrassed to tell you he lives in a car." I was so shocked because at the same time that we were buying computers and books for the school, this kid's needs were so much deeper and so much more basic. What that kid needed was—he needed a place to live—and it totally changed my view about how to think about philanthropy after that. I believe it's critical to go after the core needs first, make sure the core needs are satisfied, and then build from there.

If someone's hungry or if someone doesn't have a roof over his head, whether you buy him a computer or a book does not matter. But, of course, we as donors felt very good about giving the computers and the books to that kid. The trouble was ... that's not what he needed. I learned a humbling lesson from that experience.

I had this selfish view of how the world should be and how I should engage with these kids. It was only when I stopped talking and started listening that I discovered that they had something to say that I had not been able to hear up until then.

Was this a program where you had a long-term relationship with the kids? Were you supposed to mentor them through high school?

Every kid had a mentor assigned from the company I had worked for. So you can imagine what the problem was. First of all, people made commitments that they didn't keep because they didn't real-ize how hard it was to really be a mentor. Then there was a high turnover rate because people moved on in their jobs. This was par-ticularly difficult for the kids who had been promised a long-term mentor they could trust.

This has always been a problem with mentoring programs— whether it's Big Brother or others. It actually turns out not to be as easy as people think, and it is a much longer commitment than what a lot of people expect when they engage. I would make the follow-ing observation about volunteering that I make about giving money. Many volunteers fail because they don't do self-critical due diligence. They aren't honest with themselves, and then when they discover what the reality of volunteering is as opposed to the fantasy of vol-unteering, they discover that it doesn't meet their expectations. By that point they've already made a commitment, and then they fail to deliver on that commitment. I have seen it countless times.

And by doing an incomplete due diligence, they haven't gotten the full scope of what the task is?

There's confirmation bias. Confirmation bias is simply that we clearly hear things that support our view of the world and fail to appropriately weigh what we hear when it doesn't support our world view. So what I really want to hear is that your mentoring experience was incredibly positive and that it's been the best experience in your life. Then when you tell me something negative like, "Hey, you know, it takes up part of every weekend." I don't really hear that I have to give up my weekends because I'm so focused on the good things that support my ideal expectations.

I think that happens to most of us in our lives whether we're giving money to charities or we're volunteering. Confirmation bias is a natural human trait, and I think volunteers over commit because they don't set their own expectations realistically or because they don't want to really hear about the less desirable aspects of the experience.

You moved on careerwise. Where did that take your philanthropy?

I was fortunate to have the opportunity to join General Atlantic as a partner in 1995 and immediately became inspired by Chuck Feeney's philosophy of giving. He was a wealthy man, and the founder of Duty Free Shops, who gave away his entire multibillon-dollar fortune to charity. When I joined General Atlantic, there was a complete veil of secrecy over the fact that we were one of the primary investment vehicles for Chuck Feeney's philanthropic foundation. There's no question that we felt like the work we were doing had an additional value over and above what's experienced in a traditional private equity firm. Some of the money that we were working hard to make for our investors was going directly into the good causes that Chuck supported.

Although we all knew the truth internally, few of the specifics were known to us by virtue of the way the philanthropy was structured. But we were aware that Chuck's work was having a profound and positive social effect in many areas of the world, and there is no question that it infected us with an even more heightened sense that we should be thinking carefully about how we gave away our own money. Although to his credit, Chuck never told us how we should direct our own philanthropic energy. I was completely inspired by him and his work. He is one of the role models that I aspire to emulate.

The message at General Atlantic was that philanthropy is a very important part of our business. Every one of my partners in the firm is deeply and passionately committed to philanthropic efforts so getting back to my original comment about passion, this is something that they care about and devote time to. It's easy to write a check. It's a lot harder to spend time. I learned quickly that my partners spend significant time on philanthropic efforts that matter to them. This inspired me and really reinforced the pride I felt from my association with them.

Can you be more specific? What about Feeney influenced you?

Chuck has chosen to give away all of his billions rather than to accumulate material possessions. To me, he is the paragon of someone who had chosen to live modestly so that he can get more leverage for his philanthropy. He does all his giving anonymously and that has had a major impact on me.

Other than the public boards we sit on, my wife and I choose to do all of our giving anonymously. We make every charitable decision together. Our commitments range from organizations where they have no idea who we are and have no contact with us at all to ones where they know exactly who we are, but the ground rules of our gifts are that the donation will remain anonymous, and no credit will be given to us publicly.

I think whatever motivates people to give money away should be celebrated. If part of that motivation is public recognition, that should be celebrated; and if part of that motivation is a desire for anonymity and privacy, that too should be celebrated. I've discovered that it can be more satisfying to give away money when you don't expect to get anything in return.

There are two quotes that have changed the way I think about giving, and they both appear in the new book on Feeney. One was by Bernard Baruch who said, "It's amazing what you can get done when you don't care who gets the credit." For me that was really a life-changing quote. And the other was Andrew Carnegie who said, "He who dies rich, dies disgraced."[1]

To take a devil's advocate point of view on anonymous giving, because I was very much in agreement with you, and recently I've had someone talk me a long way out of this. It's very hard to be a force in helping an organization if you refuse to be visible in any way. By the very act of giving, you will inspire others to give. People give in packs as Tim Dibble noted; they follow other people's generosity.

I disagree. Chuck Feeney's had more affect on the world by giving anonymously. He changed the world, and no one knew he did it. You could never solicit him for money. He chose his causes carefully and then sought to maximize the leverage of every dollar. For instance, the library system in Vietnam was re-built because of anonymous financial support from Chuck Feeney. He just decided this was important. It's an amazing effort in terms of literacy and education. It was not about recognition but rather getting something important done that will affect generations of people.

I hear the argument about the giving in packs, and I guess for some organizations that matters, but I have to tell you I get a lot more leverage from my private conversations with people. So I'm willing to disclose in private where it might benefit the organization. I do think that a reason people give in packs is there's this feeling of trust, and trust is an important issue. You trust me because I know a particular organization, because of my affiliation or experience with it. For you as a potential donor, that knowledge is due diligence in one sense.

For example, you're on the boards of Peak Rescue Institute, the Cancer Research Institute, the Food Bank for New York City, and DonorsChoose. org. So I, as a donor, know that you know what's really happening in these organizations. I know that you would not sit on their boards if you were not committed to the organization's mission and the quality of its management. And when I see that you've committed your money, and you know what's happening, that gives me comfort as a donor.

I buy that. That's true. But I would say that you could accomplish that without being necessarily public about your own giving.

Fair enough. DonorsChoose.org—how did that happen for you?

This is the amazing part of the story. I read a *New York Times* article that addressed two things that I cared about. One was public education. The other was about a high potential individual, Charles Best. He graduated from one of the country's most elite prep schools and then Phi Beta Kappa from Yale but rather than choosing a career track like my own, he chose to become a New York City public school teacher, and I thought it was too good to be true.

So I called him on the phone, and I said, "I'd like to take you out for breakfast to learn more about your organization." What I expected to find was someone who was doing this as a hobby before he went to Goldman Sachs or McKinsey. Instead, what I discovered was someone who had the attributes that I had always searched for in my own giving. He had true passion for his cause, he was tireless in the work that he did, and he wasn't looking to make money. My wife and I thought this might be "the real deal," and so we asked Charles, "If someone were going to make a transformative donation to DonorsChoose.org, how would they do it?"

He responded with an inspiring idea, which was to take six of his New York City public school students and make a grant to each of them so that they could go on to the DonorsChoose.org Web site. First, these students would understand the needs of teachers better than you or I would; and second, it would empower them to understand that they could make a difference through the donations of others.

So you were going to finance the kids to fund projects that they would find through the DonorsChoose.org Web site?

Yes. We wrote a check, and each kid was allocated a certain amount of the funds, and the results were amazing. So here's what happened. We gave the money anonymously, and we gave them no direction. They were eleventh graders from an impoverished school in the Bronx, and they self-organized around things that mattered to them. One said that literacy was the most important issue. She went and found the best literacy projects on DonorsChoose.org site. Another one felt that teenage pregnancy was the most important. She went and found projects about teenage pregnancy. Another one thought that math was the most important and so on. They then allocated our money. They used our money to fund these projects.

At the time we really didn't know how this experiment would work. Yet Charles insisted that, "These kids really want to meet you. They want to tell you what they've done, and you should hear it because they're proud of what they've done, and you'll be proud." So he organized a session where I brought my wife and my then eleven-year-old son, and it was a life-changing experience for all three of us.

The first thing that happened was these kids had done a remarkable job, both of self-organizing and finding projects that ironically all maximized the impact of the money we entrusted to them. They understood intuitively that it was more important to really consider the effectiveness of each dollar they invested than it was to do something that simply felt good. I was struck by how carefully they had chosen projects that had the most bang for the buck. They had done some careful thinking and set up criteria ahead of time. For example, they had agreed on standards for a literacy project to be effective and developed a screen before they went and looked at the projects. It was unbelievable.

But the second thing, which was the best part of this whole story, is that my eleven-year-old son sat through the presentation, and at the end he turned to my wife and me and said, "I want to work here." We knew at that moment we found something that not only gave us the satisfaction and leverage that we'd been looking for, but that here was a cause that was able to touch an eleven-year-old with the power of giving through others. It literally changed our lives, and as a result, we're all very tightly connected to DonorsChoose.org now.

The other interesting experience that happened was that the NPR (National Public Radio) reporter who was there was so moved by the story that she insisted that it be aired nationally. So she told this story [with Bloom and his wife's names changed to remain anonymous donors], and it got a lot of national attention. Several important givers started to pay attention to DonorsChoose.org, and ultimately it led to an appearance by Charles on *Oprah*.

How did that lead to your greater involvement? What were the steps? You have this amazing experience with your family, but that could have been the end of it.

It was clear that the organization was at a potential tipping point in that the model was incredibly powerful and persuasive, but the organization didn't have the financial resources or the reach to be able to leverage on this fantastic program that Charles had really conceived of and built. Charles asked me to be on his board of directors, and I said, "Well, I'm pretty busy. Who else is on your board?" He said, "Me and my Aunt." [Laugh] So I said, "Yes, I'll be on your board of directors." What we both understood was that the first priority of DonorsChoose.org was to build an effective board of directors.

I think one of the lessons that I learned is nothing can transform an organization more than an effective leader. The only thing that comes close is an effective board of directors. We understood that at its core DonorsChoose.org was a Web-based technology marketplace, and it needed three things. It needed technology, guidance, and assistance. It needed market awareness and presence. And it needed a strong reservoir of financial support. We set out to build the board based on these three organizational requirements.

We have been blessed to have board members who basically fill those roles very actively. We have some world-class technology experts on our board. We have people who really understand how to get reach for the organization, either with media or with other donors. And we also have some people who have been extraordinarily generous and passionate about changing public education in America.

If you get the right board members, then you get immense leverage through their network. I am proud of the fact that every board member at DonorsChoose.org has worked continuously to leverage their network on behalf of DonorsChoose.org.

As an example, what have they done?

We now have relationships with several major companies, including Google, Yahoo, Amazon, Teach for America, and Crate and

Barrel, and they were all developed originally as the result of one of our board members committing to making an introduction and to make that relationship happen.

For you as a philanthropist, the tiny undeveloped board is in fact a huge job. It is a bigger job than had he just said, "Well, I have these twelve important powerful people in place, and you're going to be number thirteen. So just pull up a chair."

Building a board is an extremely time-consuming process. It's like getting married. There were many attractive candidates that wanted to join our board either because they were interested in our mission or because they wanted to have affiliations with the organization. And we have turned some of them down. It was not that they would not have been great, but they didn't fill requirements that we had.

The argument here is you can have a large board with people who fill many different roles, and that's okay. Or you can have a small board where everyone's time and money is highly leveraged. We chose the course of the small board.

It strikes me that you have two things going here in your decision to commit yourself in such a substantial way to DonorsChoose.org. One is the mission of the organization when you saw these kids and what the program could achieve, but presumably a huge amount of it is Charles also. You're buying a package with an executive director, because this was his dream, not initially yours. He's not somebody who was hired; he's not the seventh executive director. So you made a big bet on him.

A start-up charity is like a start-up business. A real challenge is whether the founder grows with the business. Can he develop the skills, make the decisions, and delegate to others in a way that allows the organization to reach its full potential?

I have rarely worked with a business executive who has more of those attributes than Charles Best. This is not Pollyannaish. He's a great delegator. He is one of the best listeners that I've ever encountered in my professional career. He's always interested in learning and changing his own behavior to improve the organization.

The risk in an organization like DonorsChoose.org is that you have a charismatic, energetic, young founder who can't scale with the organization. We've all heard those stories, and I got lucky. It wasn't my judgment. I was sitting at Bubby's having breakfast with this guy when he was twenty-six-years old. I mean I couldn't make that judgment of a twenty-six-year old, and now he's thirty-two, and he's made some very tough decisions and proven that he can grow as a leader while the organization grows. The fact of the matter is he is now probably one of the most innovative and effective nonprofit leaders in the country.

Two things I want to touch on that you mentioned about Charles. One is how he's listened and learned and changed and the other is the tough decisions.

Tough decisions include the one that no one likes to make. Sometimes the organization outgrows someone's ability to do the job, and you have to ask them, you have to let them know, frankly . . . well, you have to fire them. It's always a painful experience, but the reality of it is Charles recognizes that for the good of the organization, sometimes he has had to make tough personnel decisions.

There are two ways I would say that he's learned. One is to resist the seductive appeal of an immediately attractive opportunity that may not be in the best long-term interest of the organization. For example, we had a donor who was willing to make a substantial financial commitment to DonorsChoose.org in return for exercising control over how that decision was implemented. We really wrestled with the conflict between wanting the money and ceding some degree of control of our business model to someone who might have had a different agenda.

And in the end, to Charles's great credit, he understood and learned that we might have to take the less expedient course even though it meant that we would not get the money or the attachment to this person because the long-run consequences for the organization were unacceptable. That was a painful lesson because Charles initially said "yes," but the Board told him "no," and he had to basically face the music of having made a commitment that was not supported by the organization. He has subsequently learned, profoundly learned, from that harsh experience.

Then the other thing I would say is that like all start-ups the siren song of growth drives a temptation to expand in many directions all at once. We get at least one phone call a week from someone who has a great idea about how we should extend the DonorsChoose.org platform into other segments like health care, law enforcement, social service, and also outside the United States. I think initially Charles had an ambitious, perhaps overly ambitious, sense that all these things were doable. He's now learned that bringing focus and executional excellence to the core mission will eventually allow the organization to succeed. But if you succumb to the appeal of everyone who comes along and says you should expand in a different direction, you'll often fail to deliver on those commitments.

The other thing I have to say about Charles is that he understood early on the power of delegation. He has hired an extraordinary management team, and he's willing to delegate. Some founders are just unable to do that. This is a case where the leader has a natural understanding of the leverage he gets from empowering his colleagues.

In the same way that I discovered that I could get leverage through my own financial donations by doing deep due diligence, finding the right levers and the appropriate channels, Charles discovered he could get leverage through others. He has grown significantly in how he's been able to manage others to amplify his own effectiveness.

Has your role changed now that you're in a more established organization with a more established board? You were in the start up mode with him and now the board and the organization are in a different place.

It's an interesting question—so "yes" and "no." The "yes" part is as the organization has matured, the challenges have gotten larger. Now, for instance, our fund raising goals, which were quite modest when DonorsChoose.org started, have grown far beyond our original expectations. Six years ago we were operating with a budget of a couple of hundred thousand dollars a year, and now $18.4 million has flowed through the DonorsChoose.org site in the form of citizen philanthropy. The challenges have changed with scale; but as a board chair, the challenges remain the same, which is evangelizing for the organization, fund raising, and working with other board members to help set strategic direction for the organization.

The strategic direction . . . DonorsChoose.org has gone from a neighborhood, the Bronx, to the nation in just a couple of years. How did you lay out the plans for this?

I would tell you that every step of the way, like in a business, you learn new things and make lucky discoveries. Charles did not start DonorsChoose.org with the initial goal of reaching every public school in America. He started with the initial goal of providing support to the teachers he knew at his local school in the Bronx and maybe in New York City. Each step of the way we discovered that the aperture of the organization could widen particularly because of our use of the Internet.

So here's a metric for you: It took us four years to reach 50 percent of the public schools in New York City. We reached 75 percent of the public schools in Chicago in one year. And now we serve every single public school in the United States.

So that was seven years to cover 100 percent of the United States?

Yes, but it is an unpredictable growth path. The other thing that happens with organizations like this is that there are certain transformative events that you don't know are going to happen like the NPR story or Charles's interview on *Oprah*. Winning the Amazon.com/Stanford Business School Innovation Award as the most innovative charity in America was a transformative event. Then the fourth one was Pierre Omidyar's decision to give us $6 million to go national. Because without his support and the support of David Filo, the co-founder of Yahoo, and several other major donors, we could not go national.

Having major philanthropists is key, but is there a target to reach a more self-sustaining model?

There is something about the DonorsChoose.org business model that we stumbled upon that has been really significant in terms of both success of the organization and my own education as a philanthropist. We unintentionally . . . because I don't want to make us sound like we knew more than we did . . . we unintentionally split the operating expenses from the program expenses very discretely. When we go to a donor, we can say to them 100 percent of your money will go to directly providing goods and services to students and teachers. Why? Because we have a separate source of funding for our operating expenses, so we do not have to rely on our core donor base to support our operations.

This concept of discretely separating the operating fund raising from the program fund raising has been one of the most appealing aspects of DonorsChoose.org to our donors. They know without any ambiguity that their money will not end up in a black hole of fund raising or overhead expenses. In fact, this is a key lesson. At DonorsChoose.org the dollars aren't fungible. The program dollars go to programs, and the operating dollars go to operations. It's the donor's choice where the money goes, not the organizations. That is an inverted model of philanthropy that has had many positive consequences for us.

What was the impetus for separating the two pools of money?

Charles understood that we could get corporate support for operations. For instance, we're proud that Lehman Brothers provides corporate support for our New York, Chicago, and San Francisco operations. So we never have to tap a dollar of donor money because Lehman Brothers has guaranteed us that they will cover these costs as part of their corporate philanthropy. Charles has built a number of those corporate relationships around the country for our other regions including AIG, Bank of America, JP Morgan, Chase, and Lilly.

So corporate donors are funding the overhead cost of running your offices, but what about the cost of implementing the individual classroom projects?

There is a certain amount of fulfillment expense associated with each proposal. The fulfillment would be things like shipping, sales tax, and cost of the camera and developing the film to take pictures of the project for the donor. These are expenses completely associated with a particular project. If we say that we're going to deliver a hundred dollars' worth of goods to a school, the fact of the matter is that about $15 of every $100 goes to just fulfilling that project, which is not operating expense. One of the innovations Charles developed was to give donors the choice as to whether they would choose to pay for the fulfillment expense or not. Ninety-two percent of our donors voluntarily include that fulfillment expense as part of their contribution. They just check a box on the Web site when they select a project. It's kind of amazing. We never expected it to be 92 percent. Maybe we figured it would be 50 percent. It's another powerful lesson of what can happen when you empower donors to completely direct the use of their own money.

There are serendipitous discoveries you make, and afterwards you wonder why didn't you think of it. This was a serendipitous discovery that was, I think, one of the single most compelling things about our model for our donors.

How did it happen?

We understood that we were never going to be able to become a self-sustaining organization, which meant operations plus program just from citizen philanthropists making small donations. So the question was, "How do we allow our citizen philanthropist to sustain our program while we sustain our operations?"

It was the understanding that we wanted to invert the pyramid. Our goal was that many people could have a measurable impact with small donations rather than feeling like their donation didn't matter because the organization had a multimillion-dollar operating budget. This is not the traditional charity model where a donor who gives $100 often doesn't realize that the operating budget of their favorite charity is millions of dollars, and their $100 donation does nothing to "move the dial." So anyway, we eventually stumbled upon it. I wish that we could say that we sat there, and we were strategically insightful, but, in fact, we made some mistakes and eventually figured it out.

There was one other thing I was going to say about the financial model of DonorsChoose.org, and this gets back to one of my beliefs about core issues. Different issues are important to different people. The force that DonorsChoose.org unlocks is for each individual to vote with their wallet on what matters to them. I think one of the problems with traditional philanthropy is that you are enfranchising the charity to vote your money in the way they think is most effective even though—and a lot of charities are incredibly good at using your money wisely—you have still ceded your vote to somebody else.

We learned at DonorsChoose.org that most people don't want to cede their vote. They want to know that they have control over where their money goes with unambiguous transparency and accountability. And here's the consequence. We have a vital feedback loop between the donor and the recipient that leads to an ongoing relationship and deeper support. Why? Because certain things that appeal to people motivate them to stay involved with an ongoing commitment.

We have a donor who has adopted a school. He's been so impressed with the feedback that he'll fund any proposal from this school. We have other people who are very committed to certain causes. Any time a proposal appears on the site that is focused on the cause they care about, they fund it. We have some prominent people who are very private in the causes they support through DonorsChoose.org. They are consistent supporters of certain things that matter to them, but they're not seeking public recognition for their efforts. I know they value the fact that we are very protective of the identity of all of our donors.

How does a donor know what impact they have had?

They get e-mails, letters, and photographs from the teacher and the students for every proposal they fund. And the other thing . . .

have you ever seen a DonorsChoose.org impact page for individuals? I need to show you this. I'll show you my personal impact page, and you'll be blown away. We basically provide donors a real-time segmentation of how their money is being used in terms of geography, English as a second language, how many kids are below the poverty line, subject matter. When you see it—it's actually pretty amazing.

It was based on the New York City police system for measuring organizational effectiveness in precincts. It's called CompStat. Basically, the philosophy that underlies CompStat is that the more data you give to the individual police officers in a precinct, the more they're able to optimize their own results. So we literally use that model to provide data back to each individual donor. Our donors love it because basically you can give them a slice and dice capability, so they know everything about how their money is spent down to the penny.

Most organizations are either what I call retail charities or institutional charities. Retail charities depend on a large number of small contributions. Institutional charities depend on a small number of large contributions. Typically, you don't get charities that can span both. For instance, if you give $100 to a charity that is fundamentally institutional in nature, that $100 has no measurable impact on the outcome of the organization. If you have an organization that is geared towards small retail contributions, the fact is that they're often unable to efficiently manage a large institutional contribution because it doesn't fit the model. I would say that the issue isn't that neither cause is worthy or that there's a defect in the architecture; it's just that the architecture tends to be constraining because the organizations evolve as either being retail or institutional. Certain types of stakeholders get disenfranchised in either model. The DonorsChoose.org model is designed to equally enfranchise individual and institutional donors, so you can scale your level of giving at any level that works for you. We genuinely can put the $100 donor in touch with a proposal where they can make a difference. And we can put the $100,000 donor in touch with work that will truly satisfy them. So the gradient is continuous between the small donors and the large donors, and that's atypical for most traditional charities.

It strikes me that this issue of choice cuts both ways. You talked about how it's important for the donor to choose where they want their money to go and not to delegate their decision. Equally important though—when we talked about the mentor program you were involved with and not telling kids they need computers when they need homes— it is essential to listen to what the recipient really needs. The donors are not telling teachers what they need. Those who need it are making their requirements known.

That's how you get to the core foundational need. You listen. But I think the fundamental reason the people find DonorsChoose.org so appealing is that they genuinely discover that they can move the dial on something that matters to them. So even though we're providing this umbrella support for public education in the United States, the reality of it is that each individual project is effectively a vehicle by which one person or one donor can significantly influence the outcomes for kids and teachers that are focused on an issue that they care about.

I can see why DonorsChoose.org fits your vision of efficient, donor directed, personal philanthropy—the thinking piece—but tell me what you love about this program?

We process thousands of proposals every week, and the ones that have moved the staff the most go on a list. I have to tell you they will bring tears to your eyes. I'll tell you one story that literally left us speechless. We had a teacher in North Carolina who tragically lost a first grader in a fire because the family did not have a smoke detector. This teacher wrote a heartbreaking proposal first to teach fire safety to her first graders so that no one else would be at risk. But more importantly what she really wanted was to avert another tragedy by buying smoke detectors for all the kids in her class, because many couldn't afford them. A New York City firefighter read that request on DonorsChoose.org, collected the money from his firehouse, and fully funded the proposal. Those kids needed smoke detectors, and this firefighter understood that need. We get stories like that every day. I could leave you in tears with some of the stories—I mean you just wouldn't believe some of those stories. We get them from kids, teachers, and donors. We had a donor in tears. He starts telling us about this proposal, and he just starts crying because it so moved him, and I actually can't tell you the story without crying myself. Just suffice it to say that it had to do with a handicapped student who was unable to be mainstreamed because she needed some assistive technology that the school couldn't afford. When the proposal was funded, and she played with the orchestra for the first time . . . I'll tell you later, I'll just totally choke up.

One last thing, do you stay with the organizations you are working with long term, or is there a point when your job is done? When is it time as a philanthropist and a developer of an organization to move on? What are the signs? Do you have any ideas?

I have to be honest. I've never given it a thought. So I don't have an answer. When I look at the four public causes with which I am most actively involved—Search and Rescue, Hunger in New York, Cancer Research, and public education—I can't imagine that I won't have the same degree of interest, passion, and commitment to these causes in the future that I have today. These are the issues that matter to me. I can't foresee circumstances under which these wouldn't matter, and I am incredibly fortunate to be associated with four world-class organizations in these areas.

I just think there's tremendous satisfaction to be gained from helping a start-up charity to reach critical mass, but no matter what cause you choose, no matter how much money you give, if you choose wisely you can make a profound difference in the future of an organization. These organizations so mirror my own values in terms of transparency, financial efficiencies, the integrity of the staff, the quality that they bring to the recipients that I am very lucky to be associated with all four. Any one of those four would be a worthy subject for a whole book.

BERNIE AND TIM MARQUEZ
Denver Scholarship Foundation

I think life is pretty simple: people complicate it. It's the right thing to do; we have more than we need. It's pointless to accumulate money. We want to do something with it.

—Tim Marquez

IN JULY 2007, THE *WALL STREET JOURNAL* RAN AN ARTICLE about YAWNs, young and wealthy but normals. This new acronym-type was defined as those who, while still in their thirties or forties, had happened upon massive wealth but fail to purchase the private jet, yacht, and megamansions that seem to naturally go along with an elevated net worth. Instead, YAWNs have chosen to continue working, bring up their own kids (sometimes even sending them to public school), and have used their wealth to improve the lives of others. Rather than focus on their public profiles and private consumption, they have invested their wealth in giving others the opportunities they had. YAWNs, the *Journal* went on to explain, can be a bit boring for the rest of us to watch. They do not produce extramarital offspring, spin through the revolving door of rehab centers, or sit catwalk side at Paris fashion shows. The article suggested that Bill Gates was "the patron saint of yawnhood," but Bernie and Tim Marquez certainly fit the mold.

Bernie Marquez is as unpretentious a person as I ever hope to meet. The forty-eight-year-old nurse speaks with the flat midwestern accent of a girl who grew up in Portage, just outside Kalamazoo, Michigan. Her father worked at a General Motors plant, and she came from a family of eight children. Despite the fact that the Marquezes are now in possession of a very real fortune, Bernie is a suburban mom, who works part-time as a nurse at Denver's St. Luke's Medical Center and is raising three daughters, who have all attended the local East High School. She also runs Venoco's (the oil business Tim Marquez founded) community partnership overseeing the company's charitable disbursements and co-chairs the Denver Scholarship Foundation. Like all successful philanthropists, she seems to have three or four full-time jobs.

Tim Marquez is a native of Denver, and like Bernie he was raised in a large family with six children. His father taught biology in a number of the city's high schools, and his mother was a substitute teacher in the junior high schools. Tim graduated from Denver's Lincoln High School and went on to study at the Colorado College of Mines, a geological school in Golden, Colorado. His education was financed through a combination of scholarships from the school and a weekend job giving tours at the Coors plant. And while he remembers this as an unhappy period of his life, with little time for anything other than work and school, he readily admits that there are few jobs where you are paid to drink beer.

Tim Marquez learned a couple things in the thirteen years he spent as a petroleum engineer at Unocal after graduating college. He learned that big oil companies have big overhead making some drilling uneconomical for them, and that their employees can be relocated at the company's whim to undesirable locations all over the globe. Tim and his wife Bernie were tired of being transferred with their three young daughters; and since they had been relocated to Santa Barbara, it was hard to envision what would be a move up. Marquez was also itching to try something on his own, so when Unocal offered voluntary buyouts in 1992, Marquez jumped at the offer.

With his partner Ron Eson, he founded Venoco, a small independent oil company. They would not be wildcatters, searching for oil where others had failed to look, but rather they would lap up the leavings of larger oil companies, a process economically infeasible for the guys with the overhead. They would buy wells that had become inefficient or nonproductive for large oil companies, and then by updating the technology and keeping a lean infrastructure they would make these dated drill holes pay. They started on a shoestring, as Marquez explains about their first purchase made in 1994, "I cashed in everything . . . my IRA, took out a second mortgage on the house, used credit cards, and that was enough to buy it."

Marquez chose Santa Barbara as the headquarters for his new company, which was a risky choice. Santa Barbara was the site of a massive 1969 oil spill and after that was as pro-environment and anti-oil as any community in California. Marquez won the city over, with a combination of good business practices and good corporate citizenry, and in 2001 Venoco was acclaimed by Santa Barbara as the business of the year.

Part of what brought Venoco such esteem in the Santa Barbara community was Tim and Bernie's personal involvement. Their assets were largely tied up in Venoco, so that is where their philanthropy began. Tim immersed himself in serving on the boards of the Santa Barbara City College, chamber of commerce, Museum of Natural History, and Partners in Education. The Marquezes gave heavily of both their time and their company's resources.

On the surface Marquez and Eson were a perfect matchup, and for almost a decade the company thrived, as the pair bought up oil properties all over California and watched Veneco's revenue grow from $6 million in 1996 to $186 million in 2001. Yet, in reality, their partnership unraveled in a series of ousters and lawsuits.

In 2002 Marquez left Veneco and returned with his family to his hometown, Denver. Still in his forties he was far from ready to retire, and the Venoco drama was far from over. From 2002 to 2004 Eson served as CEO while Marquez ran a new eponymous oil company in Denver. Lawsuits begat lawsuits, and after a long fight among shareholders of Venoco, Marquez bought out his former partner and was once again CEO of Venoco. By June 2004 Marquez owned all the remaining shares of Venoco and explained the transition, "I saw tremendous value and they didn't."

In a little over a decade, Marquez has transformed himself from a Unocal salaryman into an oil baron worth half a billion dollars. In that time he also transformed a pile of credit card and property debts into a billion-dollar company producing twenty thousand barrels a day from oil fields in California and Texas. Yet to think that Marquez did this for the money alone would be a mistake. Having created something from nothing clearly thrills him, but to Marquez money is a means. Both he and Bernie cannot help but repeat their mantra: money is only interesting if it can do something, and the best thing that it can do is help someone.

Tim and Bernie have some different ideas about philanthropy, but their notions stem from the same three points: inherited wealth is not a desirable thing; ditto with excessive personal spending and money given carefully can irrevocably change peoples lives, for the better. "I don't see any sense in making money just to make money," Tim explains. The Marquezs seem largely untouched by their wealth, "We have a really nice lifestyle," Bernie Marquez says. "At a certain point, it's just money, and what do you do with it? You can help a lot of people with millions of dollars." Both Marquezs are suspicious at the effects that money can have on families. "In Santa Barbara, I saw a lot of kids living off trust funds." Tim says, "People need motivation. The worst thing we can do to our kids is give them a bunch of money and take away their incentive to want to do something on their own."[1]

In 2006 as Venoco's initial public offering approached, Tim hoped to reshape their philanthropy. Their $3,000 investment in Venoco in 1994 was worth close to $500 million in 2006. For the first time their family's wealth would be liquid, and he wanted to be able to focus deeply and generously on a single cause, making an impact of an entirely different magnitude. "Originally I looked at it as a duty—a company should give back to its community," Tim explains. "But I've come to find out that it's very enjoyable. I get a lot more from it than I put in."[2]

One morning in 2005 as Tim Marquez scanned through the Denver papers, he spotted an article about his alma mater, Lincoln High School. The Denver public school system has loomed large in the Marquez family life. Tim's parents both taught there, Tim and his siblings all graduated from there, and he and Bernie sent all three of their daughters there. Denver public schools have been in a state of declining enrollment for three decades. In 1980 when Marquez graduated, enrollment stood at 110,000, but it slid to 65,000 by 2006 as families fled the system for suburban or private schools. By then two-thirds of all students entering Denver public high schools were being served subsidized lunches, and few would continue their education and earn a four-year college degree.

Reading the story, Marquez learned that Scott Mendelsberg, the Lincoln High School principal, had found a way, through a twist in Colorado law, to give his students a free ride through college. Colorado law stipulated that the state provide funding for any student until high school graduation or the student's twenty-first birthday, whichever came first. Mendelsberg took the law at face value. He simply did not graduate his students once they had successfully completed all of their high school requirements. Instead, he sent them on to the local two-year college or a vocational school and provided them with a high school diploma when they had completed both programs, often at the age of twenty.

Another tiny school district in Colorado had tried the same tactic and had been shut down by the state. For Marquez it was easy to see the writing on the wall. The following day he called Mendelsberg and offered to fund the tuition of Lincoln High students should the state revoke their funding as they tried to complete their education. Marquez had learned from Mendelsberg that the rate of attendance in post-secondary education, once it was provided free of charge to Lincoln seniors, had risen from 17 to 73 percent. At this point Bernie and Tim Marquez got involved and offered not only to help the senior class at Lincoln, but also to help every student graduating from any of the nine Denver public high schools or the eighteen specialized secondary schools—for 2007 and every year going forward.

Tim knew that many of his classmates terminated their educations after graduating Lincoln High simply for lack of funds. Twenty-five years later some of their children would be in the same situation—but now he was in a position to do something about it. As Venoco approached public offering, in a mere matter of months, he and Bernie would have enough money to alter this pattern forever.

The Denver Scholarship Foundation is committed to providing the financial wherewithal for every graduate of the Denver high schools to go on to college or technical school in the state of Colorado. The program does this by placing financial aid counselors in each of the schools to help the students obtain every dollar of financial aid for which they are eligible and then funding any gap that remains. Applying to college is hard, getting into college is hard, but navigating the minefield of financial aid, perhaps with a parent who has never been to college and may not speak English, is not for the feint of heart. At the very moment when kids have overcome all the odds—they have shown their staying power with education, they have gained admittance to college, and they have found the funds to finance it—many are shocked to find that they come up short on cash from the very first day. The Denver Scholarship foundation will pay for tuition, fees, books, and the cost of a new computer. The counselors are employees of the foundation, yet they are physically located in each of the schools. "We're the most inclusive, intrusive scholarship provider ever," says Tonda Potts, the foundation's director of student services. "We're not asking students to get in the game. We're going out and grabbing them and saying, 'You will get in the game.'"[3]

Bold moves may be Tim Marquez's hallmark—and for all of his business daring, it is the Denver Scholarship Foundation that may be his boldest move. Others have gambled in oil and gas, but only one other family, operating anonymously in Kalamazoo, Michigan, has offered all of the graduates of their school system a tuition-free college education. The couple has high hopes for the changes their scholarship program can bring to both the public school system and the city of Denver itself.

The program is so big and so public that it leaves Bernie a bit wistful. A part of her wishes she could have followed the path of those who funded the Kalamazoo Promise and remained anonymous. But unlike the Michigan program, which was entirely funded by the original donors, the Marquezes kicked in a big chunk of their own fortune and committed to a huge fund raising campaign to endow the program and make it self-sustaining. Anonymity was just not an option. For this quiet, thoughtful woman, who loved her role as corporate benefactor, spreading company largess over a huge range of community projects, this was a sea change.

The Marquezes may be running one of the largest private scholarship programs in the country, but their philanthropy is just beginning. They are committed to giving away 95 percent of their fortune. The Marquez Foundation is already endowed with $50 million, and once the scholarship program is up and running (in the academic year 2007–2008), they will begin studying how best to proceed with this amazing undertaking. Tim and Bernie have thought about this for a decade, consulting with people who show real insight into giving. "With that foundation comes a lot of responsibility," Tim Marquez says. "You don't just want to give the money away. You want to be strategic. We want to have as much impact as possible. On one hand, half a billion dollars is a lot of money. On the other hand, it's not much money at all. And so the more focused we can be, the more strategic we can be, the farther that money will go."

LISA: Neither of you has a background in education, yet you have taken on one of the most ambitious scholarship programs in America. How did it happen?

TIM: There was a story in the newspaper about the principal at a high school here in Denver, Lincoln High School. Lincoln has always been and will probably always will be one of the downtrodden schools here in Denver, a real inner-city school. But it is a very different school now. When I was there, it was probably 60 to 70 percent Hispanic, and I would say for the most part it was some first-generation Hispanic students and certainly a lot like me, second and third generations. Now Lincoln is 92 percent Hispanic, and most of those are first generation. A very large percentage of the students were born in Central America and Mexico, so that's changed.

One of the interesting things is that it seems to be a safer school and a lot more student-friendly. When I was a student, there were a lot of fights, a lot of problems. Academically, it was probably a better performing school, but there were real problems. When I was a senior, several kids got killed with knives or guns. It certainly wasn't the most dangerous school in the country, but it was a pretty tough school.

In 2005 I read an article in the paper about a principal there, Scott Mendelsberg, doing something not entirely innovative, but it was pretty cool. He himself hadn't figured it out, but he had heard about another small town in Colorado where they had figured out how to game the tuition system. Colorado law says that the state will pay for public school education until the earlier of either graduating from high school or reaching the age of twenty-one. He said, "Fine, we just won't graduate the kids from high school." And he sent them off to college. It was a dual enrollment. They graduated concurrently with their high school diploma and two-year college degree, and the state paid for all of it.

Well, that's all very well and good, but he talked about it. And as soon as I read about it in the paper I said, "I know what's going to happen. I know this story. The state is going to come down on them because that wasn't the intent of the law." And sure enough that's what ultimately happened. But I thought it was really great that he was trying to help out the kids. And so I called Scott up and said, "Look, if you have a moment my wife and I would like to talk to you."

BERNIE: Scott was scamming the system. You know to be honest. . . truthfully, he was. But it was for a good cause.

Scamming the system to get kids educated?

BERNIE: Right. The kids would not have gone off to school otherwise. Do you know what happened when he started this program? Before he got the kids tuition, only 15 percent of the graduates of Lincoln went on to post-secondary education. After Scott started this plan, he got 70 percent of his graduates to continue on to some further education. That's a big jump.

So what did you do?

TIM: I called Scott up immediately at the school, and we met and I said I thought it was great what he was trying to do, and we would be very happy to fill in if there was a gap there.

Now, as it ultimately turned out, the state extended their payments for one more year, so we never ended up actually writing a check to Lincoln, but we stood ready to pay the kid's tuitions if the program was going to terminate.

At the same time, the mayor of Denver had made a promise to some kids in a Denver junior high school that he was going to figure out a way to pay for anybody who could get into college. It was fairly vague, and certainly I don't think he had calculated what the financial requirements would be. He heard about what we were trying to do, and we got together and decided we had a lot of commonality and threw in together on the Denver Scholarship Foundation, and that was about two years ago.

BERNIE: Tim always calls it a perfect storm of people coming together—us and then the principal, the mayor and the school superintendent. We all got together and started brainstorming about how we could help these students.

To go back to how we started, we were thinking about education, and then this whole thing with Lincoln just came about, and all of a sudden we understood: This is where we want to focus our money, at least right now. This was the project and the issue that mattered to us.

I don't know if in the future we'll find something else. I'm a nurse by profession, and I think the lack of health care for so many people is another crisis in our nation. We have it on the back burner for now because we're focusing on education, but I do hope that sometime we can focus in that direction.

Did Venoco always give away a percentage of the profits?

TIM: Yes, from the very beginning, from when we were a little company. I think our first year we gave away $40–50,000. We've always done that, and fortunately, as Venoco has gotten bigger, we've been able to give more money away. It's been a fun thing. It's been a good thing to get our feet wet.

BERNIE: At the time we didn't have a great deal of wealth per se, as it was all in the company. Because it was a private company, we couldn't take much out, so we gave through the corporation, and that is how we got involved with giving.

The Denver Scholarship Foundation is a big transition from where your philanthropy began.

TIM: We've been giving money away for ten or twelve years, and up until the last couple of years it's been fairly small. More recently, my company has been giving away a little more than a million bucks each year, so it is certainly not huge, but it has allowed us to learn a great deal.

It sounds pretty simple, pretty easy to give money away, and you can make it that way. You can be very reactionary; just get in the miscellaneous requests, and dole out the money. But I think the challenge is to be effective with it and try to stretch those dollars as far as you can. That's what I loved about the Scholarship Foundation. To me that was a big check we wrote out, but we never thought twice about it. It was so intuitively obvious. We did not look at it as a donation. We looked at it as an investment, as an investment in the Denver community. We think the return on that investment is going to be huge. So we didn't think twice. To be honest with you, Bernie and I probably spent five minutes talking about it. I hope we can find some other things that are that obvious to invest in.

BERNIE: Basically our goal has been to try and support the community that we lived in and we did business in. We did a lot in California, and now we're in Denver, and this year we expanded to an office in Houston. Part of the process was to not only give from the corporate side, but to get our employees involved in the community as well.

In the last few years we've been able to take more money out of the company, and our personal wealth has grown. As this happened, we've had to decide, "What do we really want to do? How do we want to make a difference?" I will give credit to Tim for focusing on this. We have a little bit of a difference of opinion about giving.

I like giving to different things. I think it's wonderful to focus on a few choice areas that you really want to give to, but I like to kind of spread it out a little bit, too. It is not that Tim doesn't like doing that, but he was the first one to start talking about doing something that really made a difference, something where you could really institute some change that gave more bang for your buck, so to speak.

As we started to move in that direction and got more focused on our personal giving, we thought, "Let's find some area where we really felt strongly about." And education emerged for us. We have three daughters, and they've done really well in school. But like everyone we have had our ups and downs.

I consider myself an educated person. I have a bachelor's degree, and so does Tim. We work, and we feel like we're people of the world. I have an eighteen-year-old daughter who is going to apply to certain universities this year. My older daughter went to Metro here in Denver, so she really didn't go through the process. I hired a college coach to help her. It's daunting what you have to do to apply to college.

If our children have struggled, you start thinking, "Well, what about the people who don't have the opportunities that we do?" How about all the kids who really have no idea or have no hope—and I'm not sure it's the best word to use but—they have no hope of really doing anything else past high school? How do you help those kids? How do we make a difference in that direction? That's really how we started thinking.

But why education? You two could have gone into so many different directions, all of them very worthy. It could have been health care. It could have been a poverty program. Why education?

TIM: I think education is the basic issue. If you can solve the education problem, that takes care of most the other problems. It takes care of homeless problems and poverty problems. People have better health care. A lot of things start taking care of themselves if . . . if we can educate our population.

I think part of it, though, is that both of my parents were teachers, and I have an affinity for education. The other reason is pretty obvious. I came from a family of very modest means—six kids with a schoolteacher for a father. You can just do the math. We weren't raised in the lap of luxury. But education has gotten me where I am today. Education is very, very powerful. With the right education and a little bit of drive, there's nothing a person can't do.

As we started getting philanthropically involved ten, twelve years ago, I was more of a generalist—involved in a lot of different things. There are a lot of great programs out there, but I kept getting drawn more and more into education. When we ended up in Santa Barbara, I was on four different boards, but they were all education-related. In Denver I'm really 100 percent focused on education.

How did the pilot program begin?

BERNIE: For the pilot program we picked three schools to focus on. First we did some research. We had our organization do some best practices research, and that's where we learned more about the Kalamazoo Promise and scholarship programs in other cities like Baltimore and Cleveland. We decided we would just do a small start-up program this first year, and we picked three high schools, and, of course, Lincoln was one of them because they were our guinea pig. Then we picked two other high schools, South and Montebello. They were the first ones to apply, and in the fall of 2007, they'll get their first scholarships.

There are a lot of merit-based programs out there, but ours is basically just based on need. Eventually, students will have to get a 2.0 grade point average to apply, and they will have to get accepted into the post-secondary education system, but it doesn't necessarily have to be a four-year college. They can do a two-year associate degree, they can do vocational training . . . whatever degree that's going to help them be successful. We'll help get them there.

We want them not just to get there, but we want them to graduate. The ultimate goal is to graduate these kids. So whatever we can do to help them get to that point, we'll put that in our program.

TIM: Scholarships are very complicated, and we have the fund raising aspect of it, negotiating tuition discounts with all the schools, and getting the kids into schools. We've done some things that we're very pleased with, and we have done something that, with twenty-twenty hindsight, we would have done differently. I've started up two different oil companies, and I know it's very difficult, and you will make mistakes when you start up new organizations. It's a guarantee. If you're not screwing up a little, then you're probably not pushing yourself that hard.

And so we've had some little screw ups, some of which have been magnified in the local papers. But all in all I think we've had a very good first year. I think the smartest thing we did is we put these financial aid counselors—we call them future center coordinators, but they're financial aid counselors—in each of the high schools. They're not really college counselors; they're purely financial aid advisors who really get real focused on the kids. And it's worked out well.

BERNIE: The district has agreed to do certain things, like provide us with space in the schools for the program. We provide the counselors and computers and scholarships when the time comes. The Future Center's job is to help those kids first of all fill out those applications and find other sources of funding. I think a lot of students don't realize that they qualify for Pell grants and all sorts of other financial aid, and a lot of them are from immigrant families for whom this is the first generation going to college, so they would have no way to know.

So we help them with that, so they can get what they're eligible for to make sure that we maximize our dollars. We pay tuition fees, books, and we're going to provide them with a computer to go off to college.

TIM: The first graduating class from our three pilot schools is just now enrolling in colleges. Well, some have already started;

some are starting in two weeks. It looks like we'll have the continuation rate of up north of 65 percent.

Sixty-five percent of the high school graduates have gone on to further education?

TIM: Yeah.

That's huge. In one year? What was it before?

TIM: At Lincoln before they started their dual enrollment thing, it was somewhere around 15–20 percent, and for the city as a whole it was something less than 50 percent. Now the three pilot schools, including Lincoln, have a continuation rate that has jumped up to over 65 percent.

It's caught us by surprise. We thought that with best practices, maybe in five, six, seven years from now, we might be able to start getting to those kind of numbers. So to do it in our first year was a very pleasant surprise.

The real secret to our success is the Future Center coordinators, our financial aid counselors. As far as I know, we're the only big city that has attempted to do this, to really have people holding kids hands as they fill out the financial aid forms. There are a lot of scholarship programs around the country, but I don't think there's any like ours that targets purely needy kids that—really ours goes to any kid—can get into any school. There's a very minimal grade point average, I think it's a 2.0 GPA. Basically, anybody who shows up for school gets a 2.0 GPA. So ours is all encompassing.

So you help them get all the financial aid they can get and then give them anything between that and what they need to live on to get through?

TIM: We don't pay room and board, but for tuition, fees and expenses we make up any shortfall. Keep in mind most of the kids that we serve are going to go to Denver metro area colleges anyway. Certainly, our first year I think about 80–90 percent or something like that are driving distance from their home, so it's not a big issue.

Do you pay for kids who are going further afield or even leaving the state?

TIM: We will pay for the student to attend any accredited school in the state of Colorado. Administratively, it was just too much to take on out-of-state schools. Maybe in a few years we can start doing that, but for right now we're just focusing on Colorado schools.

Are you going to take on all the rest of the city's schools this year, or are they staging in?

TIM: Nope, we're making a giant step forward. One of the other good things we did early last year was that we hired all of our Future Center coordinators for the whole school district, so they were able to work in our three pilot schools and get up to speed, so they'll hit the ground running. Now all these Future Center coordinators are experienced financial aid counselors, and for the most part they are very experienced. But it was all a new experience for them working directly in the high schools. Anyway, we have them all hired, and they are all in their schools, and school is already starting this week, so they're off and running.

You two have really jumped in with both feet, both in terms of the sizable financial commitment you have made and the time frame of the project. It's not like putting up a building at a university, and when you are done, you can walk away. I mean you really stepped into a long-term process here.

BERNIE: We hope to raise a $200 million endowment. We think that is the amount that will keep the program self-sustaining and generate scholarships for all the kids. We estimate that if the stars are all aligned, if I can say it that way, when we have fully four years of kids going to college, there'll be about six thousand students getting scholarships from us.

And on average how much money is that per student?

BERNIE: We're thinking about $3,000 on average. You have to take into consideration a lot of these kids will probably go to a community college for a lot less and then will move on to universities with far greater expenses. Later I imagine we are going to see a transition, with kids going directly to universities, as we hopefully change the culture across the schools, and kids are saying, "You know what? I have an opportunity that I didn't have before, so I'm going to do very well in school, so I can go on to college." Hopefully, it'll be a transformational thing that from elementary school onward Denver public schools kids will know that a financial problem is not going to be the problem to prevent them from getting into a university. It really is a long-term commitment.

It sounds like a huge fund raising endeavor. How has the community responded to that?

TIM: We haven't really kicked off our fund raising efforts. Instead of just rushing in trying to start raising money, we agreed that we wanted to get a pilot year behind us so that we can point to some success. In talking with a relatively small number of people early on, one of the push backs we got from some wealthier people was, "Well, it's a great idea, but I don't think a lot of these kids are motivated to go to school or will get accepted."

We knew that wasn't the case. Having gone to one of these lesser schools, I knew that kids wanted to better themselves, and their parents want a better life for their kids. That was never a question in my mind anyway. But now we can prove that, so we're really going to kick off our serious fund raising efforts October 1, 2007. We have had some substantial donations. On top of our $50 million matching pledge, we already have another $13 million in pledges.

Without fund raising?

TIM: Without any fund raising, that's just from our board recruitment. We have one donor who anonymously pledged $5 million. We have a couple of other people in the $1–2 million range.

BERNIE: I think when you talk about a number that large, about $200 million, people find it very daunting, but you know, it's just a matter of convincing people that this is someplace that they can make a difference. Because I think most philanthropists want to give their money to something that makes a real change in other people's lives. I think the time of just giving it to your alma mater or just giving a little here, a little bit there, is gone. I know that sounds kind of cliché, but I really do believe that the crop of philanthropists that is coming up now want to do something, and they just don't know where they can make a difference.

But it is really a process. First they have to decide for themselves what matters, what is it that they want to see happen with their money, and how they can best do something for others. And I think that's what takes time for people who have wealth. It really takes time for people who come from modest means to work through this because it's all new.

Tim and I both came from modest means. I was a child in a family of eight, and my Dad worked for GM, and Tim's parents were both teachers, so neither one of us came from families with a large amount of money. A lot of people are self-made, and that type of person wants to see that what they do makes a difference, a positive difference to other people's lives.

So we've got a start, but we still have a long way to go before we raise all the money. We know that it's not going to happen overnight. It will take three, four, five years to raise it—so we know that this is a long-term commitment. It's not just giving the money and going away. It's giving the money, raising more money, and it's also building the organization.

Two questions and they're kind of related: One is how do you think this might change the school district? And how do you think it might change the city?

TIM: I think it's going to have a very positive impact. From the time I was in school the DPS (Denver Public Schools) have lost about 40 percent of our kids, or about forty thousand students. The population hasn't declined, but a lot of things have happened in the last thirty years. One is that when I was in high school, they started busing, and that began the white flight. People started moving to the suburbs or sending their kids to private schools as busing started.

Then after that, sometime when I was out of the Denver area, they started the choicing in. You could choice into any school within driving distance. If you were in the city, you could send your kids to the suburbs or vice versa. What happened was a lot of people started sending their kids to the public schools in the suburbs and more private schools and more charter schools. That has led to a lot of bleeding.

The math is pretty simple. You lose forty thousand students, multiply that by $6,700 per student per year, and that means the public school system has to deal with a quarter billion dollars less per year. That's a lot of money, and yet they have the same infrastructure, so it's been very tough.

I think we'll definitely reverse this trend. Now that we have the scholarship program, we're hearing anecdotal stories about people sending their kids from the suburbs back into Denver. I think we're going to keep more students here. I think we're going to have higher graduation rates. Kids have a reason now to finish school. You can see the changes in attitude at Lincoln because it started that fifth-year program a few years earlier, and there was an immediate change in behavior with the students.

You mean discipline and that sort of thing?

TIM: Yes, they said prior to this they had thirteen expulsionary incidents. I think the first year after this that dropped it down to one. The fights stopped. Instead of roaming around the school, kids were sitting in the hallways studying. Teachers were more motivated. You walk around Lincoln now, and it's a good feeling. The school's got a lot of pride. In a lot of ways it's just a much better school than when I went there.

I don't expect dramatic shifts in the next year or two. I expect as we roll out citywide, and people become more aware of the program over the next four or five years, things will change. I'd be disappointed if we don't get at least 50 percent of those kids back. To get an extra twenty thousand students again multiplied by that $6,700 per student per year means the city is going to start having $125 to $130 million more a year to deal with, which is huge to the school system. So I think that's the impact it will have.

To the city I think it's very big, and to the region it's very big.

In talking to both city and state officials, we have heard this. The state's economic development director said it's very difficult to lure businesses to Denver even though we have a very educated population because our schools are not very good. We have the Colorado Paradox. We have one of the most highly educated workforces here, but we also have a very low graduation rate. And it's hard to lure businesses here for that reason.

But now the city can start touting this scholarship program. I think it's going to send a very strong message that Denver cares about education, and they can actually start luring companies and employees here. The city of Kalamazoo started a similar program to ours, but as I understand it for entirely different reasons. They did it to revitalize the city and secondarily to get the kids to college. My understanding is that they're one year ahead of us, and they've seen some dramatic changes in the nature of the city. It looks like it's really working there, but I do need to catch up on some statistics. I think it's going to have a very positive impact to the city itself and the state. We have visions, ultimate visions of trying to expand the scholarship program statewide. We're not getting carried away right now. We have to make this work in the city first.

Many people seem to have a moment in their lives where their thinking about philanthropy begins to take real shape or perhaps gets crystallized. Was there any event in your life that you can point to that might have led you here?

BERNIE: I just think that . . . let's see if I can phrase this . . . Tim and I really feel very fortunate in our lives. If we made different choices along the way, or we had married different people, things might have been different for us. So for whatever reason—if you believe in fate or whatever—that we got together, and he was successful in his business, we really feel that after a while you reach a certain point with money that it's just money.

The money doesn't make your life any better. I shouldn't say that. I mean it does. I like my life. I like not being worried about where my next dollar is coming from, and I wouldn't give that up for anything. Do I need a huge amount of money? No. Tim and I are very modest. We don't have a lot of things. We don't really aspire to spend millions of dollars buying this or that. We like to travel, and we like to ski, but we're not really extravagant with our money.

We have a very nice lifestyle, and I thank my lucky stars everyday that that's how our life has turned out. Like I said, after a while what are you going to do with that money? I mean it's just more money, and we know too many people who have trust funds for their children, and it doesn't turn out very well for the most part.

So that was part of our thinking. We're not going to leave this to our children. They'll get some help, but they're not going to get a lump sum of money when they reach twenty-one or thirty. So what do we do with it? We can't take it with us, and we're not going to give it to our family members because I think that's doing the same thing as giving it to the kids.

Our thinking just evolved over time as we got more involved in the nonprofit world. We just decided this is what we want to do. We want to use it for something that does some good. Over time it evolved and that became our belief. That's how we want to set up our lives, and we've actually communicated that to our girls.

I was going to ask you about that. One thing so many people struggle with is how you pass those values along to the kids.

BERNIE: Well, I think it helped us that when our children were younger, we did not have much money. Our life was pretty modest, and they've grown up that way. But I went to a seminar here in Denver through the Denver Foundation, and they talked about wealth and your responsibility as a family.

Tim and I have always thought that we shouldn't tell our kids what we have because we don't want them to start thinking this way. At the seminar they said, "Your kids know by the time they are eight years old. They just know. They may not know the exact dollar amount, but they know you've got money." One speaker said, "You're doing them a great disservice by not sitting down with them and talking to them and explaining to them what that means to you and what you expect of them; and as a family and if you're involved in philanthropy, you just need to talk to them about this as well."

So we sat down with our daughters last summer and had this conversation with them, and they're bright; they understand that we have a good lifestyle. They're amazing. All of them said, "We really don't care, Mom and Dad." They just said, "Well, great that's nice, you know, we're proud of you and . . ."

. . . What's for dinner?

BERNIE: Exactly. I'm hoping that as they get older, they will get more involved with our family foundation, but I really believe that you don't have to have a lot of money to help out other people.

If you give 100 bucks every year to an organization that you believe in . . . some people believe that that's not philanthropy, but I think it is. I think if you make $10,000 a year, and you give $50 away, I think that's a truly great thing. Any amount of money that you can give, or time you can volunteer, I think is important. So hopefully our daughters will get involved. Our youngest daughter is very concerned about Darfur. She thinks and reads about it, and she wants to help. I'm hoping she'll be the one to take over our foundation.

You will need her to because this is a long-term project.

BERNIE: We're hopefully raising the next crop of philanthropists that will continue to do this. Anyway, that's kind of where we are with our kids.

I don't think there was any moment that I said, "That's why I want to do this." I think it just kind of evolved over time, and as Tim and I have been able to do more financially, we have thought a lot more about how we utilize whatever donations we give to make the dollars go farther.

Maybe the moment of change was when Tim read the newspaper and didn't just fold it up, put it down, and walk away. The whole notion of scholarships at the Denver Public Schools could have been a passing thought—or one that he never even formulated.

JOHANN OLAV KOSS
Right to Play

My advice to anyone who is beginning in philanthropy, my best advice, is to just get started—because it's never going to be perfect from the start.
—*Johann Olav Koss*

A DEFINING CHARACTERISTIC OF SUCCESSFUL PHILAN-thropists seems to be the ability to hold down two, or even three, full-time jobs simultaneously. Even in this company of highly motivated souls who seemingly with ease live more than one life at the same time—Johann Olav Koss stands out. Training to be a quadruple Olympic gold medalist and eleven-time world record holder in speed skating might be seen as a full-time job, ditto training to be a physician, spearheading a national fund raising campaign, and earning an MBA. But undertaking these tasks while representing the Olympic Committee's goodwill efforts, in places as far flung as Eritrea, might be more than a single soul can handle at one time, or even in one lifetime. Yet during the time Koss was training for the Lillehammer Olympics (held in his native Norway in February 1994) and completing his medical education, he visited Eritrea on behalf of Olympic Aid, a trip that changed his life.

Eritrea had been liberated from Ethiopia in 1993 after a thirty-year civil war that had torn the country apart. The Olympic Committee for Olympic Aid, organized to bring aid and relief to the refugees, sent Koss on a humanitarian misson to Eritrea six months prior to the Olympic games. On his trip the three strands of Koss' life—his passion for sport, his interest in medicine and health care, and his deep admiration for those who devote themselves to helping others—came together. The images of that trip were so powerful for him that they became a touchstone for everything that would follow.

Six months after this visit, in the wake of winning his second gold medal of the Lillehammer games, Koss stirred the world when he announced at a press conference that he would be giving his prize money—some $30,000—to Olympic Aid and challenged Norway and his fellow Olympians to do the same. "For me, the Olympics, it's about spirit. It's absolutely inspirational. And I totally believe that the Olympics are what it was meant to be when Coubertin was mentioning it," he said referring to Pierre de Coubertin, founder of the modern competition. "It's for peace, it's for education, it's for health. When you start defining the Olympic spirit, it is actually to reach everybody in this world; it is to inspire everybody to be better people."[1]

Koss speaks English with the idiosyncrasy of a Scandinavian, the little foreign nuances amidst the phenomenal vocabulary. His accomplishments, both athletic and humanitarian, have been widely acknowledged. *Sports Illustrated* named him athlete of the year, *Time* magazine listed him as one of the 100 Future Leaders of Tomorrow, and the United Nations made him one of their ambassadors. Yet he has the unaffected charm of someone who does not take these headlines too seriously. He is far more concerned with convincing others that sport has an essential role to play in every child's life—in both developing and developed countries—than with dwelling on his own accomplishments.

Sport for Koss is both a vehicle and an end in itself. Koss formed Right to Play, out of Olympic Aid in order to bring organized athletics and games, wrapped around learning, to children all over the globe—with the heaviest emphasis on African countries that have been rocked by war or famine. Over the past fourteen years, Koss has been able to raise millions of dollars to bring sporting programs to countries as far flung as Sierra Leone, Azerbaijan, and Dubai. He has enlisted athletes with faces recognizable across the globe to help raise awareness, funds, and often to simply bring hope and inspiration to their home countries. The program is used as a positive force in children's lives and a vehicle for AIDS education, lessons on antiviolent behavior, and increased school attendance. Through programs that have evolved over a decade, Right to Play staff train locals as coaches and educators and create regular sporting events for children both to provide the health and fitness benefits that athletics brings and to be used as a vehicle for education and good will. The programs early focus was on refugee camps, where extreme stress and poor living conditions, combined with excruciating boredom, created a miserable situation. "So what happens?" Koss asks. "They pick fights, they harass women, they no longer take care of themselves. But when you introduce sports and games, something happens that you could call magic. They spontaneously rediscover a reason to live."[2] With early success, the program branched out in numerous countries and expanded far beyond the refugee camp population.

Right to Play focuses heavily on AIDS prevention and education through a program that trains local coaches to go into villages all over the countryside, interspersing educational messages with sports. Coaches are given rigorous training in prevention and health information and then are able to transmit this to the children and teenagers they work with. As one of the young participants explained, "It is more fun here than sitting in the classroom because all of the children are free to talk to the coaches, and they can sit and ask questions and be free."[3]

Despite being a speed skater, Koss's Right to Play focuses heavily on soccer and has recruited many world famous soccer players to act as ambassadors of the program to raise awareness in their home counties. Twenty Major League soccer players have enlisted, as did the Chelsea Football club. Athletes from every other area of sports have been recruited by Koss, and many of them have spent their time in Right to Play programs abroad. The same energy and drive that allowed Koss to stand on the Olympic podium has gone into giving Right to Play an international profile. To highlight the program, Adidas initiated its "red ball" campaign, selling specially designed red soccer balls throughout the world and donating all the proceeds to Right to Play. "Athletes are inspirational individuals who are looked up to," Koss explains. "They have the opportunity to leverage this status to be role models and encourage positive changes. Everyone relates to sport and games, but soccer is unique as it is the most globally recognized sport. It is loved across cultures. And soccer players are known throughout the world, so their reach and impact is that much greater."[4]

While Koss has become a hero to many, he too had his own heroes as well, particularly Fridtjof Nansen (1861–1930)—a national hero to every Norwegian schoolchild. Norway, as Koss emphasizes, is a small country with a big tradition of giving back. Nansen was an early Arctic explorer, surviving some of the most arduous conditions, as well as a widely published biologist and humanist. But his enduring legacy was as a diplomat. He was an advocate for the League of Nations, where he repatriated 450,000 prisoners of war; and later, the high commissioner for refugees following World War I. He spent the last decade of his life (1920–1930) working for the plight of millions of Russians suffering from famine and for refugees adrift in post-war Europe. Koss was always aware of Nansen and the legendary role the 1922 Nobel Peace prizewinner played in Europe. Nansen embodied everything Koss admired—the will to perform unimaginably difficult physical trials, the intellectual perseverance of a scientist, and the deep concern for humanity that spread far beyond national borders.

Koss has huge aspirations for Right to Play. He hopes to reach five million children by 2012, and that the program's effects will endure for their lifetimes. "We can develop ourselves through sports," Koss explains, "both physically and mentally. We learn to develop self-confidence. Sports teach us that there are rules, that we have to work hard and do our best. We learn how to co-operate and communicate, how to solve conflicts in a

sportsmanlike manner. I think those are essential conditions for construct-
ing a democracy."[5]

---

*LISA: I'd like to start with the people that you feel most heavily
influenced you in the early development of your thoughts on philanthropy.*

JOHANN: There are several people that have influenced me. One
of them was my grandmother on my mother's side. She lived the
rule that you should do onto others as you want them to do onto
you. She spoke about that as a major force in her life and the reason
she always worried about other people.

Were there things in her community that she was involved with?

Actually, she was very engaged in what they call the farmer's
communities. The farmwomen baked, sold cakes, and they looked
out for people when their neighbors had difficulties. That wasn't
what influenced me necessarily. It was her presence that influenced
me, more than what she was doing for others. Her values and what
she talked about with me was the important part.

In addition to that, my parents had a huge influence on me. Both
my parents are medical doctors and in Norway, that's a bit different
than it is here. We have a much more level society, a more equal
society. Historically, a medical doctor has an important role in society from being a learned person. My parents were always open to
other people and their problems. They were always helping people,
whether it was neighbors, a friend, or family. They were always
working. They even established a little medical clinic in the basement of our house so that people could come to get help whenever
they needed it.

My father also liked sports a lot, so of course this influenced me. He liked speed skating, particularly. He wasn't a speed skater, but he helped the national team, as a physician, as physiologist would do today. Doctors don't do that anymore, but he loved working with the team.

I have to say another influence was Norway and the Norwegian culture. Norway is a very tiny country, which you don't realize before you move out of it. We always think that we have an enormously high level of social conscience in the country of helping other people, and particularly outside our country. I'm not sure where this comes from, but it is understood that when you are wealthy, you should give back. I guess it comes from a social understanding within our country. We have a socialistic kind of government in many ways. It doesn't matter whether its right or left wing—it is socialistic in some ways. I think Norway's now been named the safest place to live in the world.

The heroes of our country are the people who have done something in the larger world, which is very interesting. Fridtjof Nansen in particular is one of my heroes. He was a real role model in our country. As early as the nineteenth century, he wrote about the importance of the environment and how we should protect our environment. Norway has many of these heroes, and he was a huge influence on me when I was a kid, as he was on every kid in our society.

Your life has involved being a physician, an athlete, and an ambassador, yet now it is devoted to being a philanthropist. I wondered if you could tell me a bit more about the journey. I understand it started with the Olympic Aid. Could you walk me through how Right to Play was born?

It's an interesting journey. Here I grow up in a family and a country that focuses on helping others, and I'm trying to become the best in the world in a very egocentric, repetitive, and self-absorbed way. My life was given over to skating around and around a track, and sometimes I'm wondering what I am doing here.

Is there room for self-doubt when you have a goal like an Olympic gold medal?

Yes, you have doubts. Everybody has doubt. I'm skating eight hours a day, seven days a week, and that is just training. Then I use four hours to eat, and I need to get ten hours of sleep. There's not much more time left to do other things. And everything that everyone around you does is an effort to improve your life, improve your performance. It's truly incredible. Being an athlete—there is nothing more unnatural in the world than that, which is great. Everybody should try it. [Laugh] Just think if we all had teams of people around us making us better. As I was training in 1993, I was having doubts about what I was doing. I didn't feel that I was giving back. Because of that concern, my motivation and interest suffered, of course.

Then I was asked to be an ambassador for Olympic Aid, which was a program involved with the Olympics. I was asked because I was helping out with another organization—Save the Children. I was helping Save the Children for a year with minor things in Norway, and it became part of the Olympic Aid fund raising consortium.

I was asked to be an ambassador for that consortium at the Olympics because I was one of the favorites. And they asked me to go to Eritrea, and there were things on that trip, for the very first time, that really made me believe that I was on the right path.

First of all the experience was great for me because what I saw was the help and the aid that Norway's people were giving and the things we were doing in development were really helping. You always hear about development not working. You always hear everybody's excuses—the corruption and the aid doesn't get there or that the wrong things are sent over there. But there I was, shocked, because I saw the things that Norway was doing really worked.

What did you see?

The building of new schools, particularly, and of health clinics, as well. I saw the importance of development to the kids in these communities. I met very, very dedicated people in the Eritrean government who were totally passionate about rebuilding their own country. This had a huge influence on me.

Seeing that things became a reality had a huge impact on you?

Yes. At a time when I was having self-doubt about what I was doing, I was seeing in Eritrea what was important. Then I met a group of boys, twelve year olds who were playing soccer with a rolled up shirt, because it was all that they had. The one boy who had a long-sleeved shirt was the most popular because his shirt could be rolled up and tied together to be used as a ball. You cannot play soccer without a ball. And in that moment I had the sense of all that I had been given in my life, and, as important, that these kids were not any different than I was when I was twelve. They have the same dreams, and they have the same wishes. They want just to play that game, which gave me kind of an acceptance of what I had been doing in many ways. We are more similar to others we meet than what you'd expect, even in the most devastated areas of the world.

When was this?

It was in 1993, only six months before the games. There were a number of scenes on that trip that affected me. I saw another group of kids, younger ones, boys and girls maybe eight or nine year olds, and they were looking at posters of heroes that had died in the recent war. Throughout the whole ten-day visit, I heard about these heroes. They were the ones who died for the liberation of Eritrea in the battles with the Ethiopians. There was pure admiration for the heroes of this war. At the time I was watching them looking at the posters, a group of bike riders in a race came through the streets, and these kids turned around and they yelled and screamed and cheered on the bike riders—like kids do.

I saw them admire the liberators for what they did and at the same time cheer the athletes. That was for me a moment when I said "Wow, it's good to be an athlete." I think if you can create new role models for these kids. So it's good enough to be an athlete, to be a hero of your country, if you could use this to create an alternative path of development. My humbleness in the face of all that I had received in my life and the acceptance of being an athlete motivated me again for the next six months for training.

It also gave me a little bit more of appreciation, and I stopped complaining so much about normal things, because you cannot get life in better perspective than what I saw on that trip. That took me to the Olympics. Then three, four days before the Olympics I was sitting almost crying. The athletes have mental coaches to prepare them for competition. Winning the Olympics is not physical; it's mental. Basically, it's what happens in your head. Everybody who has made it to the competition is going to be extremely fit, certainly fit enough to win. If you don't get your head right around it—you won't get there. My biggest worry was if I couldn't win, I wouldn't be successful with anything in life going forward. I had done everything possible, everything possible, to prepare the best I could for that week and that run. I don't want to say I sacrificed because you don't sacrifice when you're an athlete. You don't look at it as a sacrifice.

I'd trained, I'd been sleeping, I'd been eating the right foods, I'd been doing basically everything I thought I could do to be the best; and if I failed, I thought that couldn't do anything. And I was in the middle of medical school as well at the time. The mental coach said to me, "What is going to be the influence of your results in this race on how good a doctor you're going to be? What do your results in racing have to do with your being a doctor?" There was zero correlation between me going fast around the track and me becoming a doctor. Monday was going to come, and I was going back to medical school, he reminded me. Again, like the trip to Eritrea, it's putting everything in perspective. This limited my expectations of my own performance, which freed me to perform well. When I won the first race, I had three races to skate. When I won the first race, I was thankful to my family and team members and I asked myself why did I win? Why not any of the other great competitiors? Then I thought about my trip to Eritrea and the inspiration those children had given me. I said, "If I win the next race, I'm going to give my money away from that race. Because if I win that race, it's certainly not for me, but it's to allow me to increase recognition of the Olympic Aid and the work that we are doing around the world to eliminate poverty, and that is so important." Those kids I met had given me so much for the last six months of my preparation.

When I won my second race, I announced this at the press conference and urged everyone in Norway to give to Olympic Aid. I said everyone should give 10 Krones, or the equivalent of one and a half dollars per gold medal, and everybody did it. We raised $18 million dollars in ten days from Norwegian donors.

Was this only Norwegian money? This wasn't coming in from the rest of the world?

This was only from Norway, where there are only four million people. Everybody wanted to give, and it was a huge, huge success. I had promised those kids with the rolled-up shirt after the

Olympics I would come back. I had said to them, "I'll come back after the Olympics with the soccer balls." So two months after the Olympic games, I challenged the Norwegian children to give their used or new equipment to us, so we could collect it all and bring it down to Eritrea. This was outside of the Olympic Aid because Olympic Aid was about building schools and hospitals and things like that. This was sports-based. This is just around sports. I said to the nation that I had met kids who don't have anything, and do you guys have anything we could take to them? After two or three weeks, we had thirteen tons of equipment and 200 volunteers. I got a plane from an airline and took out all the seats from the inside so that we could fill it up like a cargo plane. We left a few seats inside for some sponsors and ten lucky Norwegian children so that we could take them with us. It was far more than I expected, and I was totally enthusiastic about this project, running around Norway talking to Norwegian kids and collecting equipment.

The day before I left, one of the largest newspapers in Norway wrote on the front page that Koss is bringing soccer balls to starving kids, what an idiot.

As opposed to food?

Yes, because that is what they needed. The president of Eritrea had called on the world to give food. There was a drought, and he knew there could be a shortage of food by the end of the year. So he had been calling for world aid at the same time I was collecting sporting equipment, and the paper picked this up and thought I was an idiot.

I had had a call with the Eritrean government about three weeks earlier and said, "Hey, I'm collecting sports equipment. Are you guys interested?" Then the minister of education and the national sport commissioner that supports the schools, said, "Yes, this would be great, we really need this, it would be wonderful, and thank you very much." And I had people on the ground there working with them getting ready to distribute what we were bringing, so I didn't think about this aspect of it.

So I called the journalist, and I said, "You're coming with me." I have never in my life been met by so many people as we were in the streets of Eritrea. There must have been 100 thousand people in the streets with Norwegian and Eritrean flags celebrating our arrival. I said, "What's happening here. This is crazy." And I was told that on the news the night before there had been a story that I was coming back after being an Olympic champion with all this sports equipment. And they showed the race in which I won a medal. When I arrived, they put me on a bike, and we rode through the streets with some of the country's young athletes. And one of the guys said, "You're so famous. I don't know why you're so famous." I said, "Well, I won the Olympics." He said he wasn't that impressed, and I said, "Why not?" And he said, "You only beat one guy—I saw the race. You were only skating with one guy." And he said, "Look at all the guys I have to beat. A bike race is so much more difficult."

Later I met with the president, and I said to him, "You have asked for food, and I'm bringing sports equipment—I must have made a mistake." He just looked at me very, very seriously, and said, "The gift we are receiving from the Norwegian children is the largest gift we have ever received. This is the first time we feel like human beings. This is something far more than just being kept alive. It's the first time my kids—he had an eight year old and a ten year old at the time—will be playing with a proper ball in their school." He said this is totally unique. "This is about respecting us as who we are." He said, "I hate that I have to go out and ask for food, because we should be able to supply our own food, but we can't. But this gift is about us being people and human beings and building new hopes and dreams for this country."

That conversation has been my inspiration since then. We have to look at each other as people and as much more equals in many ways. We have to give people an opportunity to learn and grow, and sports and play have an unbelievable power to do that in children and youth. There are so many benefits to sports that have not been appreciated by governments. This needs to be understood.

How did this lead to Right to Play?

Right to Play as an organization that uses sport and play as a tool for behavioral change. The other thing about sports and play, and I say play a lot because I think unstructured play and play activities are also an extremely important part of a child's development, noncompetitive play. What we have done is add educational outcomes to play activities. Play is fun, and if you repeat it and have a learning outcome from it, you can actually learn how to protect yourself. We have put this around health prevention tools, for instance, girls in sub-Saharan Africa learn how to protect themselves from getting HIV/AIDS. And by repeating activities and the lessons that with go with them, over time they learn about the viruses, how they should respect their own bodies, and to use a condom. The lessons are repeated through games and play, and real learning outcomes come from this. The other part of it is that it's done within the community and a group of people, so you get the lessons reinforced in a community because everyone is doing the same thing.

How did you get from Eritrea to what is now an international organization?

It took a long time because I was finishing medical school when I stopped skating. I was also asked to implement the fund raising campaign for Olympic Aid at the summer Olympics in Atlanta [where Koss raised $14 million for UNICEF], and I was working with the UN and UNICEF. Then in 2000 I started working with UNHCR [The Office of the United Nations High Commissioner for Refugees]. I worked with the Red Cross. I've worked with all these organizations, but the majority with the UN because I was asked to be an ambassador for UNICEF in 1994, and I've been one ever since.

Over these years from 1994 to 2000, I realized that I wanted the world of sports to take a greater responsibility in development because of the platform that this type of fame gives them. It was what I saw in Lillehammer, the amazing power to mobilize people, which before then I had no idea about. I wanted to do much more with sports and play and integrate it into development work. Athletes are some of the most fortunate people in the world, so we should do even more to give back. This became my passion, and when I was elected as a member of the IOC [International Olympic Committee), I tried every route. But the UN didn't think sports was very interesting, and the world of sports didn't think development was very interesting.

In 2000 I realized that there is nobody combining these two as a global organization—so I had to do it. That's when I stopped being a doctor and fully focused on building a global organization that could show the best practices in combining sports for development and education. This would be a program that would engage the development world and world of sports in giving back. So that is how this was formulated after the Sydney Olympics because I still had the relationship with the Olympics. I still used that as a platform to raise money, and fortunately that has been very successful. This is when we changed from being an organization that raised money and gave it to other programs as Olympic Aid had done, to being an organization that runs its own sports and play programs aimed at development and education.

But you changed the name from Olympic Aid?

We had to change the name because the Olympic name is very complicated. There's so much ownerships and rights and structure to it that it limited our fund raising opportunities.

As the program started to spread, what was the direction you were trying to take it? Were you focused in Africa? Were you focused on a particular sport? What educational outcomes were focused on first?

I have to say that we started to build up the program with play material with some learning objectives and health education that we put together. At first we had six sports: soccer, basketball, volleyball, netball, ultimate Frisbee, and track and field. With the play programs and lessons we had, we sent out international volunteers like the Peace Corps model to work in the local communities. They were exceptionally good people who had a great inspiration to go out there, see what they could do to work with a local team of people. They trained people in the different activities and sports. In the beginning it was very, very tough and there was very little support for the international volunteers as they mostly had to handle everything on the ground themselves. Now it has become a much larger organization with local staff implementing the program in partnership with local organizations.

You had difficulties getting established?

My advice to anyone who is beginning in philanthropy, my best advice, is to just get started—because it's never going to be perfect from the start. It is never going to be. You're going to make so many mistakes, and you're going to change the program so many times. As it goes along, you are going to understand that you have to change it. Because what you originally thought was going to be the right thing is not going to be the right thing and then you have to listen to people as time goes on to make it the best possible program.

We really moved 180 degrees. At first I believed that when we were going into refugee camps, because we focused primarily on refugee camps initially, that we would send in some international volunteers, train a couple of the local people, and pull out after three years. Refugee camps shouldn't last more than three years, but of course they do. But there were so many questions we had not answered. What about the local people? Should they be able to create their own organization? How do you make the program sustainable once international volunteers have gone? Another thing, which I hadn't thought about, was the time frame of three years. It was unrealistic. It was simply much too short. We will need a ten-, fifteen-, twenty-year perspective.

One of the impacts of the program I never anticipated was on the local coaches. We train them, they learn how to develop and plan a program, how to lead others, and they learn management skills that make them very employable, and then we lose them. This is not a negative thing. It is a very positive outcome that we had not anticipated. It's a huge benefit of the program.

Yet, it just creates more demands on the organization, and you need to put systems in place so that the people you train can train other people—train the trainer concept. Then you no longer need to send international people in because that's not necessary after a while. The goal, of course, is a self-sustaining model. And as the program has developed, we have moved further in that direction. So until 2006 we had about 100 international volunteers in the field at any time, and now we're down to about forty. Now we are using them very specifically, putting them in very specific areas, where they're needed from outside perspective.

In all those places where we had international people before, now we have local people running our programs. Everything is local. So we hired local people, and it has been an evolution. I had no idea how this evolution was going to happen. I see these things in a different light than I did before. And if I had waited to start the organization until now to find that out, I wouldn't have been able to do anything. So that's why I'm saying you have to start, and then you find out. People are afraid of starting because they are going to make mistakes. Naturally people want success, but I would say that probably the first mistake people make is that they haven't started, and it is the biggest problem.

In the last years of our lives, in the middle of this century, I don't want to look back and feel like I sat there during the greatest health care crisis of my lifetime and just watched and did little or nothing. I want to be in the game. I want to be contributing. I want to be a part of the solution.
—Anonymous, on involvement and funding of AIDS Research and Treatment Delivery Programs in KwaZulu-Natal

A NONYMOUS" LIKES TO FLY UNDER THE RADAR. FOR DEcades, he and his wife have quietly and regularly supported the local institutions in their town. Yet many people who they help do not even know who they are; even people in organizations where they have been giving for years would not be able to identify them. They are an exceptionally intelligent couple who have used their intellectual and monetary resources to serve others.

Anonymous is a male baby boomer who has enjoyed a successful career, first as a senior executive at one of Wall Street's foremost investment banks, and later as the president at an equally famous investment fund. Through both of these endeavors, he has gained a large measure of personal wealth, far outstripping his middle-class origins. During the years in which he was consumed with his career, his and his wife's giving was confined largely to their local community, and true involvement with a cause "of the heart" eluded him. Instead, he worked eighty hours a week, he focused on bringing up his kids, and he spent many years in overseas postings.

As he and his family traveled widely for work and pleasure, he viewed the world through the lens of economic opportunity for his company and his family. Despite having a first-rate education, he, like so many Americans, were not terribly knowledgeable about the economic and health care plight of the world's poor. But his life was permanently transformed by a chance encounter with Dr. Bruce Walker, a Harvard professor of medicine and a foremost expert on AIDS.

On the face of it, Anonymous and his wife resemble other highly successful middle-aged couples. They have a beautiful home, their children are thriving, and they are highly contributory members of their community. But scratch just below the surface, and you find a couple who is deeply involved in a world so far from their own idyllic suburbia that it might as well be another planet.

Each year they spend weeks or even months in some of the poorest hospitals in KwaZulu-Natal, South Africa, volunteering their own time or researching ways that they can help. Then back home they host meetings and informational dinners for community members who are blessed with both health and wealth to shed light on the greatest plague of our time. Never do they shout about the financial commitment they have made or even use it as leverage to guilt or encourage their friends and acquaintances into joining them. Rather, their guests are given the rare opportunity to dine with world-class researchers and physicians, who themselves are immersed every day in the battle that is AIDS, and to hear reports from the front lines. Unsurprisingly, the response to these fund raising dinners is overwhelming.

Anonymous giving is a subject that conflicts most of the interviewees in this book. Many said that they give anonymously some of the time but by no means all of the time.

There are a great many reasons philanthropists give anonymously. Some do so to avoid the barrage of requests that can follow the public recognition of a large gift. Others choose to shield their giving to maintain their privacy and keep the magnitude of their wealth away from public glare. There are religious beliefs that cause some to favor giving without their name attached. For others it is even simpler: They want the focus to be on the gift, not the giver.

The anonymous interviewee of this chapter falls into the final group. The monetary donations he and his wife have made are such that if they were not given anonymously, they could have their names plastered across hospital wards, buildings, and university academic chairs in Africa, Boston, and New York. But public recognition is not what motivates them to give. They have chosen to keep their philanthropic identities largely unseen by both the public and sometimes by even the grantee themselves. But the path is not always clear.

After decades of giving, Anonymous is an experienced giver. Yet like most of the others in this book, he sees himself still as a student of philanthropy. The community involvement that had dominated his giving now runs alongside a larger worldview. He and his wife have moved on without moving away. He went from sitting on a local hospital board to sitting on a major teaching hospital board and then to advising one of the premier medical institutions in the world, and he never left support for his community behind.

Anonymous's tale has so many of the threads of the others in this book. A sharp inflection point in his life, in this case two weeks in South Africa, entirely altered the path of his philanthropy. Through this chance event, a true passion took hold. His sense of his own good luck meant that he and his wife had been looking to share their fortune and were attuned to their cause the moment it crossed their path.

Listening to his story, there is a very strong sense that here is a man who has answered so many questions, and yet it is clear that important ones remain. He has given to his community, has found his philanthropic calling, and has focused like a laser on institutions and individuals that can realize that vision. But scratching below the surface of this fabulously successful businessman and philanthropist, is the nagging questions that plague anyone hoping to give money away effectively: "I am always wrestling with the question of giving to meet immediate needs, true humanitarian life-saving measures, versus looking for long-term solutions that will eliminate those needs. I also continually think about what method of giving yields the greatest leverage. As someone concerned about many issues, what is the best use of my resources and time? My thinking is always evolving."

LISA: We are having this conversation because giving has grown to be such a big part of your life and taken you so far out of your world, but it must have begun closer to home.

ANONYMOUS: My parents I think taught me great values, especially to help those less fortunate than us. I remember graduating from Harvard and just thinking I needed to contribute back to my college and that was probably the first thing I did of any meaningfulness. But I've always had this feeling that one has to make an important contribution back to your community either in the form of public service or philanthropic or charitable contributions.

So you finish college, go to work on Wall Street, and like everyone there you really don't have any time to be giving to causes. Where does your philanthropy go from there?

For the first twenty or twenty-five years out of college, a lot of people are focused on two things—their careers and families—and both can be consuming and leave little time to do anything else, especially if you want to be successful with both. And that was generally true for me. I was working eighty hours a week in my early career and very devoted to my firm and my family, and it left little time to be making any meaningful contribution to my community.

My wife was actively involved in our community and imploring me to get more involved, and I deferred doing anything until probably my early forties. At that point I was a lot more secure in my family and professional life. I had made a reasonable amount of money and just felt an overwhelming need to have more purposefulness in my life and to be more influential than I was able to be professionally. I had an enormous internal drive to contribute something back. Although that may sound insincere, it wasn't in my case. I still today feel an enormous urge to contribute back, to contribute back much of my wealth and much of my time.

Where did you begin?

We started out making annual contributions to local charities, even as we were raising our family and starting out professionally. We were trying to set a good early standard by contributing to our local libraries, fire and police departments, Boys and Girls Club, local land trusts, and various hospitals. We've been doing that for the last twenty years and contributing more each year. We have always felt that that was important beyond paying taxes because a lot of these local organizations depend very significantly on what they can extract from their communities. We wanted to be a part of it. We weren't really spending time on boards or spending a meaningful amount of time on the organizations themselves, but we were writing checks, being loyal, being consistent every year, supporting annual functions, annual galas, and actually just learning a lot. We were learning what these organizations were like, the kind of impact one can have, how to be involved, and also how to prioritize our own time. To me all of those early years where you might not be contributing such big dollars are important because you're setting a standard for your family and for yourself while learning how to prioritize.

I think that it was an obligation, a responsibility, and also a privilege to be supporting all these organizations locally, but it wasn't exhilarating enough.

Why? Because your involvement was distant?

Because I think we live in a very privileged area—and not withstanding that there are still people who are out of work, or poorly paid, who need food, shelter, after school activities, and local health care organizations—I've always felt that on a relative basis the needs here are less urgent than they are globally. In certain respects our own early giving was out of a sense of obligation and responsibility. All of our later giving has been more passionate, driven by a feeling that there are so many people in the world and causes that desperately need support, and many of these organizations aren't in areas where there's a natural philanthropic base to draw support from. So in the last six or seven years, we've thought more globally and more passionately.

How did you make that transition?

Not through any epiphany or precipitating event. As I was retiring from my first career and began to free up more time, I began to consider more thoughtfully the public policy issues confronting us, and where it made sense to try to contribute time, effort, and capital to try to solve bigger problems. And for no particular personal reason, I decided global health care is an urgent public policy issue where I thought I could begin to make a difference.

Why global public health care?

Well, there was just a confluence of things. I met someone locally who was chairman of our local hospital. He began talking to me about the hospital and the sweeping changes that he and others were making at the hospital and how fascinating it was. I always felt that the local hospital is probably the most important organization in a community to be supporting.

I also wanted to learn more about national health care and to get involved with a major New York City hospital. I talked to some friends who directed me to one of the country's top teaching hospitals, and I made an appointment to see the hospital's president one day back in 2002. I told him I had an interest in learning more about academic medical centers and about the United States health care industry. I loved the notion that this particular hospital has always been located in the middle of immigrant neighborhoods, and that anyone would be well-treated there whether they were Wall Street bankers or lawyers or immigrants from the Dominican Republic. I really admire the notion of serving the community in that way, offering excellent health care and access to everyone in a fair and transparent way.

Where did that lead?

· Well, that led very quickly to joining the hospital board. I focused all of my early efforts working with the children's hospital there. I'd never had anyone in my family who needed urgent health care services, so I wasn't being drawn into health care because of personal circumstances or some personal tragedy. I was being drawn into it because I realized that providing health care is just a very important priority for our society, and I wanted to learn about it and be a part of it.

So I liked that I was involved at a community hospital and that I was involved with a big academic medical center, but the real turning point for me came when I was working as the president of an investment firm after retiring from Goldman Sachs. One day one of my partners had invited in a group of doctors from the University of Texas and Harvard Medical School to make a presentation on infectious diseases and AIDS, in particular. I decided to join the meeting, and it was going to be one of those events, serendipitously, that would really change my life. At that presentation we listened to six doctors speak about AIDS. I had never really thought about infectious disease or global health care, and I certainly had neither understanding of, nor involvement, in the world of AIDS.

What were they talking about?

They talked about a very specific project they needed funding for, but they began by putting their project in context and explaining that millions of people were dying each year of AIDS. They made the case that although more people were dying of infectious disease than of chronic disease, problems such as malaria, tuberculosis, AIDS, and water-borne diseases really don't affect us in the West. We have excellent medical care, and we live long lives. Most of us will die of chronic diseases like diabetes, cancer, and congestive heart failure, and those are the diseases we focus on here, appropriately enough.

But we're just a small part of the global population, and most of the rest of the world, these doctors were explaining, were living in resource-scarce settings with very little income, poor shelter, poor education, not much hopefulness in their lives, and they were dying much earlier and dying from infectious diseases. I was really unaware of that until I was listening to that presentation. I had no idea that millions of people were dying each year from AIDS.

At the end of the presentation that day, I went up to one of the doctors, Bruce Walker, an infectious disease specialist at Mass General and Harvard Medical School, and I told him I'd like to learn more about AIDS. He said, "Listen, if you want to learn more about AIDS, you ought to come to South Africa with me. I'm in the process of building a lab at the University of KwaZulu-Natal in Durban, South Africa. And this lab is going to enable us to do a lot of research on pediatric AIDS." He further explained that Kwa-Zulu-Natal is one of the nine provinces of South Africa and one of the most heavily infected areas of the world. As many as one-third to one-half of the adult population in KwaZulu-Natal was infected with HIV in the late 1990s. Once he had finished building the lab in 2002, he then had the resources to start testing and treating children with AIDS.

That is actually the reason he came to visit us; on one hand, he was teaching us about the global problem of infectious diseases and AIDS in particular, and on the other hand, he was coming in to look for funding for a very specific project. He wanted to find funding for a handheld device that would allow him to test for AIDS in more rural communities outside of the hospital setting.

The handheld device that he was contemplating was an important diagnostic tool to count CD4 cells. Typically, that would be done by sophisticated technology called a flow cytometer. A flow cytometer usually sits on a desk or countertop and is very bulky and expensive. Researchers use flow cytometers to analyze and count the CD4 cells in a blood specimen. If the count is too low, it is an important indicator of AIDS. What Bruce Walker and these five other doctors wanted to create is a handheld flow cytometer that they would be able to carry around into rural villages in KwaZulu-Natal and be able to test people on-site in their own local communities. That seemed like a very interesting idea in terms of intervening at a critical stage of testing and diagnostics, and they were coming to our investment firm looking for funding.

Interestingly, we actually did fund that project. We raised about $20 million and created a company that is in the process now of making a prototype and trying to create this product for broader distribution.

Meanwhile, I had become very intrigued with Bruce Walker's work and I was about to go to South Africa for the first time. I had never been to the African continent and was very intrigued to do that.

What did the AIDS epidemic look like at this point in South Africa?

AIDS is still a very challenging issue globally. There's been good progress in the last few years as PEPFAR [President's Emergency Plan for AIDS Relief] funds, United States government funds, have been made available to countries around the world. As the price of treatments have come down dramatically, there has been a lot of progress globally.

Having said that, the AIDS virus is a very smart and complex virus and is not likely to be solved anytime soon. So a vaccine is still the Holy Grail in medicine. To create a successful vaccine against the AIDS virus will still take many years, perhaps decades, and so there's a natural growth curve to the incidence of AIDS and death rates. Some doctors and scientists have estimated that several hundred million people may eventually die of AIDS over the next few decades.

That is a staggering forecast. In the last years of my life, in the middle of this century, I don't want to look back and feel like I sat there during the greatest health care crisis of my lifetime and just watched and did little or nothing. I want to be in the game. I want to be contributing. I want to be a part of the solution. That's what I've realized over these last five or six years. These problems aren't going away; we're going to live with these problems during the rest of our lifetimes. Hundreds of millions of people could eventually die from malaria, tuberculosis, and AIDS, and I want to be engaged. I want to be in the game.

How do you do that? Here you are a banker in New York, and you have had a two-hour meeting with a Harvard physician. How does that translate into taking action in the global AIDS crisis?

I got on a plane and flew to South Africa. As you know, that's a long flight, an eighteen- or nineteen-hour flight, and I remember arriving on my first visit in Johannesburg and then connecting on to Durban. I arrived in Durban late on a Sunday night in pouring rain, and I met Bruce Walker and a local doctor, Helga Holst, who is the president and CEO at McCord Hospital. On arrival that night we jumped in a jeep and drove four hours into the Drakensberg Mountains. It is an area of KwaZulu-Natal that is very rural, and we didn't arrive at our camp until about midnight. We went right to sleep, and the next morning I awoke at 6:00 a.m. and was seeing South Africa for the first time from a spectacular vantage point, from the peak of the Drakensberg Mountains. It was an amazing panorama, just a spectacular landscape of mountains and valleys, truly beautiful. The rains and the storm from the prior night were gone, and it was just a magnificent morning.

That morning began a two-week trip through hospitals, hospices, clinics, schools, and orphanages. It was a crash course, an intensive education in the world of AIDS in a very heavily infected area of the world. During that trip I got a poignant picture of what reality is like for large populations of the world—people with very few resources facing overwhelming and urgent health care issues that alone they couldn't possibly begin to deal with.

I made that two-week tour with Bruce Walker, Helga Holst, and a number of other local doctors and nurses. It's trite to say that visit changed my life, but in so many respects it did. It opened my eyes to the way so many people in the world are actually living. It made it abundantly clear about how much we have in the United States and how grateful we ought to be for everything that we do have here, and it made me want to make a contribution in the field of global health care. I also realized on that first trip that Bruce Walker and Helga Holst were two extraordinary people. Part of the difficulty in figuring out where and how to make a contribution is finding good people to back, and Bruce and Helga were two doctors who deserved meaningful support.

My sense of both of them that developed during those first two weeks, and it's been reinforced over the last five or six years, is that they not only have amazing medical and scientific knowledge—they're both great doctors—but as importantly they have an amazing sensitivity and awareness of all of the people and problems around them. Ultimately, that's what made an even greater impression on me. They had such great empathy for their patients. The human touch that they exhibited was amazing to me. At the same time they understood the global issues; they understood the issues related to their own organizations—Bruce at Harvard Medical School and at Massachusetts General Hospital and Helga at McCord Hospital—and the complex issues related to the national and provincial government and health ministries within South Africa. They had an awareness of all of those big organizations and big bureaucracies and at the same time had this incredible rapport and dialogue with individual patients.

In those two weeks we met so many young people who were dying of AIDS. This was back in 2002 when the disease was just rampant in South Africa. We'd walk into a rural village, into modest mud huts, and the people would be deeply impoverished. Invariably there would be several people in the family dying of AIDS or tuberculosis. Bruce and Helga just had an enormous sensitivity to each of those individual patients and would talk to them confidently and with great trust. It made the biggest impression on me.

Those observations have been reinforced over and over again on many subsequent visits. They're great doctors. They're great scientists. They're great clinicians. They're leveraging their own hospitals and organizations very effectively. But at the end of the day, what they really are—they're great humanitarians. They have that personal intensity that enables them to work eighteen hours a day, seven days a week, at great personal sacrifice to care for these communities. It's amazing. They're two shining examples in my mind.

Where did that lead you?

That led me to dive deeply into a lot of work with Bruce and Helga, so it led to many visits, several times a year, back to South Africa. It led my family to help Bruce build three big AIDS clinics in South Africa. It led us to provide lots of treatment for as many as sixteen thousand patients in KwaZulu-Natal. It ultimately has led us to fund an important vaccine study at Mass General and MIT [Massachusettes Institute of Technology]. It's led me to get very involved in the field of global health care, and it's also led me on an extraordinary personal journey.

What do you think accounts for the success of the clinics that you and Bruce have established?

One of the early things that Bruce did when he first established his lab at the University of KwaZulu-Natal and then began working with two big hospitals in Durban, McCord Hospital and St. Mary's Hospital, was to form collaborations with the health minister, the local provincial government, the heads of the two hospitals, and the local university and medical school. This may sound like the usual building of important relationships, but it was very difficult to accomplish back in 2001 and 2002. South Africans were, and to a certain extent still are, understandably suspicious of western medicine, practice, and doctors.

Nonetheless, Bruce was able to form important local relationships in the early years and build trust and credibility. He also mobilized meaningful financial support from the Doris Duke Foundation, Harvard Medical School, Mass General, and private donors. He also attracted important clinical resources including lots of medical students from Harvard Medical School, residents from Mass General, and doctors and nurses from both institutions who would come over for assignments and sabbaticals that would range from a month to a year.

To work in the local labs and hospitals as clinicians?

Yes. So this meant that he was drawing support not only from the local South African communities, but also from the Harvard/ Mass General communities. He's maintained that support over the last five or six years, and it's been important. We've also been able in recent years to bring over lots of South African doctors and nurses from those hospitals to be further trained at the Harvard School of Public Health or Harvard Medical School or Mass General and then return to South Africa with even better skills and knowledge, and that's been extremely important.

One of the very best lessons I learned philanthropically working with Bruce and Helga, and maybe our greatest contribution, is that we've empowered all of the people locally. They are no longer dependent on doctors from Mass General and from Harvard, because we've trained so many young doctors, residents, and nurses. We've trained local South Africans to assume all of these positions in the clinics and hospitals. We've empowered everyone locally. It's the greatest form of philanthropy. So no one today is nearly as dependent on us financially or professionally as they were five or six years ago. They're self-sustaining.

We now have PhD students who are graduating from the University of Natal, from the Nelson Mandela School of Medicine, who work in our lab at the University. They go on to become nurses and doctors in the clinics and hospitals, they go on to do amazing research and write great papers for important medical and science journals around the world. We've empowered a new generation of young, educated, talented, South Africans who can carry on all of this work well beyond the time that we'll be there. So it's been hugely gratifying and exhilarating to be able to be a part of that.

You were saying that it's been a personal journey and made changes in you.

In my professional life as an investment banker, I was always traveling internationally. But I looked at the world through professional eyes, seeing the opportunities to make investments or create an investment banking and brokerage business overseas. I was never really looking at the human challenges globally and especially the challenges in resource-scarce settings.

Working in the field of global health care, and working with Bruce and Helga in particular, has made me realize the urgency of problems globally and particularly the complexity of those problems.

So every trip I've made to South Africa, I always think that I'm getting more out of it than I'm giving. I'm learning a lot more than the learning that I'm imparting, most certainly. Ironically, although I'm ostensibly over there to provide hope and hopefulness to people who have very little, I always come away from these trips more hopeful than ever before because of this very infectious spirit and optimism that South Africans possess. I've been able to learn so much, and that learning has made me a much better person and makes me realize how much we can give back.

When have you given anonymously and when have you not, what have been the factors in that decision?

We've given virtually all of our gifts anonymously. Early on we thought that was the right way to engage because we always thought the purpose of our gift was to help others and not to draw attention to ourselves. But there's a benefit and a "disbenefit" to that, by the way.

The benefit is just as you might imagine. When you're funding intellectual capital rather than physical activities, meaning when you're funding research rather than building a building, I feel like the importance is to be an enabler. The importance is to get funds to an individual or an organization that can be leveraged and amplified in a meaningful way. That's why I've liked working with big institutions because those organizations are scaleable. A dollar of contribution gets magnified many times.

Being the source of that funding is not important in my mind. What is far more important is how the funds are used and how the funds get leveraged. To me the heroic people are the people that are able to use the funds meaningfully, the Helga Holsts and Bruce Walkers of the world, the people who can really significantly leverage those dollars through their own science and research and medicine and that's what's most important.

The "disbenefit" I've found, especially when it comes to giving globally, is there aren't that many people who are that familiar with Africa. For example, not many Americans have traveled to Africa. Frankly, not many Americans are focused on infectious diseases. In this country we'll give to the American Cancer Society or the American Heart Association or Diabetes Association because those are diseases impacting our own families, and so we're drawn to efforts and organizations like that.

In certain ways the only way to get people aware is to publicize your own effort. So in certain respects I've regretted that we haven't made our own efforts known more broadly, especially in our local community here in the U.S. That's sort of the dilemma. We really don't want to call attention to ourselves, but we do want to call attention to the underlying issue and the urgency of addressing that issue. That's the tension that surrounds this.

Having said that, we've given most of our gifts anonymously, and it hasn't diminished how thrilling or enriching the experience has been. Ultimately, we have found the right organizations and people to be supporting, and we have been able to watch quietly from the sidelines how effectively our gifts have been used, and that is exhilarating.

Does this dilemma prompt you to change your giving at all?

You know I think philanthropy like everything else in life is a learning experience. We've made, as everyone does, mistakes philanthropically—given to the wrong organizations, given to the wrong people, given too much, too early, too quickly, or without doing enough due diligence. It's like anything else, you make mistakes, you learn, you adapt, you change, you eventually get better, and you improve over time. So we're constantly evolving in our own thinking philanthropically.

One change might be that we become a little more public about some of the gifts we make. Especially when we feel it's urgent to get follow-on interest from others. I'll tell you about an experience we just had recently, which made us appreciate the leverage in motivating others by our own actions.

Earlier this year we went to an auction for the local community center. The community center here is a food pantry, a clothing closet, and a meeting place for people who don't have many friends, or an anchor in the community. So we went to their auction at one of the local churches a few weeks ago. At the beginning of the evening, the executive director of the community center stood up and said that the community center last year had raised x thousands of dollars in their auction and that it was the most successful auction they had ever had, and they were urging people to bid aggressively enough so that the auction would exceed last year's total.

Then they showed a fifteen-minute video of the activities at the community center over the last fifteen years. It described how people who had had good careers, good families, and then by any number of circumstances—deaths in families or being fired from jobs or being struck by an illness—found themselves later in their lives in vastly changed circumstances where they ended up having very little and really desperately needed a community center to depend upon. It was very compelling.

My wife and I were really moved by the video, and as it ended, we walked up to the executive director and whispered to her, "If you can raise more than you did last year, our family will match that with $100,000." She was so touched because in their fifteen-year history the community center had never received an offer or gift like that. She immediately turned to the audience and said, "You won't believe this, but this family has just offered us $100,000 if we can exceed last year's total." She was blown away, and my wife and I were embarrassed, but actually it changed the entire evening. Everyone there was energized by our offer. All anyone could talk about for the remainder of the evening was how much money the community center, for the first time in its history, was going to be able to raise. It was a significant amount of money for them and desperately needed to provide additional food and clothing resources for the population served by the center.

We went home that evening thinking it was an exhilarating evening and fun to elicit that kind of a reaction, and it taught us that sometimes it makes sense to step forward and being more public, more visible can be a good thing. So like everything in life there's not a single straightforward answer that's applicable in every situation. In general, we believe that it's not important to have your name on a building or to be honored at galas and functions. All of that is really of secondary importance, and it's not necessary. What is important is to be supporting organizations that can leverage your time and money and magnify your own efforts and contributions.

Introduction

1 World Development Report, World Book, 1993.
2 Bill Gates address to the World Health Assembly in Geneva, May 16, 2005.
3 University of Indiana, "Patterns of Household Charitable Giving by Income Group, 2005."
4 Paul G. Schervish, Mary A. O'Herlihy, and John J. Havens, "Agent-Animated Wealth and Philanthropy: The Dynamics of Accumulation and Allocation Among High-Tech Donors," posted on Boston College Web site, May 2001.
5 Ian Wilhelm, "Melinda Gates Says Infusion of Money Is Accelerating Fund's Progress," *The Chronicle Of Philanthropy*, June 25, 2007: http://www.philanthropy.com.

Paul Tudor Jones

1 Paul Jones speech, Darden Business School, University of Virginia, January 31, 2007.
2 Meryl Gordon, "The Green Team," *New York* magazine, June 5, 2000.
3 Andy Serwer, "The Legend of Robin Hood," *Fortune* Web site, September 8, 2006.
4 "The Legend of Robin Hood," *Fortune* Web site, September 8, 2006.

Melinda Gates

1 Melinda Gates speech at Davos, *World Economic Forum*, 2007.
2 Michael Specter, "What Money Can Buy," *New Yorker* Web site, October 24, 2005.

3 Melinda Gates, Keynote Speech, XVI International AIDS Conference, Toronto, August 13, 2006.

4 Gates, Keynote Speech.

5 Edith Lederer, "Melinda Gates Takes on a Public Role," *Washington Post* Web site, January 27, 2007.

6 "What Money Can Buy."

7 Elizabeth Corcoran, "Bill Grows Up," *Forbes*, October 4, 2004.

8 Ron Chernow, *Titan: The Life of John D. Rockefeller, Sr.* (New York: Random House, 1998), p. 321.

9 Sam Howe Verhovek, "Elder Bill Gates Takes on the Role of Philanthropist," *New York Times* Web site, September 12, 1999.

10 Amanda Bower, "Riches to the Poor," *Time* Web site, October 30, 2005.

11 "What Money Can Buy."

12 "Riches to the Poor."

13 "What Money Can Buy."

14 *Charlie Rose*, June 26, 2006.

15 "What Money Can Buy."

16 "Riches to the Poor."

17 "Riches to the Poor."

18 Joel L. Fleishman, *The Foundation: A Great American Secret.* (New York: Public Affairs, 2007).

19 Ian Wilhelm, "Melinda Gates Says That Infusion of Money is Accelerating Funds' Progress," *The Chronicle of Philanthropy*, June 25, 2007; http://www.philanthropy.com.

20 The challenges, results, and key lessons from some of the Bill and Melinda Gates Foundation's major endeavors is published on its Web site: http://www.gatesfoundation.org.

Liz and Stephen Alderman

1 *NewsHour* with Jim Lehrer: http://www.pbs.org/newshour/bb/social_issues/july-dec07/alderman_09–11.html, September 11, 2007.

2 Tim Ogden, "Wise Givers: Liz and Steve Alderman Heal the Wounds of Mass Trauma," *Beyond Philanthropy* Web site, November 30, 2007.

3 *NewsHour* with Jim Lehrer: http://www.pbs.org/newshour/bb/social_issues/july-dec07/alderman_09–11.html, September 11, 2007.

Bob and Suzanne Wright

1 Bishop Fulton Sheen was the auxiliary Catholic bishop from New York who wrote some ninety books and preached on the radio and on the Emmy Award–winning television show *Life is Worth Living* in the 1950s.

Donna and Philip Berber

1 Nicole Lewis, "The Audacity of Hope," *The Chronicle Of Philanthropy*, February 22, 2007: http://www.philanthropy.com.
2 Kate Holmquist, "Digging Deep," *Irish Times*, August 25, 2007.
3 http://www.taborcommunications.com/dsstar/00/0425/101526.html.
4 Tim Ogden, "On Giving Wisely," *Beyond Philanthropy* Web site, November 26, 2007.
5 Robert Frank, *Richistan: A Journey Through the American Wealth Boom and the Lives of the New Rich.* (New York: Crown, 2007), p. 173.
6 Frank, *Richistan*, p. 177.

Peter Bloom

1 Conor O'Clery, *The Billionaire Who Wasn't: How Chuck Feeney Made and Gave Away a Fortune Without Anyone Knowing.* (New York: Public Affairs, 2007).

Bernie and Tim Marquez

1 Ben Gose, "Gambling on Education," *The Chronicle Of Philanthropy*, February 22, 2007: http://www.philanthropy.com.
2 Steve Raabe, "Tim Marquez: Oil and Opportunity," *Denver Post*, February 3, 2007.
3 Ben Gose, "Gambling on Education."

Johann Olav Koss

1 "Rediscovering the Olympic Ideal," *Washington Post*, February 27, 2006.
2 Marco Visscher, "A Man With Balls," *Ode Magazine*, April 2006.
3 Right to Play video, http://hivaids.righttoplay.com/flash/video.html.
4 Right to Play video.
5 "A Man With Balls."

acknowledgments

You never know where a walk will lead you. A simple stroll around our neighborhood led to Molly Friedrich becoming my treasured agent and this book coming into being. I'd walk anywhere with her.

Words escape me as I try to describe how honored I feel to have met all of these people who selflessly and graciously allowed me to probe them with my questions. My respect and admiration are boundless. Each in his own way has found true greatness in the gift of his time and money that he is bestowing on his fellow man. I remain in awe.

Dozens of others spent hours with me in interviews and spoke to me at length about their giving or put me onto the trail of someone who would. Thanks to Judith Aidoo, Doug Bauer, Charles Best, David Bornstein, Lowell Bryan, Frank Brosens, Gerald Chertavian, William Donaldson, John Gannon, Chuck Harris, James Jenson, Olana Khan, Jacqueline Novogratz, Chip and Jan Raymond, Chuck Slaughter, Sy Sternberg, David Tubbs, Kathy Valyi, and Bruce Walker.

Many friends and family members have let me bore them senseless on the subject of philanthropy and then in turn offered true insights on the nature of giving. For this counsel and forbearance I offer thanks to Suzy Akin, Christie Allen, Jane DeBeneducci, George Bianco, Mary Boies, Leslie Cecil, Eric Endlich, Nina Freedman, Lorrie Friedman, Martha and Rich Handler, Peter Hauspurg, Jon Kamen, Theresa Kilman, Joan Lohrfink, Michelle Miller Adams, Marcus McGilvray, Mark Malloch Brown, John Needham, Mark Schwartz, and Steve Swartzman.

Daun Paris and Hatsy Vallar have taken this journey of learning about philanthropy with me and I could have asked for no better fellow travelers than these two wonderful friends.

Without the help of my sons, Sam, Tommy, and Harry, I would have lost my interview recordings, backup files, and my mind. Their calmness and compassion in the face of my technological fiascoes and publishing pressures are a gift they must have received from their father. Each is a blessing beyond words. Everything I learned about giving came from my husband, Mark. For almost two decades I have witnessed his extraordinary generosity of spirit, be it coaching children on the soccer field or giving of time and money. He has been my first and best teacher and I hope one day our sons will feel the same.